THE GRAPHICS OF
COMMUNICATION

Typography   Layout   Design

THE GRAPHICS OF

Typography Layout Design

COMMUNICATION

ARTHUR T. TURNBULL
and
RUSSELL N. BAIRD
Ohio University

HOLT, RINEHART AND WINSTON

New York   Chicago   San Francisco   Toronto   London

THE artist in any field knows from experience that freedom in expression follows a thorough understanding of technique. Similarly, the successful journalist must have a practical knowledge of the mechanics of production as well as a keen awareness of the principles of design to function effectively in any of the diversified areas of communication.

The Graphics of Communication combines theory and discussion of techniques in such media as newspapers, magazines, books, advertising, and public relations. A strong accent has been placed on newspapers—still the basic channel of communication—but considerable attention has been given to all major branches of journalism.

The first half of the book is devoted to mechanics—and, since it is virtually impossible to discuss design and production without illustrating important steps in printing methods, action photographs of most of these methods have been coordinated with discussion.

Effective graphic communication also involves art principles. Accordingly, the second half of the book has been given over to design, layout, and make-up.

This volume itself represents the application of many design principles and many printing techniques. More than two hundred and fifty illustrations have been incorporated to bring difficult-to-acquire information to the immediate use of the reader. To create greater fluidity of design and still maintain a compact, easy-to-handle book, offset lithography has been utilized. The conjunction of freedom in design and economy of space are illustrated by the book designer's imaginative placement of chapter titles and captions; the use of wide margins and the selection of ten-point Caledonia for body type, accented by Standard for display, reflect this same pattern of legibility, utility, and visual pleasure.

In dividing the task of preparing the manuscript, the authors took advantage of their varied backgrounds and interests. Arthur Turnbull, whose major interests have been advertising, art, and typography, consequently contributed Chapters 3, 4, 5, 7, 9, 10, 13, and 16. Russell Baird, whose enthusiasms center around magazines and newspapers, wrote Chapters 1, 2, 6, 8, 11, 12, 14, and 15. Unless otherwise credited, Professor Turnbull prepared the illustrations.

...v

PREFACE

We wish to express our gratitude to the Ohio University Fund and to the Research Committee of Ohio University for financial assistance in the preparation of the manuscript and purchase of illustrative materials.

Special appreciation for their cooperation and aid in making available action photographs, type specimens, and innumerable printed materials is given to the following: Alco-Gravure Division of Publication Corporation; American Photoengraving Association; American Type Founders, Inc.; Appleton-Century-Crofts, a Division of Meredith Publishing Co.; *The Beacon* of Ohio Oil Company; Cambridge University Press; Certified Dry Mat Corporation; Edwin H. Stuart, Inc.; *Forward,* Dayton Power and Light Company; *Discovery* Magazine; The Goss Company; Harper & Row, Publishers; Intertype Corporation; The Kaumagraph Company; Kimberly-Clark Corporation; Lanston Monotype Company; The Lawhead Press, Inc.; *Life* Magazine; Lithographers National Association; Lithographic Technical Foundation; Ludlow Typograph Company; Masta Displays, Inc.; McGraw-Hill Book Company; Mergenthaler Linotype Company; *The Michigan Bell* of the Michigan Bell Telephone Company; Monotype Composition Company; Montauk Book Manufacturers; *New York Daily News,* News Syndicate Company; New York Lithographing Corporation; *The New York Times;* Stanford University Press; *Systems Magazine; The Trading Post,* Timken Roller Bearing Company; S. D. Warren Paper Company; and Xerox Corporation.

CONTENTS

MAGAZINE LAYOUT AND DESIGN 283

15

PLANNING OTHER PRINTED LITERATURE 299

16

Graphic communication today is the lifeblood of our economic, political, and cultural existence. In every waking hour we act, react, and are influenced by the reactions of others as the result of some form of the printed word.

We play watchdog to our government via the printed newspaper. We pay our printed bills with printed money or printed checks. We buy goods learned about through printed advertising, and we take those goods home in printed cartons.

Our knowledge is advanced by printed textbooks or technical or professional journals, our day brightened by printed magazines or printed books. Printed offers for countless items deluge us. The great works of art, past and present, are brought from far-off museums to our doorsteps by accurate reproductions. Libraries, drugstore magazine racks, home book shelves, and attics and basements everywhere are crammed with printed material.

So are the millions of wastebaskets emptied each night into trash cans.

In self defense, today's public must be selective in what it reads. Designers of printed media need to become increasingly skillful just to keep their work from a hasty wastebasket burial. How to win the competition for a reader's time is a vital problem found by all men and women in publishing. Newspapers, for example, must vie for attention not only against television, magazines, other newspapers, and scores of one-shot printed pieces, but against internal competition too. Most metropolitan newspapers, if folded down to the size of this textbook, would have as much if not more bulk. It cannot be assumed that the reader at his breakfast table or in his easy chair in the evening will be able to absorb that much printed matter. Consequently, each page, story, illustration, and headline must engage in its own battle for reader time and comprehension.

Only the publications and individuals offering the best in content and presentation reap the award of readership. This book, as its title indicates, must concentrate on presentation—the *graphics* of communication—alone. However, content—the *substance* of communication—must never be minimized by the student.

THE SUBSTANCE OF GRAPHIC COMMUNICATION

There is no doubt that the facts or ideas to be conveyed to people are of primary importance in communication. These are

...1

the substance to which all other aspects of communication must be related, and their importance can be seen in many ways. Readers will overcome several obstacles to get information they strongly desire. Students scan a monotonous list of scores presented in small type to find the result of their school's football game. In small communities everywhere, citizens dig into long lists of personal items to find a mention of themselves or friends. Scientists and scholars ignore the dull typography of their journals as they eagerly seek new data of importance to them. In these and hundreds of like instances, the interest in content is so great that graphics plays only a secondary role.

THE IMPORTANCE OF GRAPHICS

On the other side of the coin, however, rests the waste-basket fate of vast quantities of printed matter. Tests have proved that material of the same content has been received, read, and acted upon in one form, but discarded in another. A newspaper story may gain readership from one edition to the next simply by a change in its headline size or page placement. A direct-mail promotion piece may elicit more response with part of its message printed in red than it might with all printed in black. These examples, coupled with the knowledge that every reader is offered much more than he can ever assimilate, assert that graphic techniques are too important to be ignored.

The need for graphics in communication can be illustrated by a comparison with the theater. The designer of printed material is like the actor who gives life and expression to the lines of the playwright. The actor's performance through the use of his voice, facial expressions, and movements is akin to the designer's visual expression through typography, layout, and design. A play, poorly acted, can be a flop even if adequately written. Printed matter with solid content can also play to an empty house if it is poorly designed and produced.

WHY NOT CALL IT GRAPHIC ART?

Like the actor's, the role of the designer is a combination of communication and creativity. Because his job is creative, there is perhaps some justification for calling his work *graphic art*. This description, however, emphasizes the subordinate rather than the dominant aspect of his role.

We prefer to call it *graphic communication* because there can be no doubt that the designer of printed literature must be primarily concerned with communication and not art. His work cannot be intended as solely an expression of his artistic talent. It is not enough for what he creates to bring an exclamation about its attractiveness. Instead it must be a vehicle that successfully *transmits* the *substance* of communications. In other words, his aims cannot be toward the sake of art alone.

In his effort to get *effective* printed communication he tries to achieve these three objectives: (1) to attract attention to the message; (2) to present the message so it can be easily read and understood; and (3) to make an impression. The desired impression depends on circumstances; he may want the message to be retained as knowledge, to win the reader to a point of view, to gain acceptance for a product, or to create an emotional response. Whichever it is, the first two objectives must work toward its achievement.

WHY BOTHER WITH MECHANICS?

As he works toward his goals, the designer of effective printed communication has broad leeway but some limitation as far as mechanics and media are concerned.

Just as the actor is limited to the dimensions of the stage, the designer of graphic communication is limited to the dimensions of the page. An actor also must recognize the limits of his voice and his gestures, but he does not consider these to be unduly restrictive. It is doubtful, for example, that he bemoans that he cannot fly or change his costume magically while on stage. Instead the actor simply knows and accepts what might appear to be limitations and uses his skills to bring his performance to the highest level.

The graphic communicator must operate in similar fashion. First of all he must know the mechanics and limitations of his medium and then put his talents to work.

In this book, the mechanics involved in the visual presentation of words and illustrations are considered first. Then attention is given to specific media and the application of psychological precepts and art principles to the design of printed communication.

Needed for a true understanding of the mechanics involved in the mass production of printed materials is a background in the evolution of modern methods. Following is a brief summary of the development of currently accepted materials and means.

FIVE PROBLEMS REQUIRED SOLUTION

To provide visual communication on a mass production basis, man had to fill at least five perplexing needs:

(1) A practical set of symbols that singly and in groups could visually represent both real objects and mental creations: a workable alphabet has been the solution.

(2) Suitable materials on which these symbols might be retained for viewing: the great variety of papers in use today has met this need.

(3) Substances that could be deposited on these surfaces in the form of the symbols: inks have constituted the most common means.

(4) Labor-saving devices to make it practicable first to record these symbols easily and then to reproduce the result in great quantity: movable type, type-composition machines, and printing presses are some of the answers man has found.

(5) Mass reproduction of illustrations to supplement the symbols: photography and photoengraving are two processes that have filled this gap.

The story of man's striving to solve these problems closely follows his striving for a better life. As his efforts advanced toward a society that would grant him his spiritual and physical needs, so did his means of communication. It was no mere coincidence, for example, that the primitive method of written communication was revolutionized in the fifteenth century by Johann Gutenberg and others—this was the period of the Renaissance of Europe. It was also no coincidence that a flood of significant developments in printing occurred about four centuries later—Western civilization was in the midst of a great industrial revolution at that time. And today's flurry of changes after more than half a century of virtual inactivity, are reflecting the vast social and technological changes in our concepts of space, speed, and time.

PRIMITIVE BEGINNINGS

Too involved in a desperate struggle for survival to have much concern for communication, prehistoric man felt little need for any efficient means of recording or transmitting information in visual form.

There is evidence that he knotted cords and notched sticks to send a few messages of importance and to register the feats of tribal leaders. Eventually he also scrawled crude drawings (pictographs) on stones, weapons, utensils, and the walls of caves, but these drawings were limited to physical objects.

CONTRIBUTIONS OF EARLY CIVILIZATIONS

As he advanced to a more civilized state in some areas of the world, notably Egypt and China, man became concerned with the supernatural as well as with the world around him.

The Egyptians, for example, made substantial contributions to our alphabet with their *hieroglyphics* (sacred writings). Generally considered the forerunner of our modern alphabet, they served to provide symbols for thoughts as well as for physical objects. The Egyptians also discovered a writing surface called *papyrus*, from which our name for paper has come. Papyrus was a grasslike plant whose pith could be pressed into sheets, and its use can be traced back as far as 3500 B.C.[1]

But it was the Chinese who gave us paper as we know it today; its invention was reported to the emperor in 105 A.D.[2] How many years the Chinese may have used paper before that date is not known. This early paper was made from hemp, cotton rags, and the bark of trees. Although crude according to today's standards, it represented one of the most important steps in the evolution of printing.

The Chinese were also the first to manufacture a substance similar to ink (about 220 A.D.), and they later invented a true ink. They first used tree sap or cochineal insects to get a dyelike substance to serve the purpose. Then, during the fourth or fifth century, they used lamp black and water-soluble gums to produce what is now known as "India" ink because it was introduced to the Western world via India.

Phoenicia, a small country that lost its identity when it became a part of Syria in 64 B.C., is credited with being the source of our modern alphabet. The Phoenicians simplified the cumbersome hieroglyphics into an alphabet and gave phonetic values to their symbols (Figure 1-1). Later modifications by the Greeks, Romans, and Anglo-Saxons produced the twenty-six-letter alphabet we use today.

[1]Douglas C. McMurtrie, *The Book* (New York: Oxford University Press, 1943), p. 13.
[2]Thomas Frances Carter, *The Invention of Printing in China* (New York: Columbia University Press, 1925), p. 2.

		EGYPTIAN	Phoenician	GREEK				LATIN			Hebrew
1	Eagle . .			A	A	A	α	A	A	a a	א
2	Crane . .			B	B	B	β	B	B	B b	ב
3	Throne .			Γ	Γ	Γ	Υ	C	C	G c g	ג
4	Hand . .			Δ	Δ	Δ	δ	D	D	δ δ d	ד
5	Maeander			E	E	E	ε	E	E	e e	ה
6	Cerastes .			Y	YF	F	F	F	F	f f	ו
7	Duck . .			I	I	Z	ζ	Z	Z	z	ז
8	Sieve . .			H	H	H	η	H	H	h h	ח
9	Tongs . .			⊕	⊕	O	θ ϑ	⊗			ט
10	Parallels .			I	I	I	ι	I	I	i j	י
11	Bowl . .			K	K	K	κ	K	K	k	כ
12	Lioness .			V	Λ	λ	λ	L	L	l l	ל
13	Owl . .			M	M	M	μ μ	M	M	m m	מ
14	Water . .			N	N	N	ν ν	N	N	n n	נ
15	Chair-back			Ξ	Ξ	ξ	ε	+	+	x x	ס
16	....			O	O	O	o	O			ע
17	Shutter .			Γ	Γ	π	π ω	P	P	P	פ
18	Snake . .			Γ	Γ	M	λ	Γ			צ
19	Angle . .			φ	φ	ϙ		Q	Q	q q	ק
20	Mouth . .			Γ	Γ	P	ρ ρ	P	R	r r	ר
21	Inundated Garden			ξ	ξ	C	c σ	ξ	S	s s	ש
22	Lasso . .			T	T	T	τ	T	T	t t	ת
		I	II	III	IV	V	VI	VII	VIII	IX	X	XI

FIGURE 1-1. The Egyptian, Phoenician, Greek, and Latin contributions to the evolution of the alphabet. (Reprinted from *The Story of the Alphabet* by **Edward** Clodd, by permission of the publisher, Appleton-Century-Crofts, Inc.)

Thus, from the early civilizations of the East and Middle East came solutions for three basic communications problems—the need for a workable set of symbols, an adequate writing surface, and a printing substance. With sufficient time and labor, knowledge at last could be recorded somewhat efficiently, though slowly.

It had taken centuries for man to reach this point, and it was centuries later before any significant further advances were made. That it took so long to produce printing is remarkable. Certainly the Romans achieved a high degree of civilization as they built their empire. In government, philosophy, road building and other forms of engineering, as well as in many of the elements of culture characteristic of an advanced civilization, the Romans excelled. Certainly, as their influence spread to all parts of the world, there would have been a great opportunity for some form of printing to be introduced. Failure of the Roman Empire to provide any, however, was probably caused by the lack of a sufficiently strong need for new methods. With an ample supply of slave scribes, the

Romans could produce enough books without wanting the further efficiency of printing.

With the fall of the Roman Empire in the West during the fifth century A.D., the world underwent such vast change that little thought was given to books. The church became the dominant influence in the life of the Middle Ages, and for centuries man's attention was diverted from the mechanical innovations that would provide a way to a greater production of worldly goods. It was approximately one thousand years after the Roman Empire deteriorated that the Renaissance brought modern printing to the world.

THE RENAISSANCE AND PRINTING FROM MOVABLE TYPE

In the fourteenth and fifteenth centuries, Italian scholars started a radical shift in attention from the religious to the humanistic. Out of a spirit of rebellion against the church-dominated society of the Middle Ages, they turned to a study of the classical culture of ancient Greece and Rome. The movement, based on the past, was considered a rebirth of culture and society, and had a profound influence on art, architecture, education, and the philosophy of life itself.

The breakthrough that gave us modern printing was the invention of typography—the printing from movable types—by Johann Gutenberg of Mainz, Germany (Figure 1-2). He did not actually invent printing, for the Chinese and others had printed from wood blocks many years previously, but in about the year 1448, he perfected a method for casting and using movable pieces of type. Although some authorities say that a Laurens Coster of Haarlem, Holland, did similar printing two years before Gutenberg, there is no doubt that the latter so developed the idea as to be principally responsible for the far-reaching effect of printing on our civilization. After painstaking labors, Gutenberg found what were, for his day, satisfactory solutions to each major problem of printing: (1) a system of movable type so letters could be arranged in any order and reused as needed; (2) a method of making these pieces of type in quantity both easily and accurately; (3) a method of holding the type in place for printing; (4) a system of making the type impressions on paper; and (5) an ink that would provide a readable impression from type to paper.

Gutenberg first cut pieces of type separately from pieces of wood and held them together in lines by running wire through a hole

FIGURE 1-2. Johann Gutenberg, founder of modern printing. (Reprinted from *A New History of Stereotyping* by George A. Kubler, by permission of the Certified Dry Mat Corporation.)

drilled at the base of each piece. Then he invented a frame into which the type could be wedged and held in place. The wooden wine presses of his day gave him the idea for making impressions on paper. Type was placed on a flat bed of wood, and, by means of a lever-operated screw, a wooden platen was lowered to press the paper against the type (Figure 1-3).

When he found that ink softened his wood types and that the press wore down the letters quickly, he cut types from lead. When lead proved too soft, he tried harder metals, but these cut through the paper. At last he found a satisfactory combination of lead, tin, and antimony—still the basic components of today's types. With a satisfactory alloy in use, he turned his attention to a means of making pieces in quantity. His brass type molds were the answer, and with their use modern printing was born. Then, since earlier inks had run and blotted when used with type, he emerged with a satisfactory solution to this problem—providing his final significant contribution to all five basic aspects of modern printing. Those who followed had only to devote their talents to devising type designs, faster presses, speedier means of type compositon, and other printing methods to meet the needs and tastes of contemporary life.

Gutenberg, like so many other inventors, was an impractical person who profited little from his ingenuity. Financial backing for his work came through a partnership with John Fust, a goldsmith who was to share the profits and was given a mortgage on Gutenberg's equipment as security on his investment. Fust, after Gutenberg had devoted about five years to his famous forty-two-line Bible, brought suit against him and received virtually all the inventor owned. Together with Peter Schoeffer, an excellent printer who had worked with Gutenberg, Fust completed the 1300-page Bible in 1456, six years after its inception.

Meanwhile, Gutenberg obtained financial help from another

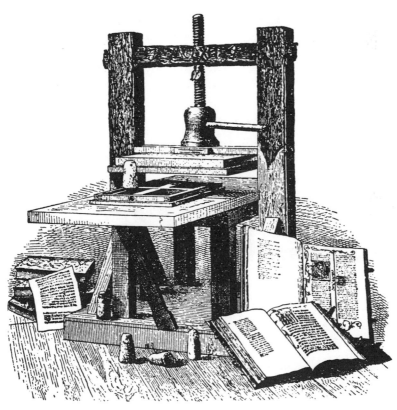

FIGURE 1-3. The Gutenberg press based on the contemporary wine press. Note the screw-operated lever used to lower the platen for pressure against the paper. (Reprinted from *A New History of Stereotyping* by George A. Kubler, by permission of the Certified Dry Mat Corporation.)

source and set up a competing shop. There he did some notable work, but died in 1468 still heavily in debt.

Printing spread to other countries soon after its introduction in Mainz, and artisans of different nationalities brought about worthy improvements in type as they created designs reflective of their backgrounds (see Chapter 3). Yet, aside from type design and a few minor changes, the printing art once again stagnated for centuries. For example, the first printing press in the United States, established as an adjunct to Harvard College by Stephen and Matthew Daye in 1638, was patterned closely after the nearly two-hundred-year-old Gutenberg press. Neither presses, type composition, nor the manufacture of paper was to change until the industrial revolution.

EFFECTS OF THE INDUSTRIAL REVOLUTION

Advances in technology, beginning around 1760, brought great changes in the way of life for the people of England, Europe, and eventually the rest of the world. Industry moved from the home workshop to the factory; machines did the work of countless men at far less cost and in much less time. New markets opened up for the increased goods, money found its way into more pockets, the desire for goods grew and in turn fostered the production of still more goods.

FIGURE 1-4. Daniel Treadwell's bed-and-platen power press, the first application of steam power to a printing press. (Reprinted from *A Short History of the Printing Press* by Robert Hoe)

FIGURE 1-5. The Hoe Type Revolving Machine. The original press used four impression cylinders; for increased production, this later model used ten cylinders. (Reprinted from *A Short History of the Printing Press*)

As prosperity spread, so did public education; literacy increased, and more and more people had the time, ability, and interest to want more and more to read.

The second phase of the industrial revolution in the 1800s brought the inventions of the telegraph, steamship, and locomotive to provide opportunities for speed of communication and transportation; but numerous factors kept the production of printed matter from taking advantage of the accelerated pace. Hand composition, the lever press, and the hand manufacture of paper were all too slow to meet the mounting demands for more printed communication. When the effects of the industrial revolution finally spread to printing, innovations helped each of these areas to catch up with amazing rapidity.

THE COMING OF STEAM POWER AND THE CYLINDER PRESS. The magic of steam was first put to use in printing in Boston by Daniel Treadwell in 1822 and by Isaac Adams in 1830. Both men applied power to the familiar Gutenberg bed-and-platen presses. Treadwell's press (Figure 1-4) met with little success, but Adams' was used extensively for book work for several years.

This application of steam power to an inherently slow method was not enough for newspapers, whose circulations were mounting rapidly. Too much time was wasted in lifting the platen away from the type or in moving the type away from the platen under the old system, and a basic change was called for.

It was answered by the substitution of a cylinder for the platen. The first steam-powered cylinder press came from Friedrich Koenig, a German who received financial backing for his work in England. Koenig's press, with a cylinder to pick up the paper and carry it over a moving type bed, was patented in 1810, and was first used for newspaper work by the *London Times* on November 28, 1814. By using two cylinders, Koenig made his presses *perfecting;* that is, they printed on both sides of the sheet. Two of his steam-driven two-cylinder presses were used by the *Times* to produce 1100 copies an hour, a quite remarkable achievement for that day.

Many improvements have since been made in the flat-bed presses, including the use of *web feeding*, whereby paper is fed from a continuous roll instead of in sheets. Flat-bed, web-perfecting presses are still used for some newspapers today, but even in the late 1800s, the circulation giants of large cities required still faster presses.

THE TYPE-REVOLVING PRESS. The first press based on the principle now used for highest-speed newspaper production was built by R. Hoe & Company and put into operation at the *Philadelphia Public Ledger* in 1846. Called the Hoe Type Revolving Machine, the new press was designed to rotate the type, instead of to hold it stationary. Type was locked into place on a large cylinder by means of wedge-shaped rules between columns. In miraculous fashion, the cylinder could revolve at rather high speeds without the type flying in all directions.

Hoe's first type-revolving press used four impression cylinders around the central type cylinder and was capable of turning out 2000 sheets per hour for each impression cylinder, or a total of 8000 per hour. One man was required to feed each impression cylinder and corresponding type bed, and the press printed one side of a sheet. To increase output, Hoe eventually grouped as many as ten impression cylinders around the type cylinder (Figure 1-5).

The Hoe Type Revolving Machine was important because of its rotary principle. It cleared the way for *stereotyping*, a process that led to the modern rotary newspaper presses, which put printed impressions on paper about as fast as an electric-powered cylinder can rotate and paper can be fed to it.

STEREOTYPING AND PRESENT-DAY WEB-PERFECTING ROTARY PRESSES. A disadvantage of the Hoe type-revolving press was the necessity of locking countless type pieces onto the main cylinder. This cut speed and restricted type display to one-column widths because of the wedge-shaped column rules. Although long lines of display type in advertising and headlines that can spread across columns are commonly accepted as necessities today, it was the demand for still greater speed—not large headlines—that encouraged the experimentation resulting in the use of stereotype plates in newspaper printing.

Briefly, *stereotyping* is a method of making, with type metal, "perfect facsimiles of the faces of pages composed of movable type."[3] Knowledge and use of modern stereotyping methods existed as early as 1690 in Germany and other parts of Europe.[4] Credit for its invention is generally given, however, to Claude Gennoux, a French printer who obtained a patent for it on July 24, 1829.[5]

Gennoux used the "papier mâché" or "wet mat" process for making duplicate plates. By pressing the wet mat made of several layers of paper against the type area, Gennoux made a mold that when dried was used to cast the plate from molten metal. Today's dry mats came into use in this country after 1890.

In 1849, Jacob Warms of Paris obtained a patent for making curved stereotype plates by placing a wet mat in a curved mold.[6] The idea was introduced in this country by Charles Craske, a New York engraver who made the first curved stereotype plate for a rotary press of the *New York Herald* in 1854. His first attempt was not entirely successful, but in 1861 he started stereotyping the regular editions of four New York newspapers, and the process has been used regularly since that time.

Stereotyping made it possible to put full newspaper pages, in the form of single curved pieces of metal, on press cylinders that could then revolve at tremendous speeds, making impressions on paper as they went. To be fully efficient, rotary presses using stereotype plates had to be improved to: (1) make it possible to print both sides of the paper at once; and (2) make it possible to feed paper from a continuous roll instead of from sheets. The first rotary press to incorporate these two features was devised by William

---

[3]George A. Kubler, *A New History of Stereotyping* (New York: privately published, 1941), p. 23.
[4]*Ibid.*, p. 34.
[5]*Ibid.*, p. 75.
[6]*Ibid.*, p. 262.

Bullock of Philadelphia in 1865. His press was said to be web-perfecting because paper was fed from a roll (web) and printed both sides of the sheet (perfecting). As is the case with most inventions, it contained some unreliable mechanical features. A greatly improved web-fed rotary press was introduced by R. Hoe & Company in 1871 and was widely accepted after being put to use at *Lloyd's Weekly Newspaper* in London and the *New York Tribune*.

The Hoe company pioneered in other notable improvements in rotary presses, including the manufacture of presses that used several units to multiply production capacity. Its Double Supplement Rotary Press installed at the *New York Herald* in 1882 consisted of two units and could print 24,000 twelve-page papers an hour. The Hoe Quadruple Newspaper Press installed at the *New York World* five years later produced sixteen-page papers at the same rate.

IMPROVEMENTS IN COMPOSITION METHODS

As presses were developed to meet the mounting pressures for increased production of newspapers and other printed material, attempts were also made to eliminate the three shortcomings of hand composition of type: (1) the matter of time and effort needed to get the pieces of type from their storage places and set them into lines; (2) the tedious problem of spacing between words and/or letters to fill out lines flush on the right; and (3) the distribution of the type back to its storage places.

Most of the early machines succeeded in speeding up only one or two parts of the typesetting operation. The mechanization of the setting phase seemed to cause the least difficulty: machines that would eject type pieces from their storage places when an operator pressed a key on a keyboard were quickly devised. A solution to the distribution problem was presented by the Unitype, manufactured in 1870 by the Wood Nathan Company. As a substantial improvement over other machines, it was used in many newspaper plants for years. Although justification still had to be done manually, the Unitype was said to be able to do the work of four hand compositors.[7] Its operation was keyed to two cylinders, one above the other. The top cylinder automatically distributed the type into proper positions in the lower cylinder, from which the pieces could respond to keyboard action.

[7]Kenneth E. Olson, *Typography and Mechanics of the Newspaper* (New York: Appleton-Century-Crofts, Inc., 1930), p. 98.

FIGURE 1-6. Ottmar Mergenthaler, inventor of the Linotype. (Courtesy Mergenthaler Linotype Corporation.)

MERGENTHALER AND THE LINOTYPE. Several completely automatic composing machines were introduced with enthusiastic praise by their backers in the 1890s, but most of them failed to meet production tests. Manufacture of a device called the Paige machine, for example, was supported by Mark Twain to the extent of $190,000. According to Twain, it could do everything but drink, swear and go on strike.[8] But when tested in the Chicago *Times-Herald* office in 1894, it failed to perform satisfactorily.

On July 3, 1886, a man named Ottmar Mergenthaler (Figure 1-6), in the *New York Tribune* building, set the first line of type on a machine that was to be christened the Linotype (Figure 1-7) and was destined to provide machine composition practical in every respect. Mergenthaler, its chief inventor, was a German-born watchmaker who had been working in Baltimore as a skilled constructor of patent models. His work in perfecting a type-casting machine had been financed by a group of publishers including Whitelaw Reid of the *Tribune*, in whose building the Linotype was introduced.

Mergenthaler's machine was based on a new principle that involved the casting of lines of type by injecting molten metal into brass molds during the setting process. It met all the requirements

[8]Frank Luther Mott, *American Journalism* (New York: The MacMillan Company, 1962), p. 499.

FIGURE 1-7.
The original
Linotype.
(Courtesy
Mergenthaler
Linotype Cor-
poration.)

for a typesetting machine: casting was performed by hitting a keyboard; both the distribution of the molds and the justification of
lines with expandable spacebands were automatic. In addition,
using molds instead of pieces of type was an added bonus: because
every line that came from the machine was newly cast, type was
saved from constant wear.

Although several of the first Linotypes were installed in the
shops of newspapers, it was not until 1890 that improvements made
the machine function efficiently. For example, when it was first
introduced, the Linotype used blasts of air to move type molds;
the later models let the force of gravity pull the molds into position.

OTHER EARLY TYPE-CASTING MACHINES. The Intertype
machine, chief competitor for the Linotype today, was produced
by Herman Ridder, publisher of the *New Yorker Staats-Zeitung*,
and was first put into operation at the New York *Journal of Commerce* in 1913. It is a line-casting machine similar to the Linotype.

The Monotype, invented by Tolbert Lanston in 1887 and employed for production in 1898, gets its name from the fact that it
casts single letters instead of line slugs. It also differs from Lino-

type and Intertype because it consists of two machines: one is a typewriterlike device that makes a perforated tape; the other does the casting as the tape is fed to it, much like a roller piano.

Still another machine, the Ludlow Typograph, was introduced by Washington I. Ludlow in 1909 and later developed by William A. Reade. Designed mainly to produce the large sizes of type that had previously been set most economically by hand, the Ludlow system is widely used today. Although it is not an automatic system (molds are handset and then cast into lines), it offers some important improvements over hand composition. Each line is fresh new type in one piece and is, consequently, easier to handle.

FOURNIER AND THE POINT SYSTEM. Early type designers and founders made no attempt to base type sizes on any uniform set of measurements. For printers the result was at times utterly confusing. Type from one founder could not be mixed with that from another; the fact that spacing materials were different made each incoming order of type a new puzzle to be solved.

A French printer, Pierre Simon Fournier, is mainly responsible for bringing order to type measurement. In his *Manuel Typographique* of 1764, he tells of his efforts:[9]

To clear this chaos and to give ... typography an order which never before reigned there, is the subject which has gained my attention. Through the invention of *typographic points,* I think that I have been fortunate enough to succeed with an exactness and precision ... The typographic point is nothing more than the separation of the bodies of types by equal and definite degrees, which I call points ... I have divided the standard scale into two inches; the inch into twelve lines, and the line into six typographic points; making altogether 144 points in two inches ... The invention of these points is the first service that I rendered to typography in 1737.

The introduction of the point system by Fournier was indeed a service and a major step forward. But more than a century passed before the point system came into use in the United States in 1878. In that year the foundry of Harder, Luse & Co. of Chicago was destroyed by fire. When it rebuilt, the company decided to introduce the point system for all the type it manufactured. Finally, in

[9]Quoted in Hugo Jahn, *Hand Composition* (New York: John Wiley & Sons, Inc., 1931), pp. 202-203.

1887, The United States Type Founders' Association adopted a system using points equal to 0.01384 inch, a modification on Fournier's plan. It is standard in this country today.

MACHINE PAPERMAKING

Until it was mechanized during the Industrial Revolution, the manufacture of paper was a slow, tedious hand process. The first papermaking machine was invented by Nicolas Robért at Essonnes, France, in 1798. Henry and Sealy Fourdrinier bought his patent and, with the aid of an engineer, introduced the first practical paper machine in 1803; this marked the real beginning of large-volume mechanical papermaking.

REPRODUCTION OF PHOTOGRAPHS

Early American letterpress printers and publishers had to content themselves with woodcuts for illustrations until the 1870s, when zincographs (line illustrations etched by acid on zinc) came into use in this country. Introduced in Paris in 1859, these were an improvement over woodcuts, but did not provide a means for reproducing on a plate all the tones of a photograph.

Authorities differ as to the discoverer of the halftone photoengraving process which eventually overcame this obstacle. Undoubtedly many men from several countries were instrumental in perfecting the process. William Talbot, an Englishman, is said to have made the first halftone in 1852 by using a cloth screen and sensitized coatings to put a continuous tone image on a relief printing plate. Frederic Ives of Philadelphia, with successive inventions in 1878 and 1886, is generally given credit for the modern halftone process of photoengraving. In experimentation at Cornell University, Ives produced a crossline screen on glass similar to the screens used today. At about the same time, Stephen H. Horgan made a halftone plate that was the first to be used by an American newspaper. His reproduction of "Shantytown" was used by the New York *Daily Graphic* on March 4, 1880.

But the work of these men would not have been possible, of course, were it not for the basic idea of photography itself. This had made its debut when Joseph Niepce produced the first photographs around 1827 in Europe.

DISCOVERY OF OFFSET PRINTING

Two accidental discoveries set the stage for what might be called the "age of competition" in graphic communication. Both incidents, though many years apart, brought about a new printing process, called *photo-offset lithography,* now coming to the fore as a strong competitor for the traditional letterpress system of Johann Gutenberg.

In 1796, a little-known but imaginative Bavarian actor and playwright named Alois Senefelder discovered that he could print from the flat surface of a stone. Senefelder, because he could not afford to make expensive engravings for printing his plays, was trying to learn the art himself by practicing to write backwards. For his practice he substituted a flat stone for engraver's copper because the stone could be more easily scraped and used again.

One day as he was polishing a stone slab, his mother came into his workshop and asked him to write a list of linens to be washed before the laundress, who was outside waiting, took the clothes with her. With neither paper nor ink at hand, Senefelder used a greasy substance he had been working with to scrawl the laundry list on the stone. Later he noticed that when the stone was coated with water, the greasy inscription repelled the water.

This basic principle—the greasy surfaces accepting only ink and rejecting water, and vice versa—is still the basis for lithographic printing. It is however, about the only aspect of commercial lithography that has not changed.

Even in primitive form the new process revealed some special advantages. Any number of images, for example, could be applied to the stone, thus providing for the printing of several copies at once. And, generally speaking, the process provided a faster, more economical method for producing illustrations than did designing on copper plates, the competing method of the day.

In 1825 when Goya did his famous "Bullfighter" lithographs, he established lithography as an artist's medium. Commercial work in color by the new process soon followed, and lithography began to develop into a printing process known for giving color in various tones economically.

Among the early users of lithography in this country was Nathaniel Currier, who learned the technique as an apprentice to William and John Pendleton of Boston. Currier set up his own shop in New York in 1835 and hired an artist, J. M. Ives. Ives later became a partner in the firm, and under the name Currier & Ives it produced lithographic prints that are still popular.

The first lithography presses were of the hand-operated, flat-bed variety. R. Hoe & Company introduced a power press in 1869, but real progress was delayed for twenty years until thin sheets of zinc replaced stones as the printing surface, and a direct rotary lithography press became possible. Actually, the switch to zinc plates wrapped around a cylinder made the term lithography (taken from *lithos*, "drawing," and *graphos*, "stone") a misnomer.

The process picked up its most common name, *offset* printing, as the result of the second accidental discovery. Ira Rubel, a New Jersey lithographer, was feeding paper into his press when he noticed that occasionally a surprisingly precise image would show up on the back of a sheet. This occurred when a sheet first failed to feed; the image was then transferred onto the impression cylinder and would appear with amazing clarity on the back of the next sheet.

Rubel incorporated the transfer, or offset, idea into a press he introduced in 1905. A special cylinder covered with a rubber blanket was used to receive the image from the plate and in turn to "offset" the image onto paper. The Harris brothers of Niles, Ohio, who were manufacturers of a rotary letterpress machine, also introduced a press with the plate-to-rubber-blanket principle in 1906.

First commercial use of an offset press was in the plant of the Republic Bank Note Company of Pittsburgh in 1906. This press and others to follow showed that offset lithography was an excellent means for producing quality illustrations on even the roughest papers. The resilient rubber blanket, because it squeezed the image into, rather than just on, the paper, made quality work possible on any surface.

About the same time the offset principle was added to presses, photography was adopted as a means of making lithographic plates. The ability to put the image on the press plate photographically was a giant step forward, but offset was slow to gain wide acceptance. Since World War II, however, it has been turning the printing world upside down.

One of the developments that spurred the recent use of offset was the introduction of *cold type* methods for setting type. Called cold type because they avoid the necessity of casting type from hot metal, these systems often rely on photography or are typewriter-like in nature.

THE ERA OF COMPETITION AND CHANGE

Offset's emergence as a behemoth of the printing industry is one of the significant current developments that mark post-1950 as an era of competition and change for graphic communication.

In 1950, for example, only one daily newspaper in the United States was produced on a web offset press; it was the Opelousas,

Louisiana, *World* with a circulation of about 10,000. By 1962, there were forty-two dailies and four hundred thirty-one weeklies pouring from web offset presses.

Scores of small magazines are printed by offset, as are some editions of major magazines. The five international editions of *Time*, twenty-one of the twenty-eight *Reader's Digest* foreign editions, and about 25 percent of each United States edition of the *Digest* are offset printed.[10]

In 1962 *Grit,* a weekly newspaper-format magazine with 900,000 subscribers across the country, put into use a three-hundred-fifty-ton, $2,000,000 offset press capable of producing 50,000 copies an hour of a seventy-two-page four-color newspaper.

Letterpress printing, however, continues to be the major process for mass production of words and pictures on paper, although offset is not its only competitor. Other processes, many of them with unique superiority for certain types of work, also call for the attention of users of printing.

The increasing importance of one method of printing is, of course, not the only consequential current development in the graphics of communication. It does exemplify the need that now exists for a greater breadth and depth of knowledge about techniques of producing printed materials. Anyone who plans a career with any medium of communication must be prepared to use any system skillfully. His finished product must also meet higher standards than ever before.

To be successful today, any printed material—newspaper, magazine, brochure, poster, newsletter, or what-have-you—must be prepared with a talent and finesse never previously asked for with such urgency. This demand stems, as did events during the Renaissance and Industrial Revolution, from the necessities of a society in the midst of great flux.

Television's booming voice and powerful image have changed many living habits of Americans, as well as the role in society that other communication media must play. Satellites, like Telestar, soaring in outer space, bring the promise and challenge of a global flow of information with consequences difficult to imagine for the world in general and communications in particular. The ever-growing population is making ever-widening demands for quick distribution of information. New industries and vastly altered old ones are requiring a continuing system of education via media of communications. In engineering and other professions graduates

[10]*Time,* March 16, 1962, p. 43.

are discovering, before the ink is dry on their diplomas, that significant new knowledge already outdates what they have just learned.

These developments mean that designers of printed literature must learn new methods and use old ones with dexterity in order to get the printed word into the minds of their readers faster and easier. The following chapters provide a foundation of knowledge necessary for the preparation of efficient, functional graphic communication.

Gutenberg's method remains the most-used system of printing today. However, his pressing of raised inked elements against paper or other surfaces to reproduce words and illustrations in quantity is only one of several processes available to publishers, advertisers, promotion men, and all users of printing. The development of a great variety of specialized needs plus technological advancements in other processes have pushed other methods to the fore as alternatives to traditional letterpress printing.

Photo-offset lithography is already a strong challenger, but many processes have their own particular value in graphic communications. To all journalism students, regardless of their specialized interests, each process is important because of its direct competitive relationship with the rest. Certainly future advertising and promotion men and magazine editors must be able to make comparisons and select printing systems in their work; and a growing number of newspaper publishers are conducting exhaustive studies concerning the feasibility of making basic changes.

the basic principles of common graphic reproduction processes

To understand the commercial systems in use today, it is necessary to give some attention to their basic mechanical or chemical principles (Figure 2-1). One or more of these five

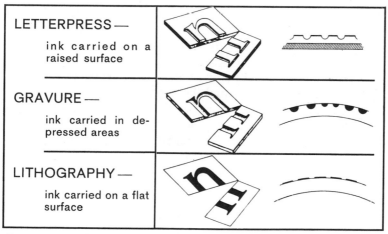

LETTERPRESS— ink carried on a raised surface

GRAVURE— ink carried in depressed areas

LITHOGRAPHY— ink carried on a flat surface

FIGURE 2–1. The three major printing systems. (Courtesy Lithographic Technical Foundation.)

principles serve as the basis for each printing method with a commercial application:

(1) Inking obtained by pressure against *relief* (raised) surface.

(2) Inking obtained by chemical action from a *planographic* (flat) surface.

(3) Inking obtained by lifting ink from an *intaglio* (engraved or depressed) area.

(4) Inking obtained by seepage through a stencil or screen.

(5) Images created on light sensitive surfaces through *photography*.

RELIEF, OR LETTERPRESS, SYSTEM OF PRINTING

Because it is the traditional system of printing, letterpress perhaps requires less explanation than other methods. There are, however, a number of characteristics of the system, and their ramifications, which must be noted.

It takes only a moment's thought to realize that letterpress can be defined as a direct, mechanical system of printing from raised surfaces. But the words *mechanical* and *raised* point to characteristics that are of considerable significance to anyone either preparing material for reproduction by letterpress or considering the system's quality and cost levels.

PRODUCTION STEPS IN THE LETTERPRESS PROCESS. For printing to be done directly from a raised surface, words and illustrations must, in some way, be "carved" or molded in relief in a substance sufficiently hard to withstand wear from constant applications of pressure. It should also be apparent that equality of pressure against the sheet being printed for all elements becomes a matter of necessity for a high level of quality in this process.

These two requirements point directly to three matters of importance to users of the letterpress process:

(1) In general, words and letters must be cast in metal to be reproduced.

(2) Any illustrations must be separately manufactured in plate form to be reproduced.

(3) Time and skill are required in "making ready" these elements so that the impressions obtained will be of high quality.

Let us look at each of these items to see how they are of importance to the journalist who works with the letterpress process.

Type Composition. The mechanical preparation of copy starts with a skilled technician called a *compositor.* He may operate a machine, such as the Linotype, Intertype, Monotype, or Ludlow type-caster, or he may set by hand the pieces of type stored in *cases* (drawers) in the composing room. *Hot Type* (molded from hot metal) is used mainly because of the cost factor. Compositors, who serve an extensive apprenticeship, are paid wages commensurate to their skill.

Plates for Illustrations. The manufacture of metal or plastic plates for reproducing illustrations by letterpress is another consideration of cost and procedure. Each photographic or other illustrative area in a letterpress-printed piece is reproduced from a *halftone* or *line* plate, or from a combination of the two. Illustrations in material prepared by letterpress thus constitute a significant variable where cost is concerned, for as plates increase in number, size, or complexity, so does expense.

Procedurally, platemaking requires the services of an engraver in addition to the printer and user. Copy for illustrations must be channeled through him, and his schedule must be correlated to the deadlines of the printer. Some printers have complete mechanical facilities, including equipment, so engraving can be taken care of on the same premises.

Much letterpress printing is done from *duplicate* plates—*stereotypes* or *electrotypes.* Publications using rotary presses, for example, are printed from stereotype castings made to fit over rotary cylinders. Molds for these castings are usually of papier mâché, shaped by pressure against the printing form. Thus, the impression of all the type faces and illustrations appear in the papier mâché *mat,* or *matrix.* Molten metal, when injected against the mat, hardens and forms a duplicate printing surface of the original page or form.

Also in use today are a number of electronic machines that produce plastic plates. Best known of these are products of Fairchild Graphic Equipment, Inc., called *Scan-A-Graver* or *Scan-A-Sizer.* Several similar machines available now make metal as well as plastic plates, both of which may be used directly or as originals for stereotypes.

Because they are usually leased and not sold, the machines let users (notably the publishers of small newspapers) include many large photographs in their publications at a virtually constant cost for materials and rental with no initial investment.

Importance of Make-Ready in Letterpress Printing. Theoretically, type set for letterpress printing is *exactly* 0.918 inches high, and all plates are mounted at *exactly* the same height. Perfect impressions depend upon these two factors. Perfection, of course, is seldom attainable, but it is sought in letterpress printing through a process of adjusting type and plates called make-ready. This is an extremely important part of the operation because it definitely establishes the level of reproduction quality and because it is so costly, requiring skilled labor and time.

When printing is done from type and original plates, fine press-work can be obtained only by carefully adding tissue paper under low areas and by cutting away packing where impressions are too heavy. This painstaking procedure is worthwhile for it insures results of the finest quality. Although operations similar to make-ready are involved in other processes, it is of far greater value to letterpress.

USES AND CAPABILITIES OF LETTERPRESS PRINTING. For several reasons, letterpress is a system of utmost importance to the student. It is the process used for the majority of printing in the United States; almost all newspapers and magazines are reproduced by it. In smaller communities letterpress may be the only commercial printing source available. Because of this, the methods of platemaking, types of presses, and other details of letterpress printing will be covered in separate chapters later in this volume. Meanwhile the student needs to be aware of its basic characteristics in order to compare it with others less commonly used but suitable for quite specialized purposes.

PHOTO-OFFSET LITHOGRAPHY

Photo-offset lithography, of increasing interest to everyone in the field of communications, differs from letterpress because it is: (1) *photographic;* (2) *planographic* (printing is done from a flat surface); (3) *chemical* in nature rather than mechanical; and (4) usually *indirect* rather than direct. Each of these can have an effect on editorial, as well as mechanical, procedures.

For example, the fact that it relies on photography for the preparation of copy prior to actual press operation means offset can employ several systems of type composition. Anything that can be photographed can serve as copy for offset lithography. Hence a typewriter or similar machine can be a composing machine; material so composed is generally called *cold type* because it did not have to be cast from molten metal. The traditional hot type may also be used provided a proof is taken so it can be photographed.

Why this feature is preferable for some editorial operations should be obvious: instead of being done by a skilled craftsman at some printer's shop, type for offset may be composed in a publication office. As typewriterlike machines become better adapted for such work, this feature becomes increasingly significant.

Combined with its photographic characteristic, the planographic nature of offset has a direct bearing on the use of illustrations. When an offset cameraman takes his photograph of copy, he is not concerned if line illustrations are on the same sheet with type material. Therefore such illustrations can be used in any quantity with no resultant effect on cost.

Other illustrations, such as photographs, must be handled separately because they have shades of tones and are not merely made up of line (full tone) or white (no tone) areas. Halftone negatives, made by exposing the original illustration through a screen onto film, must be made, but the planographic characteristic eliminates the need for etching separate metal plates with acid as is done for letterpress. This separate handling means some additional cost, but generally less than that for letterpress plates. Special treatments (unusual shapes, silhouettes, and the like) also can be achieved with greater ease. These and other characteristics of the offset process should become clear to the student as he understands the various steps in this system of printing (Figure 2-2).

Steps Involved in the Offset Process. The work of the offset printer may start with any one of several stages of copy preparation. For simplification, we shall assume until a later chapter that all art work and copy preparation prior to the photographic step has been completed by the buyer. Camera-ready copy for offset is usually in two part: Line material and halftone illustrations.

Making Line Negatives. The line work includes all headlines or titles, body copy, captions, and any line drawings or decorative devices. As they go to the cameraman, these items have been pasted with rubber cement to a piece of white cardboard. Each is in its proper position on the page or pages included in the paste-up, the halftone areas marked by guidelines or blacked in with India ink. The paste-up is then ready to be photographed the same size, enlarged, or reduced.

Cameras used to make negatives for offset are the same as those used by makers of photoengravings for letterpress printers. To photograph a paste-up of line copy, the cameraman simply loads

a. Line copy is pasted up.

b. Paste-up and halftone copy are photographed separately.

c. Negatives are developed.

d. Negatives are opaqued to eliminate undesired clear spots.

e. Negatives (line and halftone) are stripped into the goldenrod sheet.

f. Plate is cleaned.

g. Plate is coated (steps f and g are eliminated when presensitized plates are used).

h. Goldenrod containing negatives is placed over plate and exposed to light.

i. Plate is inked.

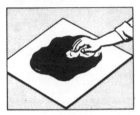

j. Plate is developed.

k. Plate is put on press cylinder.

l. Paper goes between rubber blanket and impression cylinder to receive ink.

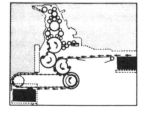

FIGURE 2–2. Principal steps in offset lithography. (Reprinted from *Printer 1 & C*, Navy Training Courses, U. S. Government Printing Office.)

the camera with film, puts the paste-up on the copy board in front of the lens, and makes his exposure. Thus a full page or pages, minus photographs, can be produced as a negative in a matter of seconds. The negative is then developed and dried.

Making Halftone Negatives. The photographs or other illustrations that must be made as halftones are treated separately, but in much the same manner. Before halftone copy can be photographed, a screen must be placed in the camera between the lens and the film. The screen breaks the image on the film into dots. One exposure is needed for line copy; halftones require several. The timing of the exposures and the development of the film are critical; it takes considerable skill to make halftone negatives that will give a clear, accurate reproduction of the subtle gradations of tones.

Preparation of the Flat. Once the halftone and line negatives have been made, they must be *stripped* into position in a sheet of opaque, ruled paper usually called a *flat* or *goldenrod*. An opening large enough to accommodate the line negative is cut from the flat, and the negative is fastened in place with cellophane tape.

At this point it should be recalled that the areas to be taken up by halftones may have been blackened on the paste-up. If so, they appear as clear spaces on the negative, for black reflects no light onto the negative, and, when developed, the film remains transparent. Therefore, the halftone can be taped into position behind these "windows," as they are called, completing the final step prior to the platemaking. If only guidelines are used to designate halftone areas, two other alternatives can be followed. The halftone area may be cut out of the line negative and the halftone taped in the hole. Or, if there is no room for tape around the cut-out window, a separate flat may be used for the halftone. In the latter case, the opening in the separate flat must be perfectly positioned so the halftone will be in its proper place on the plate.

Making the Plates. Platemaking is the next and final step before material goes on the press. Flat metal plates, usually of aluminum or zinc and about the thickness of the tin in tin cans, are used in offset. They are made light sensitive by either the manufacturer or the lithographer. The flat is fastened to the plate with cellophane tape and then "printed" in the photographic sense. Light is exposed to the plate through the negatives in the flat. If halftones are in a separate flat, the plate must be "double burned" by exposing one flat onto the plate after the other.

The burned plate is then developed. Any of several techniques may be used, depending upon the type of plate, but in principle it is much like developing a photograph. Rubbing the plate with chemicals hardens the emulsion in the exposed areas and causes the image to emerge.

Offset-Press Operation. Offset presses are rotary in nature and use the principle that grease and water do not mix to deliver the desired impressions on paper.

The printing section of the press includes a *plate* cylinder, an *impression* cylinder, a *blanket* cylinder, inking rollers, a moisture system, and a plate-adjustment (registration) device (Figure 2-3). In addition, of course, it has a *feeder* system to move the paper into the press and a *delivery* system for the finished work.

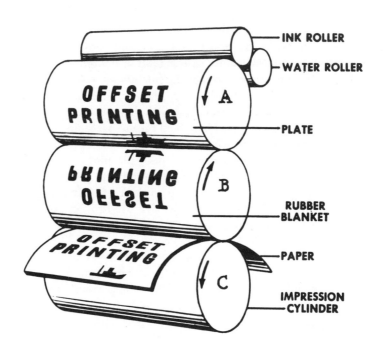

FIGURE 2–3. Principle of offset-press operation. As press cylinder (A) rotates, it is coated with water in the nonimage area and with greasy ink in the image area. The ink image is transferred to the rubber blanket on cylinder (B) and then to the paper as the latter passes between the blanket and impression cylinder (C). (Reprinted from *Printer 1 & C*, Navy Training Courses, U. S. Government Printing Office.)

That all material to be printed is on one thin, flat, and pliable plate is one of the virtues of the offset process. Make-ready is no problem, and the plate is easily wrapped around the plate cylinder much in the fashion that a mimeograph stencil is applied.

Once the plate is on the press, the operator must apply the moisture (water plus an additive) to the surface of the plate. The water adheres to the nonimage area of the plate and is repelled in the image areas. When ink, a grease, is applied, it adheres only to the image area and is repelled by the water-wet portions. Because of the water-grease action and its photographic nature, offset lithography is considered a chemical process.

It is called an *indirect* process because impressions are not made directly from the plate. The plate never touches the paper; instead it deposits the inked image on the blanket cylinder with each revolution. The paper receives the image from the blanket as the sheet or web goes through the press between the blanket and impression cylinders. The impression cylinder is simply the surface backing up the paper as the blanket squeezes against it—serving the same function as the platen in a typewriter or the bed of a traditional flat-bed press.

The student should be reminded that the original copy for an offset job is first converted to a negative, then to a positive image on the plate (type reads from left to right), and then to a reversed image on the blanket.

Each revolution of an offset press therefore consists of:

(1) Application of water to the nonimage area of the plate.
(2) Application of greasy ink to the image area of the plate.
(3) Transfer of the inked image to a rubber-blanketed cylinder.
(4) Pickup of the paper by the feeding system of the press, which inserts the paper between the blanket and the impression cylinders.
(5) Deposit of the image from the blanket to the paper.
(6) Delivery of the sheets or web of paper.

Although this may seem to be a lengthy series of details, it is accomplished instantaneously. Because offset presses operate on the rotary principle, they are capable of extremely high speeds. In general their speeds are basically determined by the efficiency of their feeding and delivery systems; the cylinders can rotate as fast as an electric motor can turn a drive shaft.

The most frequent problem in connection with offset press operation is the maintenance of a proper balance of moisture and ink. Changes in humidity sometime give pressmen a great deal of difficulty in this regard.

SOME ADVANTAGES AND USES OF OFFSET LITHOGRAPHY. Offset lithography's growing popularity is due to some advantages inherent to the process. These are most evident when complicated office forms, charts, or the like have to be duplicated from a job completed at a previous time. In these cases, type composition and the preparation of rules and certain kinds of illustration can be skipped entirely. All that must be done is to place one copy of the required form or chart in front of a camera and photograph it. Even with original jobs, this process has its advantages. The use of cold-type composition makes it increasingly adaptive to some types of work, particularly as cold-type machines become perfected.

Inexpensive illustrations, the ability to reproduce halftones on rough stock, the virtual nonexistence of make-ready as a time factor, high press speeds, and ease of plate storage are additional strong points. Plates can be coated and filed for future use with little effort; the flats can also be saved without taking up much shop space.

Offset printing has achieved perhaps its most spectacular gains in the widespread use of small presses by business concerns all over the country. Small offset duplicators turn out great quantities of letterheads, forms, price lists, sales letters, and similar items in offices everywhere, as well as in commercial printing plants. The process has also shown considerable growth in the production of magazines, direct-mail promotion pieces, and newspapers. Perfecting presses fed with sheets or from a web are fast and efficient and are gaining acceptance by many suburban and community newspapers.

GRAVURE PRINTING

The terms "gravure" and "intaglio" are used to describe the printing process in which images are transferred to paper from ink-filled depressions in a surface rather than from inked lines in relief or material on a flat surface.

A typical application of the process in its simplest form is the reproduction of calling cards or formal invitations. The lines to be printed are cut into the surface of a plate, the plate is coated with ink, then wiped clean, leaving ink only in the depressed areas. When paper is pressed against the plate, it picks the ink out of the depressed areas, thus coating the image in relief on the paper.

The simple engraved invitation can be considered only a distant relative, however, to the fine reproductions of works of art achieved by gravure printing. These are the result of adding photography to the process (*photogravure*); the ability to make these reproductions with high speed has come from the adaptation of the rotary-press principle to the process (*rotogravure*).

Photogravure is not as commonly used as letterpress or lithography because of the high initial cost for plates, but for long runs with a demand for great fidelity of reproduction of photographs and similar art work, it offers unique advantages. Generally speaking, the use of photogravure is not feasible for runs of less than 5000; for rotogravure the quantity needed should ordinarily be 100,000 or more.

PRODUCTION STEPS OF GRAVURE PRINTING. In some respects the steps involved in photogravure printing are similar to those of photo-offset lithography, at least in the early stages when photographic procedures are followed.

Making Negatives for Gravure. The first step in preparing gravure copy is to photograph the original. Different films are used for line copy and for halftone copy; a film that provides maximum contrast for line copy and solids; a minimum-contrast film for continuous tone copy. The negatives are then combined to form a film positive—a reproduction of the copy on a clear piece of film.

Transferring the Image to the Plate. In photogravure printing, a sensitized gelatin transfer sheet called a *carbon tissue* is usually used to transfer an image from the film to the plate. The carbon tissue is prescreened; that is, it is exposed to light through a screen in a contact printer before any attempt is made to transfer an image to a plate. The prescreening points up the difference in the function of the screen in gravure as compared to that in offset or letterpress platemaking. Here the screen performs only a mechanical task: it creates walls between ink wells to be etched on the plate and has no part in producing tonal qualities.

Screens used for gravure plates vary as to the number of lines per square inch, as do offset and photoengraving screens, but they differ in that the lines are transparent. The screen pattern made on the carbon tissue is, therefore, composed of opaque lines.

After this pattern has been exposed on the carbon tissue, the screen is removed from the contact printer, the film positive is put in its place, and light is directed through it. The gelatin surface hardens to the degree of the intensity of light that strikes it. The exposed carbon tissue then has ridges of completely hardened gelatin in the pattern of the screen (light of full intensity went through the transparent screen lines in the preprinting), and other

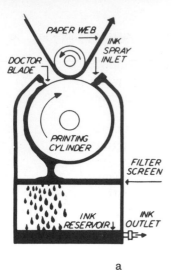

a

FIGURE 2–4. Production steps of gravure printing. (a) Basic principle of operation. Note how doctor blade scrapes excess ink from cylinder before ink is carried to paper from depressed areas. (b) Photographing copy. (c) Developing copy. (d) Retouching negatives and positives. (e) Sensitizing carbon tissue. (f) Cylinder with carbon tissue laid down preparatory to etching. (g) Staging a cylinder (painting out parts to be etched). (h) Etching a cylinder. (i) Engraving a cylinder. (j) Proving a cylinder to determine quality of etching. (k) A high-speed Goss Rotogravure Perfecting Press. This press contains 12 units, is 118 feet long, 22 feet high, 14 feet wide. (Courtesy of Alco-Gravure Division of Publication Corporation, Hoboken. N. J.)

b

c

d

e

f

g

h

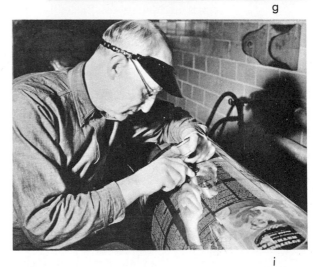

i

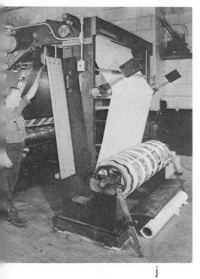

j

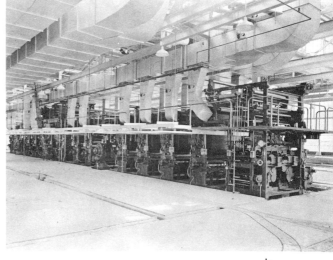

k

raised areas of gelatin of varying hardness according to the amount of light released through the film positive.

The gelatin deposits on the carbon tissues are transferred, in position, to a copper plate. The plate is then etched with acids that eat into the metal at depths determined by the hardness of the gelatin. The plate surface is thus composed of uniform, rectangular ink wells formed by the thin walls created by the screen pattern. These wells are shallow for light tones, deep for dark.

The plates described are conventional; some gravure plates are now made so that the ink wells vary in size instead of depth or, through a process called "News-Dultgen," both in size and depth. The latter process has been used particularly for color work.

Gravure Press Operation. High-speed rotogravure presses work on the same principle as that used in making simple calling cards or invitations. Basically, it is a matter of filling the wells with ink, scraping the excess ink from the surface, and applying paper to the plate with pressure (Figure 2-4a).

The rotary press plate is cylindrical and receives a watery, fast-drying ink as it revolves in an ink bath. The plate is scraped clean by a steel knife known as a "doctor blade" before it receives the paper, thus leaving ink only in the wells of the image area. Gravure presses are both sheet-fed and web-fed and vary in size and speed of operation.

USES AND CAPABILITIES OF GRAVURE PRINTING. The picture sections of Sunday newspapers, magazines, reproductions of paintings, and a great variety of product containers and wrappings are among the items printed by the gravure process. Its chief asset of reproducing highly faithful copies of photographs and paintings (both monotone and color) happens because the thin ink in the wells of the plate spreads enough during printing virtually to eliminate any screen or dot pattern. Also, because variations in tone result from the thickness of the ink deposit instead of from a dot pattern, photographs are reproduced with a special quality that cannot be otherwise achieved.

Type reproduction by photogravure is another matter. As pointed out earlier, type matter and illustrations are transferred together from a prescreened carbon tissue to the plate. Type matter is screened at the same time. Because of this and the watery consistency of gravure inks, the text material of a gravure job is less sharp than it would be if prepared by other systems. As a matter of fact, one of the means for discovering if a piece was printed by gravure is to check the fuzziness of type matter.

The use of gravure in commercial printing has expanded with the call for more printing on materials such as cellophane, new plastic films, and foil. But to the prospective journalist, gravure's special forte in printing remains the quality reproduction of photographs, usually in large runs.

SILK-SCREEN PRINTING

Based on a principle completely different from the three commercial printing methods discussed so far, silk-screen printing is relatively new. All the equipment needed for the most elementary kind is a wooden frame, some stencil silk, a material to block the pores in the silk, a squeegee, and paint or ink (Figure 2-5).

The silk, stretched tightly over the bottom of the frame and fastened, constitutes the printing form. A solid area is printed by putting paper under the screen and forcing ink through it with the squeegee. To form any desired image besides a solid, it is necessary only to block up the pores of the screen in any of the areas where ink should be withheld. A silk screen so prepared is called a *stencil*. It can be prepared in several ways.

PREPARING SILK-SCREEN STENCILS. The most common method involves the use of transparent paper to which has been bonded a film of lacquer. This can be used as a tracing medium by placing it over the material to be reproduced. A cutter traces the outline of the material with a knife, cutting and stripping from the paper the lacquer film in the areas that must be printed. The sheet is then bonded with a solvent to the silk screen, and the backing paper is pulled away, leaving the lacquer film to plug the screen in all nonprinting areas.

The main advantages of the lacquer-film method of stencil preparation are durability (runs of up to 20,000 are possible), ease of preparation, and a relatively high quality of result.

Some stencils, however, are prepared by hand painting with a brush, by photographic development, and with lithographic crayons and materials. The first is especially suited for stipple and dry-brush effects and requires great skill from the painter. The second is the most complicated of the methods, but is particularly effective for halftone and fine line reproduction. Lithographic materials are used mainly by artists for self-expression and for fine art reproductions; stencils so prepared result in beautiful work but are not suitable for long, commercially feasible runs.

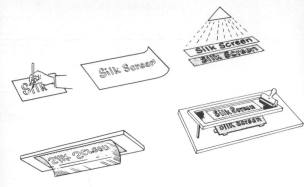

a

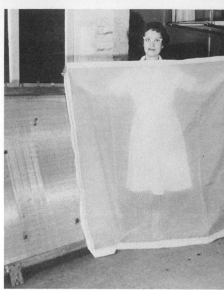

b

FIGURE 2–5. Silk-screen printing. (a) Basic process: Stencils are cut by hand or done photographically, stencil is adhered to underside of stretched fabric and backing sheet is peeled off; squeegee forces ink through stencil to paper underneath. (Courtesy Masta Display, Inc.) (b) A screen of porous silk. Various metallic-wire materials also are used for screens. (c) A photographically produced stencil has been applied to a screen and non-printing areas are being opaqued by a skilled craftsman (Photo-Art picture). (d) Here a stencil is being hand cut—open parts will become printing areas (Photo-Art picture). (e) Screen-process ink—often called paint—has the consistency of syrup. An ink man is shown measuring to a precise color formula. (f) A simple screen press. Ink in frame is pressed through silk by a hand drawn squeegee blade (Photo-Art picture). (g) A semiautomatic screen press requires positioning of paper by the operator but actual printing cycle is automatic. Note drying rack. (h) A 30- by 44-inch fully automatic screen-process press capable of printing up to 3000 sheets an hour. Unit is over 60 feet long. (i) The heart of the 30- by 40-inch screen press is the frame and squeegee, similar to the simple hand press in principle but fully automated. (j) The 30- by 44-inch press delivers printed sheets into a wicket dryer. Sheets can be air dried or baked dry in the heat tunnel through which the wicket passes. (Photographs b, e, g–j courtesy Kaumagraph Co., Wilmington, Del.)

e

i

e

d

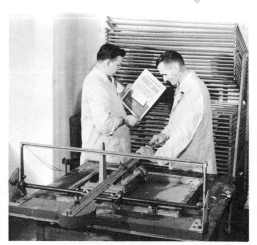

f

g

h

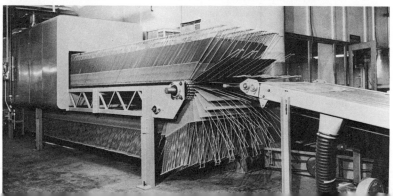

j

USES AND CAPABILITIES OF SILK-SCREEN PRINTING. Posters, displays, and fine art reproductions are perhaps the best-known uses of the silk-screen process, but it serves many other purposes. Because virtually any surface of any thickness may be printed on by this process (bottles, decalcomanias, machinery dials, wallpaper, and fabrics, to name a few), silk screen is considered whenever difficult problems with the other processes are present in a printing job.

The process has decided limitations. Although halftones can be reproduced by silk screen, the other processes offer much better results. One of its basic advantages, the ability to lay down heavy opaque layers of ink, is also a disadvantage because difficulty in drying occurs. Copies may have to hang individually on racks for as long as twenty-four hours before they can be stacked; consequently, the production rate may be extremely slow.

Although every effort is being made to mechanize the process and speed production, silk-screen printing remains, at least for the present, a process best suited for short-run work.

PHOTOGELATIN PRINTING

Although it differs because it does not require a screen for the reproduction of halftones and is a direct process, photogelatin printing is similar to photo-offset lithography in that it is photographic, chemical, and planographic.

PRODUCTION STEPS FOR PHOTOGELATIN PRINTING. Except for the omission of the screen as continuous-tone negatives are made, the first steps of photogelatin production are the same as those of photo-offset lithography.

Line work and photographs are handled separately and then stripped into position in a mask. After any needed retouching or opaquing, the mask is placed over a plate in a vacuum frame and light is directed through the negatives. Plates used in this process are coated with a thin film of light-sensitive gelatin. As light goes through the negatives and strikes the plate, the gelatin coating undergoes a chemical change that makes it moisture-repellent according to the amount of light received. It is this characteristic that makes photogelatin unique.

Instead of achieving variations of tones by a dot pattern or by the depth of ink receptacles, photogelatin gets its tonal range according to how much water the plate repels. In clear areas (not light-struck) the plates take a full coating of water that completely repels the thick ink. In areas struck by full light, all water is repelled and all ink received. Exact reproduction of the tones between these extremes is obtained as varying amounts of ink adhere to varying exposures on the plate.

USES, CAPABILITIES, AND LIMITATIONS OF THE PHOTOGELA-TIN PROCESS. Photogelatin printing is equal to or better than any of the other processes for the exact reproduction of photographs, paintings, and the like. Because it is a screenless process, it can produce true duplicates of the original. This is especially apparent, for example, in copies of old documents made by photogelatin—every flaw or symptom of age is faithfully reproduced. Photographs duplicated by photogelatin and glossed with varnish cannot be told from the original and can be used as original copy for the other printing processes.

Advertisers who want to show their products in the very finest detail consider the photogelatin process. Book publishers who want especially good reproduction of illustrations in a quality book turn to it. Some catalogues and sales or public relations presentations are also done by this process. In fact, photogelatin becomes an alternative to other printing methods whenever faithful reproduction of photographs or works of art is essential.

Its use is restricted mainly because it is slow and because plates cannot be carried over from one day to another, limiting the number of impressions. The cost involved in making a new plate daily for a long press run tends to make other systems cheaper for large jobs; with other printing systems the cost per copy goes down substantially as the number of copies increases.

Most photogelatin presses in the United States accommodate large plates (40 in. by 60 in.), but they produce only about eight-hundred impressions an hour. Although the rate of turning out small printed pieces can be increased by putting several on one plate, the photogelatin process is still slower than other systems.

XEROGRAPHY, A DRY PROCESS OF PRINTING

Xerography, a dry system of printing based on electrostatic principles, was demonstrated publicly for the first time in 1948. Although its early commercial applications have been mainly restricted to office photocopying machines, the process represents a revolutionary concept that may have considerable importance in the future.

Xerography uses no ink, no pressure, and no chemicals for getting reproductions on paper or other surfaces. Instead, a dry powder and the principles of photoconductivity and electrical attraction are used to create the duplicate images (Figure 2-6). Plates made of an electrically conductive material, such as sheet metal or foil, that have been coated with a photoconductive material are used to transfer images to paper. Sprayed with electrons, these plates become electrically charged and sensitive to light. They are exposed to an image pattern under a projection lens or in a camera or contact printing frame in the same way that standard photographic film or paper is exposed. Wherever light hits the plate, the electrostatic charge is discharged; wherever light is withheld (in the printing area), the charge remains. Powder is then applied to the plate, adhering to the charged area and falling away from the nonprinting (discharged) area.

The transfer of the image from plate to paper is accomplished first by charging the paper; as it contacts the plate, it attracts the powder; then heat is applied, melting the powder and fusing it to the paper. Thus the desired image is transferred (printed).

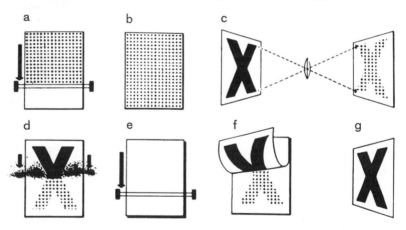

Figure 2–6. Principle of Xerography. (a) The surface of a specially coated plate is charged as it passes under wires. (b) Plate, when charged with positive electricity, has coating. (c) Copy (X) is projected through camera lens. Xs show projected image with positive charges. Positive charges disappear in areas exposed to light as shown by white space. (d) A negatively charged powder adheres to the positively charged image. (e) After powder treatment, a sheet of paper is placed over the plate and receives a positive charge. (f) Positively charged paper attracts powder from the plate forming a direct positive image. (g) The print is heated for a few seconds to fuse the powder and form a permanent print. (Courtesy Xerox Corporation, Rochester, N. Y.)

Complicated as it sounds, the xerographic process makes it possible to photograph a subject on a plate, develop the plate, and produce a positive print in less than a minute. It has been applied successfully to machines for copying letters, documents, plans, charts, and other such material, but it still must be considered in the developmental stage as a printing process.

It is important mainly to illustrate that new developments in the graphic arts are always possible and can have far-reaching effects in the future.

SOME MISCELLANEOUS REPRODUCTION PROCESSES

The preceding reproduction processes represent only a few of the total number, although they account for the bulk of large-quantity printing.

The term "printing" in its broadest sense includes the work of the photographer as he turns out photographs from negatives and of the typist as she uses carbon paper to make six copies of written material. These and other activities are often ignored or treated separately because their production capacity is minimal. But actually, any person who engages in communication through graphic means should view these and other limited processes as integral to the whole field.

Mimeographing, for example, is a duplicating system of considerable potential. A stencil process, it can fulfill many communication needs, such as newsletters, high school newspapers, instruction manuals, sales pieces, and interoffice communications.

Spirit duplicating is also used for similar purposes. It employs an aniline-dye carbon paper beneath a sheet of coated paper to make master copies that, when moistened with an alcohol-base liquid, deposit impressions on paper.

Used within their natural limitations, all duplicating processes are important means of transmitting messages. Choosing a process for any situation is a vital action because both effectiveness of communication and resultant cost are affected.

 selection of the process

The wide range of processes would seem to make the selection of one a rather difficult chore. In most cases, however, there are factors that immediately pare down the possibilities.

These include: (1) availability; (2) cost; (3) deadline; (4) number of copies; (5) type of paper; (6) use of photographs; and (7) quality level.

Many items are mimeographed simply because a machine is available, and the job can be turned out in a short time. Letterpress printing is used on occasion because it is the only process available locally for a job requiring top quality in both words and pictures. Offset lithography is used in a given instance because good quality reproduction of photographs on a textured paper is a necessity, and the press run is large. A newspaper publisher continues to use letterpress printing when a shift to offset might seem feasible because the change-over would require a greater investment than he can afford.

These examples merely give an indication of the various factors that influence process selection; they are not intended to represent a complete list of possibilities by any means. Nor can this chapter make the student professionally adept at deciding a process for a publication or a major printing job. It is hoped, however, that it has provided the descriptions essential for a communicator to work effectively with any of the processes.

3 Spoken and written words have always shaped the history of man. As a purveyor of this power, typography acts like the voice of an orator. Accents, emphasis, tones, and modulation let the speaker put across his ideas; the manipulation of printing materials serves exactly the same end.

As long as movable metal type was used for all printing needs, typography could be defined as the arrangement of printing materials to make effective printed communication. But the introduction of other means, such as photographic composition, as in offset lithography, necessitates a broader definition: *Typography is the planning of how printing materials should appear in order to make effective printed communication.*

Type is the primary element in typography. It is the medium for shaping words, which in turn convey thoughts. Certain secondary elements, illustration and decoration, supplement and reinforce the type, but the latter can stand alone, capable of delivering a completely effective message without auxiliaries.

Metal type, little changed from the time of Gutenberg, is still used for the majority of printing. Today, of course, it is cast by machine rather than by hand and is available in a great variety of faces.

For some time after the invention of printing, printers found one style of type in one size sufficient for their purposes. Then, with the passing of time came an ever-increasing demand for additional sizes and designs to enhance printed literature. As the expanding craft spread to other countries, changes reflecting the different cultures were effected by a sort of natural evolution. In Italy, for example, letter forms were developed that resembled the graceful characters in manuscripts prepared by Italian scribes. The basic Roman form, through the decades, has passed through so many mutations that today there are literally hundreds of type-face styles basically Roman yet subtly individualized.

Estimates abound but, to guess conservatively, there are 1200 to 1500 different faces. Counting variations in designs and sizes, the number can reach several thousands. No single printer or typographer can supply all, naturally, but a search of various firms will turn up any desired face.

The number continues to grow. Advertisers search constantly for fresh designs to give their efforts a distinction in their highly competitive field. People in the printed media are also interested in developing new faces to improve readability (legibility) and, at

...45

TYPE AND TYPE FACES

the same time, to cut costs by devising ways to get many printed characters in small spaces.

Selection of type is an important aspect of planning how printing should look. If a man's typographic design activities are limited to a single newspaper, he may need to familiarize himself with fifteen to twenty-five different type faces. On the other hand, a specialist in typography, dealing with large printing and typographic service houses, may make selections from literally thousands of faces.

Study and experience are the only ways to become proficient in selection. As a student broadens his familiarity with different faces, he soon realizes that certain characteristics assist him in distinguishing among them. As the capacity to recognize these grows, the ability to make sound selection develops.

The fundamentals that aid identification appear later in this chapter. Needed first is a consideration of the physical properties of type, the way it is measured, and its make-up.

 ## type materials

Type is made of metal or wood. The latter, generally maple or other hardwood, is used for *poster type*, so called because its major application is the composition of posters. Metal, most commonly used, may be divided roughly into two kinds: (1) foundry; and (2) casting-machine metal.

Foundry metal is used in *foundry type*, also called *hand-set type*. Not surprisingly, such type is cast in foundries and is purchased there by printers. Each letter and character is on a separate piece of type, except for *ligatures*—combinations such as fi, fl, ffi, ffl, and ff.

A printer's purchase consists of assorted letters and characters bought by the pound. He places them in type cases that contain storage compartments. When needed, foundry type is taken from its case, is composed, printed from, cleaned, and returned till the next use.

Because it wears in the printing process and because its distribution is time-consuming, most printing is done from type cast by the printer in his own shop from casting-machine metal. This is "melted down"—returned to original metal form—after use. It is then used again for casting other type. Thus "new" type is available for each printing, and the distribution problem is eliminated.

Casting-machine metals are lead, antimony, and tin, compounded in various percentages depending somewhat on machine requirements and particular shop practices. The same metals, often supplemented with other metals to increase hardness and dura- bility, are used in foundry type.

measurement of type

The face of a piece of type is the portion that receives ink and makes contact with the paper. It is raised above the *body* of the type, as shown in Figure 3-1. Note also that the body on which the face, *H*, rests is longer than the letter itself. The body length determines type size, and *points* are the unit of measure-

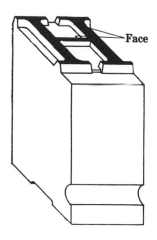

FIGURE 3-1. Type face and body. (Courtesy Ameri- can Type Found- ers Co., Inc.)

ment. Although 12 inches times 72 points is 4 points less than 1 foot, printers say there are 72 points to an inch for convenience sake.

Figure 3-2 shows the special rule that decides type size and other printing dimensions. It is called a "line gauge," "pica rule," or "pica gauge" and is made of wood, metal (steel, brass, alu- minum), or Vinylite. Along the edges are various units of gradu- ated measures needed by the printer and typographer. Usually this means inches by sixteenths are ticked off on one edge and *picas* and *nonpareils* (half picas) are on another.

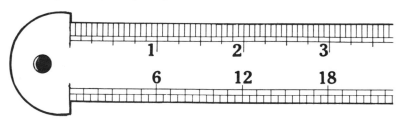

FIGURE 3-2. Type gauge.

Based on the point system, 1 pica equals 12 points, 1 nonpareil 6 points; 6 picas equals 1 inch. The pica is called upon to measure the following:

(1) Length of lines; that is, from left to right (horizontally).

(2) Width of columns; also a horizontal measurement.

(3) Depth of columns; that is, from top to bottom (vertically).

(4) Size of margins.

(5) Size of illustrations.

Illustrations are also referred to in terms of inches. Thus the reproduction of a photograph, printed size 4½ inches wide and 3 inches deep, can be spoken of as either 4½ by 3 inches or 27 by 18 picas. Note that width is expressed first.

DETERMINING TYPE SIZE

The procedure of measuring metal type with a line gauge is portrayed in Figure 3-3. The type is placed in the notch at the top of the gauge and measurement is taken along the proper edge. In this case the type is 5 picas (60 points) deep and can be referred to as 60-point type.

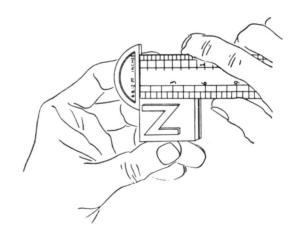

FIGURE 3-3.
Measuring type
size.

Different faces on bodies with the same number of points can vary in size because type size is the measure of body not of face. For example, the type on the left side of Figure 3-4 appears larger than that on the right side; indeed, its *center-body letters, s, a, c,* and *e* are, by design, greater than the center-body letters *a, c, e, i,* and *m* in the right side. Both faces are cast on 18-point bodies and are thus the same size.

This type face   abcdefghijklm

FIGURE 3-4. Both faces are 18-point, but one appears larger.

Another variant among faces with the same type size is the length of *ascenders* and *descenders*. The former is the portion of a face rising above the center body (as in *b, d, h*); the latter, the portion that falls below (*g, j, p*). The proportion that ascenders and descenders bear to the center body is not standard by any means and can differ from design to design as much as center-body letters.

In measuring by the pica rule, which is graduated in 6-point units, some considerations need to be kept in mind. Metal type ranges from 4-point to 144-point bodies. It is graduated by 2 points up to 14, jumps to 18, and thereafter increases by 6 until 60 points are reached; then units are added generally by 12 points at a time. This can be tabulated as follows:

6	18	48	96
8	24	54	120
10	30	60	144
12	36	72	
14	42	84	

Type sizes divisible by 6 are readily determined by measuring with the gauge. An 8-point body is slightly more than a nonpareil; 10-point is slightly less than 1 pica, 14-point slightly more.

Some of the commonly used type faces are available in 7-, 9-, and 11-point sizes. It would obviously be impractical to use the line gauge to distinguish 6-point from 7-point, 7-point from 8-point, and so on.

In addition to the above sizes, which are considered usual, there are occasional "odd" sizes available. Among these are 16-, 20-, 21-, 22-, 28-, and 34-point. These oddities can be found especially in the newspaper field. Many newspapers use a 5½-point size—called agate type—for classified ads, finding the size convenient for getting a large number of words into a minimum space. For editorial content, sizes such as 6¼-, 6¾-, 7½-, and 8½-point are available. These sizes have been introduced with faces specially designed to provide legibility while getting many words into little space.

Wood Type Sizes. Wood type size is the measure of capital letters. The height of the face itself determines the size, since the face fills the entire body with no extra space above or below the letter. Size is expressed in picas or more commonly in *pica lines.* Often reference is simply made to size as so many lines. Thus 5-line type is 60-point—but remember that this is when speaking of the measurement of the capital letter only. Other common sizes are 8-, 10-, 12-, 15-, and 24-line.

Determining Size of Type in Print. Frequently it is necessary to discover the size of type already in print. This can be done by taking a line of the printed specimen, placing a line gauge at the top of the highest ascender and measuring to the bottom of the lowest descender.

This indicates type size, but not whether it has been *set solid* (without extra space between lines) or *leaded* (with extra space between lines). Before one has an eye experienced enough to discern the difference between, say, leading of 1 or 2 points, it is best to decide the identity of the face and compare spacing between the lines of the printed material with the samples in a printer's *specimen book.* This is a catalogue of available faces, and samples are quite apt to be shown with and without various leadings.

 the type body

Helpful to anyone learning the art of typography is an understanding of the terminology relating to the parts of a piece of type (Figure 3-5).

The *face* is the letter or character that stands in relief atop the *body* of the piece of type.

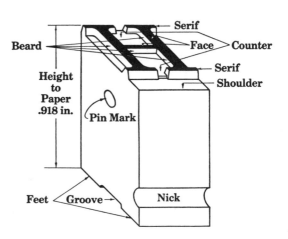

FIGURE 3-5. Parts of a piece of foundry type. (Courtesy American Type Founders Co., Inc.)

The type stands on two *feet* separated by the *groove*. The body must rest firmly on its base when printing. If type is "off its feet," as the printer expresses it, it leans to the side and does not print properly, since only a part of the surface of the face contacts the paper.

The top of the body is divided into *counters* and *shoulder*. The former refers to the areas within and around the face. The latter is the portion of the top below the face and above the *nicks*.

The *nicks* are sections cut across the body. There may be one, as in Figure 3-5, or several on one body. They serve a dual purpose:

 (1) To assist in identifying various faces. Type of a given size and face has the same nick or combination of nicks.

 (2) To indicate the bottom of a face, thereby preventing a letter from being placed upside down in a line.

The *beard* is the beveled part of the type between the face and the body, and the *pin mark* is made by the tool that separates the type from its mold at the time of casting.

Some type faces are cast so that an element of certain letters overhangs the body on which the face rests. This part is called the *kern* (Figure 3-6). Usually found in certain Italic and Script types, these are made so that the kern on a letter overlaps the next letter to achieve better spacing. (Italic and Script faces slant to the right and appear in greater detail later in this chapter.)

FIGURE 3-6.
Kerned letter.

The words "Height to Paper .918 in." appear in Figure 3-5 and refer to the distance from the bottom of the body at the feet to the surface of the face. This measurement is referred to as *type high*. All printing materials—type and auxiliary elements—must be at this height for proper printing.

Keep in mind that the terminology in this section applies to foundry or hand-set type. Type composed on casting machines is structurally different, as will be discussed later.

type classification

Obviously the qualified typographer should be able to identify type faces. But there are thousands available. To learn to recognize all—or even any substantial number—is an overwhelming task, especially if one tried to memorize them.

To facilitate recognition the typographer must familiarize himself with how type is organized. Once he understands this system, he is able to locate the faces that will serve his needs. Moreover, a knowledge of type organization enables him—through the experience of dealing with different faces—to learn to recognize many type designs.

Type is organized into (1) groups or races; (2) families; (3) fonts; and (4) series.

TYPE GROUPS

In the first classification of type faces, by races or groups, authorities are not agreed on how many divisions there should be. Some indicate four, others divide types into as many as eleven. But regardless of number, all are based on two considerations: the historical development of the faces and their structural form.

In this text type is divided into the following five groups or races, some with subdivisions: (1) Text; (2) Roman; (3) Gothic; (4) Script and Cursive; and (5) Decorative and Novelty.

TEXT. Today's type faces have their origins deep in the past. Early designers were inclined to fashion their faces on hand lettering. Gutenberg, Fust, and Schoeffer designed their type after the calligraphy found in German ecclesiastical manuscripts, and their adaptation of this characterized by heavy angular strokes, was used in the forty-two-line Bible, a portion of which is reproduced in Figure 3-7.

Many designs have evolved from the Gutenberg style and have become known as *Black Letter* and as *Text* types, since their source was the German texts. They have been used for centuries in German books and newspapers. The influence of Gothic architecture, too, can readily be seen in Text type faces. But the student should not call them Gothic, although the letter form echoes this style.

William Caxton (1422?–1491), the first English printer, used types fashioned after the German. For years thereafter these were the only faces used in England. There is, in fact, a Text face called

Old English Text and it is not uncommon to hear Text type faces described as having "an Old English look."

Quod cũ audisset david: descendit in
presidiũ. Philistijm autem venientes
diffusi sunt in valle raphaim. Et cõ-
suluit david dñm dicens. Si ascendã
ad philistijm· et si dabis eos ĩ manu
mea? Et dixit dñs ad david. Ascende:
q̃a tradens dabo philistijm in manu
tua. Venit ergo david ad baalphara-

FIGURE 3-7. Portion of the Gutenberg Bible.

Caxton was a merchant who became interested in printing as he carried on trading activities with the Germans and the Dutch. He introduced it to Britain, establishing a print shop and producing in 1475 the first book published in English—*Histories of Troy*.

A look at Figure 3-8, which shows a Text face, Cloister Black, explains why the use of Text faces is limited today and why only a few variations are extant: several lines are difficult to read. For this reason it is generally called upon for the following special purposes: (1) formal announcements such as weddings, graduations, and so on; and (2) headlines, short enough to be readable, in cases where the "feel" of Text is desired, such as in religious publications. The use of Text elsewhere seems out of place and typographically weak.

ABCDEFGHIJKLMNOPQRS

abcdefghijklmnopqrstuvwxyz

FIGURE 3-8. A Text face, Cloister Black.

It should never be used "all caps," as the printer expresses it, for such faces are designed specifically for printing upper and lower case (capitals and small letters). Legibility of words in all caps is greatly reduced, as indicated in Figure 3-9.

HARD TO READ

FIGURE 3-9. Head in all-cap Text is difficult to read.

ROMAN. Roman faces are a gradual development of Text based on the manuscripts of Italian scribes, who wrote lighter, more graceful characters than the Germans. Another strong influence, that of alphabets carved on ancient Roman buildings, is apparent in the capital letters of Roman faces. These alphabets consisted of capital letters only, but in copying them the Italian scribes developed a variation, a sort of lower case, in order to make their writing quicker and easier. These letters, known as miniscules, were adapted into the design of Roman faces.

A face cast in 1465 by Sweynheym and Pannartz, German printers who migrated to Italy, is said by some authorities to be the first Roman type, but other writers point out that their face, while a departure from Text, bore noted resemblances to it, particularly in respect to color and tone (see Figure 3-10).

FIGURE 3-10. Adaptation of Text by Sweynheym and Pannartz.

Murice iam croceo matabit uellera`luto.
Sponte fua fandix pafcentefueftiet agnof.
Ipfe lacte domum referent diftenta capelle.

This face also resembles that developed by Nicolas Jenson (or Janson) five years later. Jenson, who learned the art of printing at Mainz, set up a shop in Venice. His type face is generally credited as the first Roman type. Perhaps the dispute can be resolved by saying the Jenson face, shown in Figure 3-11, is the first *pure* Roman type. His types have been a model ever since. Cloister Old Style of the American Type Founders is an accurate reproduction of Jenson's type.

The earliest type designers looked upon printing as a method for giving greater dissemination to the work of those who lettered by hand. Thus it was only natural that they tried to make type faces resemble letters made by hand. But in 1524 a French printer and type founder named Claude Garamond produced a face basically original in style. Using the Roman and Italic letters of the day, he added distinctive touches of beauty that made his product preferred by most typographers. Because of its attractive and functional qualities, Garamond is still produced by type foundries and is in wide use.

William Caslon, an engraver, is also noteworthy for his contributions to the development of early Roman faces. Printing as an art took its greatest step forward in England in the early 1700s when he began designing and making type. His flair for lettering caught

VNC Autem teſtimonia etiam exteriorum de ipſis
diligenter citabimus. Illuſtriſſimi enim etiã græcorũ
nõ imperiti omnino iudaicæ philoſophiæ alii uitam
eorũ ſcriptis ſuis approbaſſe uidentur:alii theologiã
quantũ potuere ſecuti ſũt.Sic eim diſces nõ temere
ſed abſoluta exquiſitaq; ratione iudaicã philoſophiã gentilibus nugis
præpoſitam a nobis fuiſſe.Primum igit´ea ponã quæ de uita iudæorũ
præclariſſimi græcorum teſtantur.Theophraſtum igitur audias:cuius
nõnullos textus Porphyrius in his libris poſuit quos de abſtinendo a
carnibus cõſcripſit:his uerbis iudæi ad hæc uſq; tépora Theophraſtus
ait animalia quomodo ſacrificant? ut ſiquis nos ad imitatione illorũ
hortaretur audire non pateremur . Non enim comedũt ex ſacrificatis:
ſed mel atq; uinum noctu infũdunt holocauſta facientes:nihilq; inde
relinquentes:ut nec ille qui omnia perſpicit rem tam prauam iſpicere
poſſit:quod faciũt interim ieiunantes:ac quoniam philoſophi natura
ſunt de deo inter ſe colloquétes noctu aũt ſtellas aſpiciétes oratioibus
deum inuocãt.Primi enim iſti omninm hominum & bruta & ſe ipſos
offerre cœperũt:nulla neceſſitate aut cupiditate id faciétes.Et i quarto
eiuſdé negocii hæc a ſe ipſo ſcribit Porphyrius.Eſſæi iudæi genere ſũt:
hi alter alterum magis diligunt q̃ cæteri homines faciant:& uoluptaté

FIGURE 3-11. Roman face developed by Nicolas Jenson.

the attention of English printers. The types they had been using
were legible and adequate, but were mainly imports from Holland
and did not truly reflect the artistic traits of the English.

In 1722 Caslon gave English printers a type style that had all
the practical advantages of the Dutch types while adding characteristics that were strictly English. Now known as Caslon Old Style,
the new type rapidly gained acceptance in England and was put
to wide use on the continent. It is still a popular choice for all types
of printing in the United States and Europe. Its versatility has
caused many printers to follow the rule of "when in doubt, use
Caslon."

Faces of Roman letter form are the most numerous of the five
groups and literally hundreds have been developed. While they
are essentially similar in form, they may be subdivided into three
kinds: (1) Old Style; (2) Modern; and (3) Transitional.

Like Text faces, Roman faces have *serifs*. These are the short
crosslines placed at the ends of unconnected strokes of various
letters. A close examination reveals that they differ broadly from
face to face. They may be horizontal or inclined; generally the latter
in lower-case letters such as *m*, *n*, *u*, *r*, and *p*. Serifs may be heavy
or light, bracketed or unbracketed (the bracketed serif is curved
into the stroke to which it is attached), large or small.

Except for retaining the serifs, Roman faces differ from Text in that they are lighter in tone and have greater contrast of strokes within letters. Certain refinements distinguish Old Style, Modern, and Transitional.

Old Style. When compared to Modern Roman, Old Style faces are less formal in design. Contrast between thick and thin strokes is less pronounced. Comparison is made in Figure 3-12, with Caslon Old Style above, and Bodoni, an excellent example of Modern Roman, below.

FIGURE 3-12. Caslon, an Old Style face (above) and Bodoni, a Modern face (below).

ABCDEFGHIJKLMNOPQRSTUVWXYZ&
ABCDEFGHIJKLMNOPQRSTUVWXYZ&
abcdefghijklmnopqrstuvwxyz

ABCDEFGHIJKLMNOPQRSTUVWXYZ&
ABCDEFGHIJKLMNOPQRSTUVWXYZ&
abcdefghijklmnopqrstuvwxyz

It should be noted that Old Style serifs are rounded or oblique and curve into the strokes. They are, in the language of the typographer, bracketed.

Modern. The most notable difference between Old Style and Modern is in the serifs. In Modern faces they are straight and thin, and unbracketed. In general, they present a geometric appearance, seem "squared off" and formal. It is as if they were studied or mechanical in design, while Old Style faces seem to be more hand-drawn or less restricted.

Giambattista (John the Baptist) Bodoni, an Italian, brought type design to what many consider the ultimate of perfection about the time of the American Revolution. He had learned printing at an early age in his father's shop and later apprenticed in Rome at the printing plant of the Catholic church. After he set up his own shop, his fine work won the attention and support of the Duke of Parma, who brought Bodoni to that city to direct its printing activities. The face we call Bodoni was developed there.

In its day Bodoni was thought of as a classical face. The term "Modern" is meaningless in the real sense of the word, for it was modern more than a century and a half ago, but the term persists in the Anglo-American trade.

Transitional. These Roman faces have characteristics of the Old Style and the Modern. Because of this, many authorities do not classify them separately, placing some of them in the Old Style group, others in the Modern, depending upon which they seem most closely to resemble.

It is often difficult to distinguish transitional from the other two. Historically they developed when designers, in an attempt to improve legibility of the Old Style faces, redesigned the alphabets by concentrating on increasing contrast between thick and thin strokes.

Baskerville is one of the most popular transitional faces. It was developed about 1752 by John Baskerville, an Englishman, who remodeled Caslon Old Style. His work was not too widely accepted in England, and Bodoni adapted certain features of it to develop a pseudoclassical style in keeping with French decor at the time of Napoleon.

In Figure 3-13 Caslon is shown above and Baskerville below. Increased contrast between the two faces is obvious. It will be noted, however, in referring back to Bodoni (Figure 3-12), that Baskerville does not have so sharp a contrast as the Modern Roman face.

Other transitional types include Century, Scotch Roman, Bell, Bulmer, Nicolas Cochin, De Vinne, and Electra.

ABCDEFGHIJKLMNOPQRSTUVWXYZ&
ABCDEFGHIJKLMNOPQRSTUVWXYZ&
abcdefghijklmnopqrstuvwxyz

ABCDEFGHIJKLMNOPQRSTUVWXYZ&
ABCDEFGHIJKLMNOPQRSTUVWXYZ&
abcdefghijklmnopqrstuvwxyz

FIGURE 3-13. Caslon (above) and Baskerville, a transitional face (below).

GOTHIC. The so-called Gothic faces are second only to Roman, both in number and frequency of use. Their general appearance is *not* Gothic, however, for, as noted earlier, it is the Text faces that reflect the Gothic style of architecture. The name persists despite its inaccuracy.

Gothic faces are monotone and skeletal in appearance. Introduced early in the 1800s, it originated as a symbol of protest against the traditional face of Caslon and the neoclassicism of Bodoni. These faces, or adaptations of them, were widely used in Europe and America.

Inspiration for the development of Gothic faces came with the Industrial Revolution. When the shift from manpower to machine power made its impact on the printing industry with the introduction of the steam press, a number of Gothic faces were cast between 1800 and 1850. The first was called "Doric," and it is interesting to note that it was introduced by the H. W. Caslon & Company, originally founded by the William Caslon mentioned above.

Letter form for Doric was in the style of classic Greek characters, which bore strokes of uniform width. It is no accident that the designer turned to classical Greek as an expression of a new mood. It was at this time, 1801, that the Seventh Earl of Elgin dispatched portions of the frieze and sculpture from the ruins of the Parthenon to be housed in the British Museum. Architects and artists of the day set about to marvel at and study the basic simplicity of Doric structure.

It was not until the 1920s that the simple purity of Gothic faces caught the fancy of designers. Gothic then became the letter form best capable of expressing the tempo of functional modernism in the arts. This term refers to a "new" style of expression, independent of the historic and the traditional. It is a movement still alive in the various arts—music, painting, architecture, sculpture, and literature.

The effects of functionalism were brought to bear on typography through the Bauhaus Institute. Established in Germany in 1919, this school was dedicated to revitalization of design, primarily in the areas of architecture, painting, sculpture, typography, and industrial design.

The Bauhaus was devoted to a break with tradition. Its advocates proclaimed that the spirit of the machine age—as contrasted with the age of handicraft—should be essentially scientific, for the machine is best capable of producing, economically and artistically, simply structured, unadorned surfaces.

In actuality, however, the Bauhaus break with tradition is not a break at all. As we have seen, each period in history produces a typographic style that bespeaks its time. The mood of the twentieth century is in the Gothic faces. Bodoni, too, also found favor with the Bauhaus evangelists whose expression has also been felt in the broader area of printing design.

There are several other labels applied to the Gothic group or race, used as synonyms for Gothic. They are *Sans-serif, Block Letter,* and sometimes *Contemporary.* Sans-serif is the French for "without serifs." This term is frequently used, since it describes one of the major characteristics of these faces. Another major characteristic is found in the strokes of approximately the same weight. The marked contrasts of thick and thin strokes in Roman faces are missing in the Gothics. Figure 3-14, showing Vogue type, illustrates a typical face. Although some Gothic faces carry slight variations in strokes, the over-all monotone effect is retained (see Futura, Figure 3-15).

ABCDEFGHIJKLMNOPQRSTUVWXYZ
IIII2222333344445555666677778888899990000$$$$

ABCDEFGHIJKLMNOPQRSTUVWXYZ&
abcdefghijklmnopqrstuvwxyz

FIGURE 3-15. Futura.

Gothic faces are popular in display or headline use, but when used in smaller sizes for presenting the body message, they give a monotone appearance in the large area and tend to become un-inviting. They are, therefore, apt to be used for the text of short messages only.

Square Serif Types. There are several faces available that might be described as Gothic types with serifs added. These faces present something of a problem in classification. Because of the basic evenness of strokes and serifs, we shall consider them a variation of Gothic. Shown in Figure 3-16 is a sample of Stymie, one such face.

ABCDEFGHIJKLMNOPQRSTUVWXYZ&
abcdefghijklmnopqrstuvwxyz

FIGURE 3-16. Stymie, a square-serif Gothic.

SCRIPTS AND CURSIVES. These faces imitate handwriting by pen or brush; the most distinctive difference between them is that Cursive letters are not joined, while Script letters appear to be.

The latter are carefully designed so that when any two letters fall side by side, the gap between is scarcely discernible. In Figure 3-17 a Cursive type face, Coronet, is shown above, and a Script, Commercial Script, below.

Most of the faces in this group slant to the right, as is the case with most handwriting. A few, however, are upright.

ABCDEFGHIJKLMNOPQRSTUVWXYZ&
abcdefghijklmnopqrstuvwxyz

ABCEFGHIJKLMNOPQRSTUVWXYZ&
abcdefghijklmnopqrstuvwxyz

FIGURE 3-17. Coronet (above) and Commercial Script (below), examples of Cursive and Script faces.

Like Text faces, they are difficult to read in large areas. Consequently, they are generally used for display when an air of grace and charm is desired. In addition, because of the atmosphere of personal intimacy they engender, they are often used on letterheads, social invitations, and calling cards.

DECORATIVE AND NOVELTY. This group cannot be defined so that a face with required characteristics can be placed in it. It is, rather, a catch-all bin into which faces that cannot be classified as Text, Roman, Gothic, or Script-Cursive are tossed.

A number of these faces might be called "mood" faces in that they give a period, place, or mood connotation. Examples, shown in Figure 3-18, are Legend, P. T. Barnum, and Typewriter.

FIGURE 3-18. Legend, P. T. Barnum, and Typewriter, examples of "mood" faces.

The remaining types might be referred to as Novelty faces. Their design characteristics vary so widely from those of the other four groups that Novelty remains the only logical classification. Lydian, Hobo, Cartoon, Neuland, and Broadway, shown in Figure 3-19, are examples. Lydian is often classified as sans-serif.

FIGURE 3-19. Lydian, Hobo, Cartoon, Neuland, and Broadway, "novelty" faces.

It is, however, better qualified for placement here because of the notable contrast between strokes. It lacks the simple skeletal structure of Gothic.

TYPE FAMILIES

Families must be mentioned in a discussion of type groups. For example, our consideration of Roman included Caslon, Bodoni, Baskerville, Century, Scotch Roman, Bell, Bulmer, Nicolas Cochin, De Vinne, and Electra. Likewise, several Gothic faces were named.

How the various design elements, or parts of the type face, are handled sets one family apart from another, for they are manipulated in the same way for every family member. An adequate definition of family might be: a group of type faces closely related in design, such as the "Caslon family" or the "Bodoni family."

FAMILY VARIATIONS. Within type families may be a number of variations, but regardless of members, the basic family design characteristics remain, related to width, weight, and posture. Width variations refer to the extension or condension of letters and include *condensed, extra condensed,* and *extended* (or *wide* and *expanded*).

Several degrees of weight—that is, whether strokes are relatively light or heavy—range through *light, medium, demibold, bold,* and *extrabold* (*heavy*).

Types with postures that slant right are called *italic,* except in the Script or Cursive families.

Because of these three factors, type faces are more specifically labeled according to their variations in the family. In other words, it is common to speak of a particular face as Futura Bold Condensed Italic.

Some authorities list italic as a separate race or group; in this book it is termed a family variation. Its name was derived from Italy, its country of origin, and Aldus Manutius is credited with its first use in 1501. He was a teacher, as well as a printer, and he used the new style of type to provide reading matter for those who could not afford the high prices then charged for books. Because the letters in this new type style were spaced much closer together than other types, he could get more on a page and reduce the size and cost of his books.

In the original form italic was composed of lower-case letters of slanting posture. Capitals remained upright. Later designers gave the slanting posture to the capitals also, and today the term "italic" is used to describe faces of either derivation—Gothic or Roman —provided only that they be characterized by the slanting strokes.

For decades italics were separate type faces. We term italic a family variation now since in practically every case the italics have been designed by adapting them to already existing faces.

The term "oblique" is applied to some faces in lieu of the word "italic."

The upright version of a face is called "roman" by printers. This is true regardless of group; that is, there may be Cheltenham roman, as well as Futura roman. The latter seems to be inconsistent, since Futura is obviously a Gothic face. But trade practice dictates that "roman" is the opposite of italic. This enables one to say to a printer, "Set this in Futura roman," rather than to say the confusing "Do not set Futura italic."

All the possible variations do not exist within any one family. The Cheltenham family has perhaps the largest number. Following are many faces that exist under this name:

Cheltenham Old Style

Cheltenham Old Style Italic

Cheltenham Old Style Condensed

Cheltenham Wide (Monotype)

Cheltenham Wide Italic

Cheltenham Wide (Linotype)

Cheltenham Medium

Cheltenham Medium Italic

Cheltenham Bold (Linotype)

Cheltenham Bold (Foundry)

Cheltenham Bold Italic

Cheltenham Bold Condensed

Cheltenham Bold Condensed Italic

Cheltenham Bold Extra Condensed

Cheltenham Bold Extended

Cheltenham Bold Outline

FONTS

A *font* consists of the assortment of letters, figures, and punctuation marks that constitute a branch of a family in one size. By branch we refer to a variation. Thus, the printer speaks of a font of Cheltenham Bold or of Cheltenham Medium Italic, for example.

Occasionally a character from another font will appear in type matter, due to a mechanical error. Usually it is obvious, since its design is likely to be incompatible with the family with which it appears. The printer terms this out-of-place character a "wrong font," (or simply "wf") a term that denotes an error to be corrected.

SERIES

The range of sizes in a family branch available from a printer or compositor is termed his "series." Thus, in Cheltenham Bold, the printer may say his series consists of 5-, 6-, 7-, 8-, 10-, 12-, 14-, 18-, 30-, 36-, 42-, and 60-point.

how to identify type

Pinpointing the name of a given face—that is, identifying it—is often a difficult task, even for an old pro. Though type faces may often seem to be alike, they are not. The differences exist in the design elements of the faces.

Clues to identity may be found in examining any of the letters of the alphabet, and a good typographer will do just that when necessary. But it is reasonably safe to make the generalization that a study of the upper case *T* and *A* and lower case *g, e, r, t,* and *a* will suffice. These letters will stay in mind if one can remember that together they spell *TAgerta.*

Serifs, too, are often helpful. So are ascenders and descenders. As discussed earlier, the former rise above the center body or *x-height* letters of the font, as in *d, b, l,* and *h.* The latter fall below, as in *q* and *p.* The size of the x-height and the comparative length of ascenders and descenders are particularly significant in type identification.

The *set* of letters in a font may be helpful. Set is *close* when there is little space between letters in a composed line. This is due to the fact that the letters fill—or nearly fill—the top of the body laterally. Some types have a *wide* set and at the same time a small face.

Contrast between *thick strokes* and *thin strokes* may aid.

Treatment of the *bowl*—the rounded portion—of the letters *a* and *e* varies notably among type faces as does that of the two bowls in the letter *g*. And the position of the *hook* or *ear* on the top bowl of the latter may offer another clue.

 ## conclusion

To the beginner in typography, type faces may seem to look alike. Even after an introduction to the methods of type classification, he is likely to feel overwhelmed by what seems a bewildering complexity.

But with experience the student discovers an increasing capacity to recognize various faces. He is helped by clipping type samples from current publications, checking them against type specimen books, and noting their established identities in a file.

Sometimes identification can be found only after most careful study of several letters of the alphabet, matching them against specimens, comparing the design elements, or parts of the type face, mentioned in this chapter.

There is no point, of course, in learning to recognize a large number of faces simply as a feat of memory. After all, recognition is a means to an end. The typographer is constantly faced with the situation in which he must match a face previously printed, or choose faces to carry a printed message purposefully. His ability to identify facilitates his selections.

Type helps to create a feeling or atmosphere in printed material —a significant factor in building effective communications. It is more than a gray mass, for it has texture and color as the result of its design. Only through a knowledge of the different faces can the typographer qualify to select the proper faces for the task at hand.

4 To give instructions to the printer concerning his plans, the typographer must have a full knowledge of the measurement system standard throughout the industry. In the previous chapter points and picas, basic units of measurement, were introduced. They now must appear in further detail.

the point system

All type measurement is based on the point system. The point is the smallest unit in the system, about 1/72d of an inch. Actually it is 0.013837 inches, which means that 72.46 points are required for one inch, but for general purposes it is sufficiently accurate to say 72 points equal one inch.

Two other units of measure are part of the system. They are the nonpareil and the pica. Six points equal a nonpareil and 12 points equal a pica. There are, therefore, six picas in an inch.

THE EM

The *em* is related to the point system although it is not, in a strict sense, a part of it. Moreover, it is a unit of measurement of *quantity of type,* rather than a unit of linear measure, as are the pica and the point. A typographer will sometimes use the term "em" to express linear measurement, but his reference is actually to the pica.

An em is a square of the type size. There are 6-point ems, which are six points square; 8-point ems, which are eight points square, and so on.

The term "em" came about when the lower-case letter "m" was usually cast on a square body having the dimensions of the type size. This is not usually the case today. The bodies of various letters in a font vary in width but share the same depth. For example, an *m, i, u,* in 8-point are all eight points in depth of the body, but their widths are different. An em of the same font, however, is always as wide as it is deep.

At one time printers referred to type sizes by name rather than by points. For example, 5½-point was known as *agate* type; 6-point was referred to as *nonpareil,* and 12-point was called *pica* type. It was the pica em (12-point) which became the standard unit of linear measure. Because of this, in referring to

... 65

various measurements the typographer and printer may refer to a column as being 11½ picas wide or 11½ ems wide.

As stated above, the em can be used as a measure of quantity of type. This does not mean pica ems but ems of a specific type face, or, as they are sometimes called, *set ems*. Machine composition is often calculated and sold on the basis of so much per 1000 ems (set ems). One would calculate the number of ems in a space 15 picas wide and 7½ inches deep, 10-point composition, as follows:

$$15 \times 12 = 180 \text{ points}$$
$$180 \div 10 = 18 \text{ (10-point ems in a line)}$$
$$7½ \times 72 \text{ (points per inch)} = 50$$
$$540 \div 10 = 54$$
$$54 \times 18 = 972 \text{ ems (set ems)}$$

If there had been 15 inches of depth, there would have been 1944 ems, or 1.94 units of 1000 ems. This method of calculation is useful for so-called *straight matter,* which is type composed in regular running paragraphs, requiring no special make-up as would be required in setting in headlines or making up tables. Set ems are also useful in copy fitting, which is calculating how much space is needed for a given number of words when they are set in type. This will be discussed later.

To summarize, the word "em" has two meanings:

(1) The square of the type in question (a set em).

(2) The standard unit of linear measure, when used as a synonym for pica. This can usually be discerned from context.

THE AGATE LINE

Another unit of measurement used by the printer bears mention here, although, like the em, it is less related to type measurement than to the point system. It is the *agate line* and appears on many line gauges.

Actually the agate line, sometimes called simply the *line,* is a measure of advertising space. Cost of advertising is often quoted by the agate line. It might be defined as being 1 column wide and 1/14 inch in depth. The term "agate" comes from the name for 5½-point type, mentioned above. Although 14 x 5½ is more than 72, the number of points in an inch, the custom of computing 14 per inch prevails.

The student should be on guard against confusing agate lines and lines of type. When, for example, we refer to an ad of 28 lines, we mean an ad 2 inches deep and 1 column wide—written 28 x 1— or 1 inch deep and 2 columns wide—14 x 2, spoken of as "fourteen on two."

OTHER USES OF THE POINT

The point is also used by the printer to measure the size of *line-spacing materials;* that is, the strips placed between lines of type to provide additional space. There are three kinds: *leads* (pronounced "leds"), *slugs,* and *reglets.* The first two are made of type metal and may be cut to any desired pica length. Leads are 1-, 2-, or 4-points thick, most frequently 2-points; slugs are usually 6-points.

Reglets are made of kiln-dried hardwood, treated to resist moisture. They are usually 6- and 12-points thick and are available in yard lengths, from which desired pica length can be cut. They are used instead of leads and slugs, and are also available in fonts, which consist of 6- and 12-point reglets, cut to various pica lengths.

Reglets, leads, and slugs are nonprinting and have to be less than type-high so that they will not pick up ink.

The point is also used in measuring *rules* and *border,* both of which are printing materials and are, consequently, type-high. Rules are used for printing lines of various thicknesses. They are usually made of type metal but are also available in brass, steel, or plastic. There are many styles—a single line, double line, multiple line, and dotted line. The latter are often called *leaders.* Special steel rules with fine teeth may also be used for perforating. These are slightly above type-high and press into the paper during printing. The perforated line is ordinarily inked.

Another special rule, known as *scoring* rule is available for creasing heavy papers to make exact folding possible. Also made of steel, these rules, like perforating rules, stand slightly above type-high. Unlike perforating rules, they do not cut into the paper but compress it.

Hairline—6 pt. Body

1½ pt.—6 pt. Body

3 pt.—6 pt. Body

6 pt.—6 pt. Body

Hairline—2 pt. Body

1½ pt.—2 pt. Body

2 pt.—2 pt. Body

FIGURE 4-1. Various size rules.

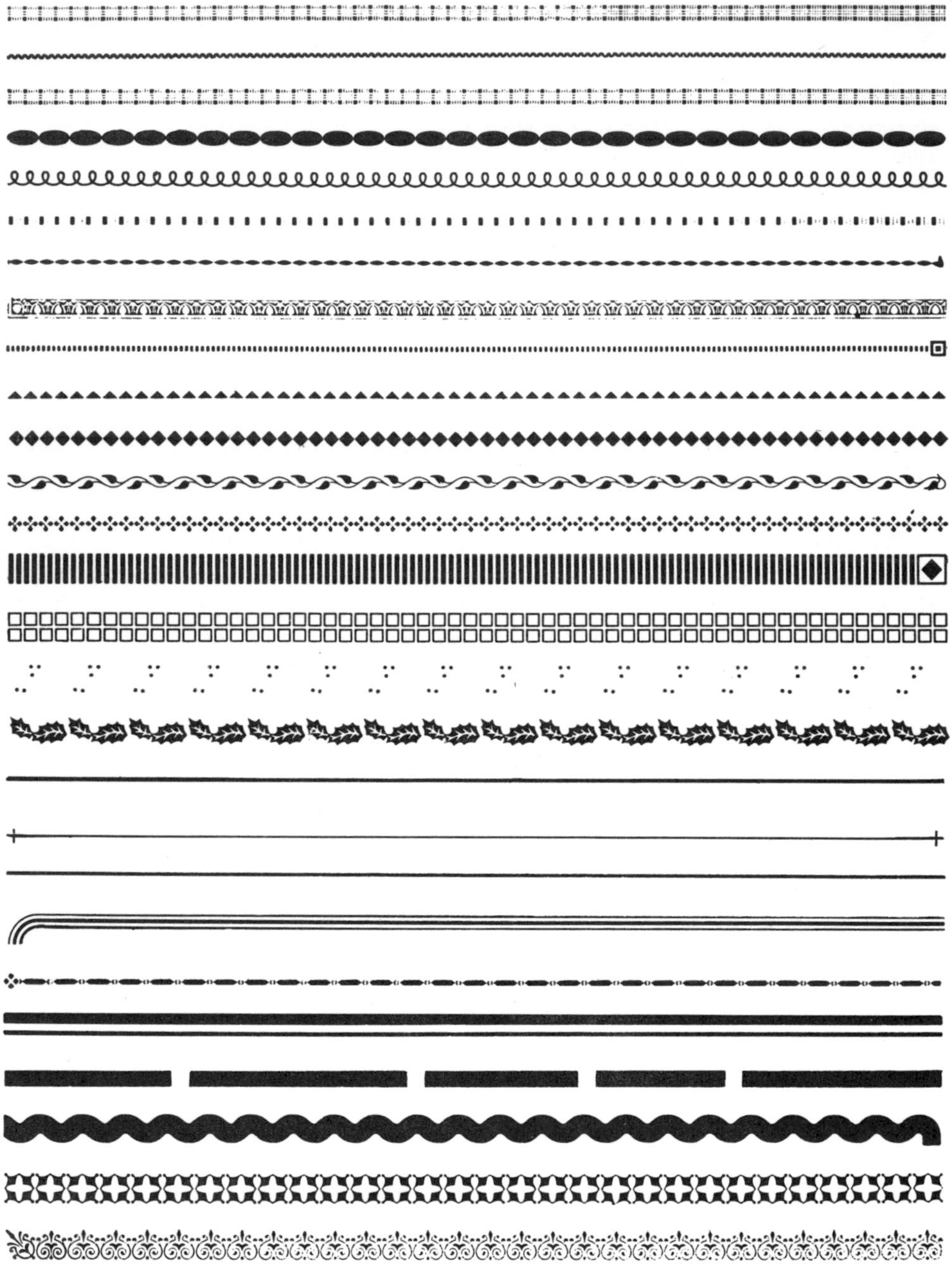

FIGURE 4-2. Border materials.

In designating the size of rules, the printer usually refers to two measurements, the size of the printed line and the size of the body of the rule which supports the printed surface (Figure 4-1). Note that the line may be as thick as the body but is not always so.

Borders, like rules, are available in strips, to be cut to desired pica lengths as needed. Border materials are more decorative than ruled lines (Figure 4-2). Measurement of a border rule indicates the thickness of the body.

The point is also used for indicating the size of *dashes, braces, parentheses, brackets, ornaments, initial letters, special characters,* and *logotypes.*

Dashes have a wide variety of uses in typography. Newspapers occasionally use them to separate the decks in a headline, and both magazines and newspapers may use them between stories and articles. They are cast on either the Linotype or Intertype composing machines on column-wide slugs of varying point thicknesses to and including 24-point.

    ———————   Figure 4-3. The jim dash.

    ————————————   The 30 dash.

    ————————————   The ornamental dash.

Three kinds of dashes are shown in Figure 4-3. At the top is a *jim dash,* used to separate headlines from stories or to insert between related items. In the middle is a *30 dash* or *finish dash,* generally used to separate unrelated items, as does the *ornamental dash,* shown at the bottom. The use of dashes is on the decline, as white space becomes increasingly popular for separating items.

Examples of *braces, parentheses,* and *brackets* are shown left to right in Figure 4-4.

Figure 4-4. Braces, parentheses, and brackets (left to right).

Many *ornaments* are available for printing, but few printers stock a wide variety because so many of them take the form of florets and embellishments, used seldom in modern typography.

Initial letters may be conventional or decorative, as shown in Figure 4-5. Again, their use is restricted today.

The term "special characters" covers a wide range of symbols

Figure 4-5. Decorative initial letters.

and characters. For example, advertising figures (large numerals), fractions, *percent* symbols, dollar and cents marks, prescription marks, number marks, and playing card indicators are stocked by many printers.

The word *logotype* here refers to whole words set on one body, sometimes combined with a design to identify a product, a firm, or an organization. Various logotypes are available in different sizes from type foundries or in matrix form for use in casting machines. Frequently used words may also be available in logotype form.[1]

As a final observation concerning the point—the printer may refer to the thickness of heavy-weight cover paper as being so many points thick. In this application the term "point" refers to 1/1000th of an inch and should not be confused with the point as used in type measurement.

 hand composition

For more than four centuries, from the time Gutenberg developed movable type until the coming of typesetting machines, hand composition was the only method of preparing printed matter for publication.

Even today hand composition remains a significant method of setting type. In fact, as reported by Jackson, ". . . the production of foundry type, made to be set by hand, is greater today than ever before—even greater in tonnage than it was before machines were invented, when all type was set by hand."[2]

Most type is set today by machine, of course, but hand composition remains important primarily because of the demands of advertisers. They are in constant search for display (headline) faces

[1]Logotype also refers to any type body or any matrix on which two or more letters appear together. The letters are frequently used combinations, and unlike ligatures, are not joined.

The term also refers to the name of an organization or product made into an engraving. While the latter or even a duplicate of it—such as an electrotype or stereotype—is not a piece of type, it may be referred to as a logotype.

Naturally, the term is applied to a print from any of the above.

[2]Hartley E. Jackson, *Newspaper Typography* (Stanford, Cal.: Stanford University Press, 1947), p. 42.

that are "out of the ordinary." Consequently, many printers and composition houses[3] carry styles of foundry type not available on machines.

The typographic rules that govern machine composition are basically the same as those for hand composition. Many students of typography become acquainted with type and the rules governing its use through training and actual practice in hand composition. Since there is no better way to learn than by doing, many schools with courses in printed communications require lab work in hand composition.

THE JOB CASE

Hand-set type is stored in metal or wooden trays, called cases. Each case contains a font and is divided into a number of different-sized compartments—the larger ones for storage of characters that occur frequently, and the smaller ones for those needed less often. The hand compositor must know the location of each character within the case. That is, he must know the *lay of the case* before he can set type by hand efficiently.

The *California job case* is most generally used today throughout the printing trade (see Figure 4-6). Note that capital, or upper-case letters,[4] are stored to the right and lower-case letters to the left. The caps (capital letters) are in alphabetical order, except for

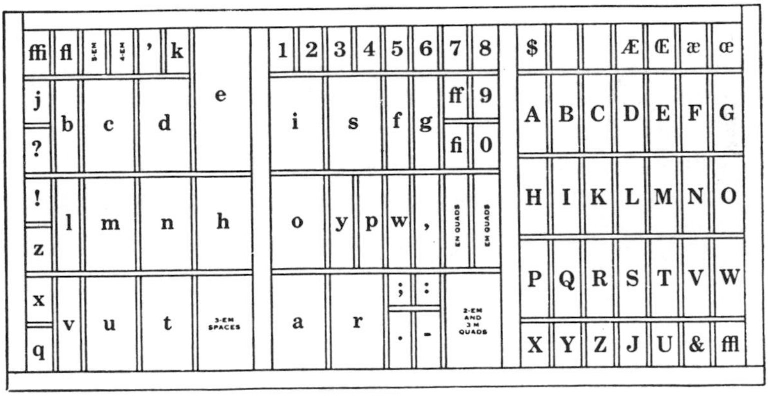

FIGURE 4-6. The California job case. (Courtesy American Type Founders Co., Inc.)

[3]The composition house does no printing but sets type to order for printers and advertisers and stocks more faces than the typical printer can supply.

[4]Prior to machine composition, type was set from two *news cases*, one containing capitals, the other small letters. They were arranged on a stand, one above the other. The caps, at the top, were known as *upper-case* letters; placed below, small letters were called *lower case*. The California job case is a combination of the pair of news cases.

J and *U*, which follow the *Z*. This arrangement exsists because these letters were added to our alphabet after it had previously been set at 24 letters.

The layout of the lower-case letters is arranged so that type selection can be made most efficiently, just as a typewriter keyboard is arranged so that letter combinations that appear most regularly can be struck with a minimum of effort.

Lay of the case can be learned by keeping a copy of it handy for reference while setting type. The student will find that after a few sessions the copy is no longer necessary. As he becomes acquainted with the case, he will find that he can expedite memorization by mentally grouping letters as they appear in the case; for example: "*b, c, d, e*"; "*i, s, f, g*"; "*l, m, n, h*"; "*o, y, p, w*."

Most students find that careful attention must be given to remembering the location of punctuation marks, infrequently used letters "*j,*" "*z,*" "*x,*" and "*q,*" and the ligatures.

STORAGE OF THE CASES. The cases are stored in *type cabinets* that accommodate a number of fonts in tiers. The top of the cabinet is usually a slanted working surface, called a *sloping bank*. Above the bank may be found a case in which leads and slugs of varying lengths can be stored. Storage is organized so that fonts in a series are grouped together.

SPACING MATERIALS. The job case contains *spaces* and *quads*, used for filling in nonprinting areas within a line of type as it is being composed. Spaces are used between words and are found in the compartments labeled in Figure 4-6 as "3-em spaces," "5-em," and "4-em."

Quads are used to fill out wide nonprinting areas and are found in the compartments designated "en quads," "em quads," and "2-em and 3-em quads."

Earlier in this chapter we mentioned line-spacing materials, used to increase space between lines. Thus, leads, slugs, and reglets can be referred to as *vertical spacing materials*, since they are utilized to increase space up and down.

Quads and spaces, used intraline, are thus *horizontal spacing materials*, for they increase space across, rather than up and down.

Other spacing materials are found in a composing room, although they are *not* stored in the type case. These include *thin spaces* for horizontal spacing. They can be combined with 3-, 4-, or 5-em spaces between words, and sometimes are utilized for *letter spacing*, between letters within a word. Thin spaces are made of brass, copper, or lead and are 1-point, ½-point, or 2-points in thickness respectively. They come in various sizes and are stored in *thin space cases.*

Furniture is another kind of spacing material. It is made of wood or metal and is used to fill in nonprinting areas around composed type. Thus it is difficult to classify as either horizontal or vertical, since it may be used at the sides or above or below composed matter. Furniture comes in various lengths and widths, both dimensions being multiples of 12-point, or 1 pica. It is stored in *furniture cabinets.*

The spacing materials in a case all have a relationship to the em. Bear in mind that the em is a square blank body found in every size. In examining a case containing 12-point type, the em is found to be a square 12 points on each side. Twelve points, then, is the base figure for determining the size of other spacing units.

The em itself is a quad and is often referred to as a *monkey quad* or *mollie quad* to distinguish it from the *nut quad* or en quad. The latter is 12 points in size but only 6 wide, since an en is one half an em. Stated another way, it requires 2 ens to equal 1 em.

In the lone case of 12-point type, the en is a nonpareil. This is true because by definition a nonpareil is half a pica. A nut quad in 8-point is 4-points wide.

The 2-em quad and 3-em quad are two and three times wider than the mollie.

Three-em spaces are one third as wide as an em; 4-em and 5-em spaces found in the case to the left of the lower case *k* are one fourth and one fifth as wide as the em. Or, it takes three 3-em spaces, four 4-em spaces, and five 5-em spaces to equal a mollie.

These relationships are all clearly shown in Figure 4-7.

FIGURE 4-7. Comparative sizes of spaces and quads. (Reprinted from *Typography, Layout and Advertising Production* by Edwin H. Stuart and Grace Stuart Gardner, by permission of the publisher, Edwin H. Stuart, Inc.)

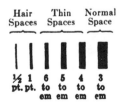

Hair Spaces	Thin Spaces	Normal Space
½ pt. 1 pt.	6 to em 5 to em	4 to em 3 to em

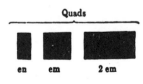

Quads

en   em   2 em

THE COMPOSING STICK

Type characters are selected from the case and placed in a *composing stick.*[5] This is a metal frame with a movable part, called the *knee*, that can be adjusted to pica or half pica measure-

[5]Originally these were carved from a piece of wood; hence the name "stick."

ments, which are marked along the outside edge or *foot* of the stick. The distance between the knee, also called the *slide*, and the *side plate*, which is opposite the knee, is the measure of the line of type that is composed.

SETTING THE TYPE

Before composition begins, the compositor places a lead, slug, or reglet the same length as the measure to be set, against the *back plate* or *head* of the stick, opposite the foot. This gives an even surface for the pieces of type to rest against.

The stick is held in the left hand so that it rests on the finger joints. The fingers should be curved underneath, the tips barely touching the lead or slug that rests against the back plate. The thumb can be utilized to keep each succeeding piece of type on its feet as it is placed in the stick. Figure 4-8 shows how the stick should be held. Note that the foot is away from the compositor and the head closer to him.

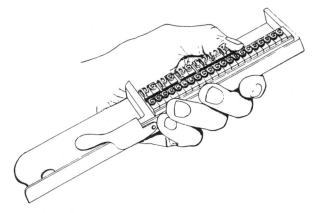

FIGURE 4-8. Proper method of holding the composing stick. (Courtesy American Type Founders Co., Inc.)

Type is selected from the case with the right hand; this is true even for left-handed persons. With the nicks of letters pointed *away* from him, the compositor drops them in place, one after the other, starting in the left-hand corner of the stick.

This means that the lines of type are upside down when the compositor looks at the stick. But they will read from left to right, as on the printed page. It is important to be able to read type matter upside down and backwards, for that is how the printer works with it. Particularly in newspaper work, and often in the magazine fields, the journalist supervises in person the make-up of type matter into pages.

As soon as a line is completed, the compositor places a lead or other line-spacing material at the bottom and sets the next line against it. If the matter is to be set solid, no line-spacing material is used.

JUSTIFYING THE TYPE

All lines of type must be the same length. If not, there is no retaining pressure on the short ones, and they fall sideways or drop out when the composed matter is lifted from the stick. The process of making each line the same length is called justification, or *justifying the line.*

If indention is called for at the beginning of a paragraph, the em quad is generally used. And also as a general rule, the 3-em space, sometimes called a *common space,* is used between words.

Only rarely in composition does a line come exactly to full measure at the end of a word or sentence. Most likely the final word falls short of the end of the line, or it is too long for the space remaining in the line.

If the former case exists, extra space must be placed between words, and occasionally within words (letterspacing); in the latter case, space between words must be reduced, or the last word must be hyphenated and continued on the following line. The varying degrees of spacing required for justifying are achieved by using different combinations of the horizontal spacing materials, including the thin spaces.

SPACING. Proper spacing is the most important factor in hand composition, and, for that matter, in machine composition as well. It is an art, and there are a number of principles to be observed if the resulting composition is to please the eye. Let us examine some of these fundamentals.

(1) As stated above, a common space is generally used between words. But the general rules in any art form can be broken when conditions warrant. There are occasions when less—or perhaps more—than a 3-em space can be used between words.

In Figure 4-9 the top line is spaced with common spaces, but there appears to be too much space. Since the example is 24-point type, spaces are 8-points wide. In the second line spaces used are

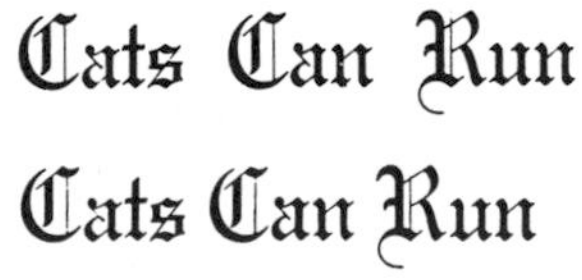

𝕮𝖆𝖙𝖘 𝕮𝖆𝖓 𝕽𝖚𝖓

𝕮𝖆𝖙𝖘 𝕮𝖆𝖓 𝕽𝖚𝖓

FIGURE 4-9. Incorrect and correct spacing between words. (Figures 4-9–4-12 from *Typography, Layout and Advertising Production* by Edwin H. Stuart and Grace Stuart Gardner, courtesy Edwin H. Stuart, Inc., Publisher.)

4-points wide, and spacing seems more attractive thanks to the 50 percent reduction. This is accomplished by using two lead hair spaces or four brass thin spaces.

(2) If the face being set has small center-body letters less space is required between words (see Figure 4-10). The type used is Caslon 471, and in the top line this 18-point sample is spaced with common spaces. The second line, with 4-point spacing between

Cats Can Run

Cats Can Run

Caslon   Caslon

FIGURE 4-10. Incorrect and correct spacing between words.

words, gives a better appearance. The third line shows Caslon 471 to the left and Caslon 540 to the right. Note both are set in 18-point type to indicate the difference of the size of the letters on the body.

(3) "Fat" letters may call for more than common spaces. In Figure 4-11 the top line is set in Nubian and a common space is used. The second line, spaced with a nut quad which is 50 percent wider, seems more balanced.

NEW FAT

NEW FAT

FIGURE 4-11. Incorrect and correct spacing between words set in "fat" letters.

(4) A common space following a period may or may not be adequate, depending upon what capital letter starts the next sentence. Remember that the period itself admits white space. If the following cap is T, W, V, Y, or A, a thin space in addition to the period will appear sufficient, since these caps also admit white space.

As mentioned several times previously, what appears most pleasing to the eye is the standard for judging proper spacing. When the compositor keeps this in mind as he works, he finds that the print from his effort seems to have uniform spacing.

These subtle nuances can be supplied through machine composition, too, but the extra time and consequent cost are usually foregone in favor of speed. This explains further why advertisers may prefer hand composition.

In any case there is little excuse for what typographers refer to as *rivers of white*, shown to the left in Figure 4-12. More careful spacing could happily have eliminated this situation, as was done

RIVERS OF WHITE

Among them were: Mr. and Mrs. Samuel Goldwyn, Mr. and Mrs. Florenz Ziegfeld, Mr. and Mrs. Louis B. Mayer, Mr. and Mrs. Irving Thalberg, Mr. and Mrs. Jack Mulhall, Dr. Harry Martin, Luella O. Parsons, Mr. and Mrs. Paul Buckermann, Mr. and Mrs. Hugh Murray, Mr. and Mrs. Ben Jackson, Mr. and Mrs. Edgar Selwyn.

SEE THE RIVERS

Among them were: Mr. and Mrs. Samuel Goldwyn, Mr. and Mrs. Florenz Ziegfeld, Mr. and Mrs. Louis B. Mayer, Mr. and Mrs. Irving Thalberg, Mr. and Mrs. Jack Mulhall, Dr. Harry Martin, Luella O. Parsons, Mr. and Mrs. Paul Zuckerman, Mr. and Mrs. Hugh Murray, Mr. and Mrs. Ben Jackson, Mr. and Mrs. Edgar Selwyn.

RIVERS OMITTED

FIGURE 4-12. Rivers of white eliminated through proper spacing.

in the right-hand column.

One final suggestion is in order. Space at the end of a paragraph should exceed one em; otherwise, the line should be spaced out full. And in justifying a short line, quads should be used to the outside, with necessary spacing materials to the inside. A thin space placed at the end of the measure lacks support and can drop out when the type is removed from the stick.

LETTERSPACING OF CAPS

When words are set all caps, they can look crowded unless they are letterspaced as, for example, LETTERSPACING. To give a more pleasing appearance, thin spaces may be inserted between letters, so that the word now appears:

LETTERSPACING.

Consideration must be given to the fact that some letters admit white space by the nature of their design. Thus, letterspacing the word "TAG" requires, let us say, 1-point or 2-point spacing between A and G and none between the T and A. Or, again, in letterspacing the word "SPACING" less is required between P and A than between the other letters.

READING THE STICK

It is a good idea for the compositor to "read the stick" before justifying a line. He should be on guard against errors that occur in composition; specifically, wrong font letters, type placed "upside down," and transpositions. It is best to catch these at the time a line is set *before it is justified.* Assume that a word is omitted from the fourth line of a seven-line paragraph. When the error is discovered, after the paragraph is completed and proofed, insertion may require resetting all of the last four lines of the paragraph.

The beginner will find difficulty with the so-called *four demons* of type: *d, b, p,* and *q.* The surest way to identify each is to hold the piece of type, nick away from you, and to remember that the bowl is in the same direction as it will be in print, but the ascender or descender will be in the opposite direction.

Not all fonts contain quotation marks. If type has been composed from a case that does not, opening quotes can be made with inverted commas and closing quotes with apostrophes. Quotes should be carefully checked in reading the stick.

Word division should also be watched carefully. In general, hyphenation is done according to pronunciation. Thus, it is a sound practice to have a dictionary available for reference whenever a question arises during composition. These special situations ought to be retained by the student:

(1) Do not hyphenate words of one syllable.
(2) Do not hyphenate four-letter words, such as "un-to."
(3) Do not hyphenate plurals of one syllable words.
(4) Do not divide the last word on a page and carry it to another page.
(5) Do not hyphenate one-letter syllables such as "a-bove."
(6) Avoid hyphenating hyphenated words such as "color-bearer," unless division can be made at the hyphen between the two words.
(7) Avoid hyphenating amounts stated in figures. If division is necessary hyphenate following a comma.

REMOVING TYPE FROM THE STICK

When composition is completed, type must be removed from the stick and transferred to a *galley.* This process is called "dumping the stick."

The galley is a metal (brass or steel) tray with a rim, less than type-high, on two sides and at the *head end.* The end opposite the head end has no rim. The galley holds and stores type. Composed material is put in it and inked so that a proof can be made. First, the galley is set on the working top, or sloping bank, of the cabinet, open end to the left. Then the stick is placed in the galley, back plate against the edge of the galley nearest the compositor. Before removing the type a lead, slug, or reglet of the line length is dropped in the stick below the bottom line. This gives the compositor firm support both above and below the type. Remember that one was also placed against the back plate before composition began.

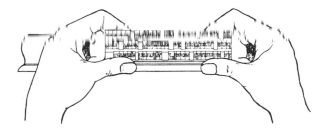

FIGURE 4-13. The proper technique for holding type when removing it from the stick. (Courtesy American Type Founders Co., Inc.)

The proper way to remove type is shown in Figure 4-13. Forefingers and thumbs are pressed against top and bottom supporting materials, middle fingers against the sides of the composition. Type matter is moved forward from the stick onto the galley without lifting, and is slid to the head end.

The task is completed when the type is tied with cotton string. A length sufficient for five or six turns is cut. Starting in the upper left corner of the type matter, as shown in Figure 4-14, allow an inch or so of string to overlap the corner. Then wind the string around the form clockwise. Be sure that the first turn around crosses the end held in the left hand at the starting point. When the end

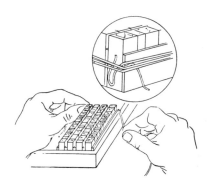

FIGURE 4-14. Tying type for storage. (Courtesy American Type Founders Co., Inc.)

of the string is reached, hold the free end tightly around the corner of the type matter with the forefinger of the left hand. Next, push a loop of the end of the string behind all the layers of twine. Draw the loop back toward the corner, where it will be secure. Leave the end slightly above the layers. By pulling on this later, unwinding will begin. Refer again to Figure 4-14 to see how the loop can be fastened.

TAKING A PROOF

After tying the type, the compositor is ready to *take, pull,* or *draw a proof.* The type is carried in the galley to the *proof press* and laid on the bed, head end toward the cylinder of the press. Ink is applied with a *brayer,* which is run back and forth two or three times on the *ink plate* and is then rolled two or three times over the type. A piece of paper is laid on the type and the press cylinder is rolled over it. When lifting the proof paper, care should be taken to avoid smearing. Cylinder should cross type only once.

There are many kinds of proof presses. The student typographer should become acquainted with the kind he will be using before attempting to operate it.

THE HAND PROOF. Not all proofs are pulled on proof presses, even in commercial establishments. The *hand proof,* also known as a *stone proof* or *planer proof,* is often used. The type is slid from the galley onto the *stone,* a large flat working table, also called an *imposing table,* where type forms are assembled prior to being placed on printing presses. Typography labs are likely to have such working areas even if they lack a printing press. These tables were originally called "stones" because they had smooth stone tops. Although they are likely to be constructed of steel today, the men who work at them are still referred to as stonemen.

The form is made level with a wood block called a *planer.* It is placed on top of the form and is gently struck with a *mallet.* Then the form is inked. The proof paper may be placed on it either dry or moistened with a sponge and laid dry side down on the inked type. A *proof planer* (wooden block with a felt covering) is laid, felt against paper, on the form and struck gently with a mallet as often as necessary to cover the entire form.

CLEANING THE TYPE

As soon as proofs are drawn, type must be cleaned by a rag moistened with a type-cleaning solvent or gasoline. Cleaner should not be allowed to run down into the type.

MAKING CORRECTIONS

After a proof has been pulled, it is read for errors by carefully checking it against the original copy. Mistakes are indicated on a proof by standard proofreading marks understood throughout the printing industry. A knowledge of these marks and their proper use is of utmost importance to anyone dealing with printers, and they are covered elsewhere in this text.

To make corrections the compositor returns to his bank with type matter properly placed in the galley. First, the form is untied. Then the lines below the line containing an error are moved several inches toward the open end of the galley. To secure them a piece of metal furniture is placed above these lines, another below. A piece of spacing material the same measure as the type line is placed above the line containing the error and another piece below it. Then the line is placed in the stick, corrections are made, the line rejustified and returned to the proper place in the galley.

This process is repeated for each line containing an error. Note that some corrections are possible without the removal of the line from the form. This can be the case when a worn letter is replaced or a transposition righted.

When separating lines of type in the form the *make-up rule,* or *hump-back* rule as it is also known, is a handy device. This is a thin (2-point) polished steel strip with a curved top. The bottom edge is sharpened to facilitate placement between the lines of type. If lines are leaded, this rule is not needed.

In making corrections, type lines should be handled with great care to prevent spilling. Printers call type that has been so disarranged "pi."

After all corrections are made, another proof, called a *revise,* or *revise proof,* is pulled. This is compared by a proofreader to the first proof. If errors remain, new ones were committed, or the type was pied, a *second revise* may be needed before the final "O.K."

DISTRIBUTING TYPE

With corrections in order, it is time to print. In most laboratories the final proof is the last use of the type, since printing is impossible. Type no longer needed is said to be *dead matter,* and the process of putting it back in the cases is called *distributing the type.*

Proper distribution insures against *pied,* or *dirty, cases.* If the compositor follows these steps carefully he can be sure the case is left clean for the next person to use it:

(1) Return the galley to the bank and untie the form. Move it carefully to the open end.

(2) Place a piece of spacing material on either side of the bottom line. Lift it in the left hand and hold it between the thumb and the middle finger with the nicks up and steady it with the forefinger underneath the bottom slug, as shown in Figure 4-15.

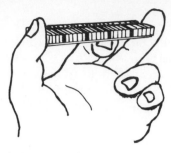

FIGURE 4-15. Holding a line of type for distribution. (Courtesy American Type Founders Co., Inc.)

(3) Remove the top spacing material and with the right hand pick up the first word at the *right side of the line,* holding it between right thumb and index finger. Drop the word, a letter at a time, into the various compartments, spelling the word as you proceed. Repeat these procedures for each word and each line.

(4) Place all spacing materials aside in the galley as you come to them. When storage of type is complete, replace spacing materials where they belong.

FIGURE 4-16. Distributing type. (Courtesy American Type Founders Co., Inc.)

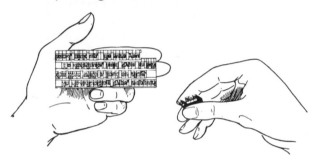

Figure 4-16 indicates how type should be held while being distributed. It is advisable to work a line at a time at first. As proficiency develops, one can then hold several lines at a time in the left hand, as shown.

 conclusion

The student typographer should not expect to become a qualified compositor by practicing the art of hand composition in a college laboratory. He can reasonably expect to get a "feel" for type and learn something of the possibilities in its use. He will acquire a background for fuller comprehension of the other methods of composition and of the various methods of printing.

And he cannot avoid a full appreciation of the accuracy with which the printer works. Even the copper thin space used in final justification teaches this appreciation by a mere consideration of its size. It is ½-point thick, or approximately 0.007 inches.

5 Because foundry type is set by hand, it is time- and money-consuming. Therefore, most composition for periodicals, books, and commercial jobs is done by machines today, and the saving in time and money is substantial. It is advisable for the typographer to understand the composition and limitations of the several machines involved so that he may make the most economical use of them.

In broad terms, the methods of composition can be divided into two classes: hot metal and cold type.

 ## hot-metal composition

Hot-metal composition is done on various type-casting machines. None of them assembles individual pieces of type into words and sentences in the manner of hand composition. Rather, they manufacture type as they are operated, either as one justified line of words on one type body (called a *slug*), or as single letters, which come from the machine composed and justified.

The following machines cast lines of type on a slug: the Linotype, the Intertype, the Ludlow Typograph, and the APL (All-Purpose Linotype). The Monotype is a single-letter-casting machine. Like foundry type, the faces of letters cast on all these machines stand in relief. In fact, the hot-metal type-casting machines can be grouped with foundry type and called the *traditional methods of type composition.*

The reader should remember that printing by pressing paper against the inked faces can directly follow composition done with any of these traditional methods.

THE LINOTYPE AND INTERTYPE

The Linotype and Intertype machines are fundamentally similar. Their differences are in mechanical details. Newspapers are composed almost exclusively on either the Linotype or its competitor the Intertype. Periodical, book, and job work is also their domain, although in these latter fields they share the composition task with the Monotype, to be discussed later.

At the Linotype (Figure 5-1), the operator sits at the keyboard, labeled 1. As he punches the keys in much the manner that a typewriter is operated, brass molds, called *mats* or *matrices* (plural of matrix), are released from their position of storage in the *maga-*

...**83**

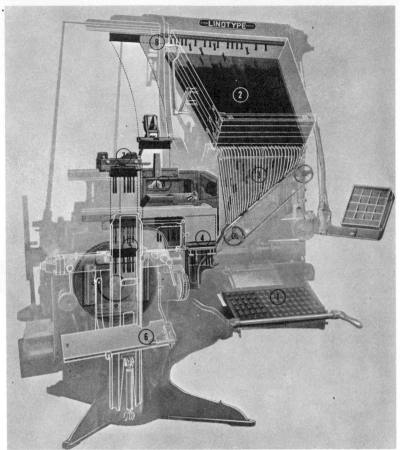

FIGURE 5-1. The Linotype. (Courtesy Mergenthaler Linotype Company.)

zine, 2. They drop through the delivery channels, 3, and are then carried to the *assembly elevator*, 4. At this point *spacebands* are dropped between words.

The line of mats and bands is then moved to the casting mechanism, 5, where molten metal is flushed against it, thus casting a type slug. Completed slugs are trimmed to proper thickness and type height before dropping into the galley, 6.

After casting, the mats and spacebands are raised by the *first elevator*, 7, to a point where they are transferred to the *distributing elevator*, 8. From here they are lifted to the top of the machine to the *distributor bar*, 9. Spacebands were left at 8, from which they are returned to their storage box, ready to be used again.

Mats are "keyed" by teeth to notches in the distributor bar. They move along the bar until they reach the proper point where they are released and dropped into the correct compartment in the magazine.

In summary, then, there are four major sections of the Linotype and Intertype machine: (1) the keyboard; (2) the magazine; (3) the casting mechanism; and (4) the distribution system.

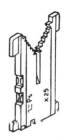

THE MATS AND SPACEBANDS. The matrix (Figure 5-2) has been called the heart of the Linotype. Mats are made of brass and are of varying thicknesses, depending on the width of the letters they are to mold. Since the face to be cast must stand in relief and reverse in position, the face is indented in the mat and "reads forward."

FIGURE 5-2.
The Matrix.

Mats are generally "two-letter mats," particularly in the small-size faces. The mat in Figure 5-2 carries an upper case I, one in a roman version, the other in italic. Roman and boldface letters are another combination frequently found on two-letter mats. This makes it possible for the operator to set roman with italic or roman with boldface from one magazine. Such "duplexed faces" are available in sizes as large as 24-point.

Spacebands make justification of the composed lines possible. As noted above, these are dropped by the operator between words. When his line is nearly full, he is able to expand the spacebands, thereby filling the line completely. This happens because of the ingenious design of the spaceband. Actually it is composed of two wedges tapering in opposite directions; when they are pushed together, the spacebands expand. Matrices of varying widths are also available to the operator for spacing. Frequently he will set these at the end of a line and distribute them manually within the line to supplement the spacing of the spacebands or to letterspace where needed. This is done, of course, before the assembled mats are transferred to the casting mechanism.

ADVANTAGES AND LIMITATIONS. Obviously it is advantageous for the person ordering type composition to understand what Linotype and Intertype machines can deliver economically. Here are some major pros and cons:

(1) These machines offer exceptionally rapid delivery of straight matter. The flow of mats from assembly through casting and distribution can be constant and uninterrupted. A machine operator is capable of setting type five or six times faster than a hand compositor. Moreover, duplicate slugs can be made simply by recasting. The machines can save the time required for leading (placing strips of metal between lines), for the operator can cast

a face on a slug wider than normal for the face. Thus, 10-point type can be set on a 12-point slug, the equivalent of 2-point leading.

(2) The range of faces stocked by compositors varies widely. Basically a separate magazine is required for each font of type, but remember that two different faces may be cast from each mat, at least up to 24-point. Magazines are quickly interchangeable, and most modern machines carry four, some eight—any one of which can easily be brought into play by the operator.

Special thought should be given to using a face found in a *split magazine,* which is half the size of a regular magazine and thus contains fewer mats. It is well to avoid setting copy in long measure (lengthy copy) in such a face, since the machine is likely to run short of certain mats, thereby forcing the operator to sit idle as he waits for them to run the cycle of his machine.

Linotype and Intertype machines set faces as large as 36-point; some fonts up to 60-point can be accommodated. Most printers, however, prefer to restrict their available faces to 24- or possibly some 30-point type, composing larger sizes by hand or on the Ludlow, to be discussed later.

There are definite limitations to combining two different faces in one line (other than the two found on one mat), since the operator can usually compose from only one magazine at a time. A third face can be brought into a line by setting another slug from a different magazine and then using the needed portions of the two slugs. Obviously, this means time and expense.

Many printers and compositors have special machines capable of setting different faces in one line. These are known as *mixer machines* or *double distributor machines.*

(3) There are restrictions on the length of line that can be composed, most machines being limited to 30-pica or 30-em slugs, with only an exceptional one setting as wide as 42 ems. This does not mean that one cannot order, for example, 14-point Century set 36-picas wide. But it entails extra cost, since the compositor has to use *butted slugs* in composing each line. This means that for each line two slugs are set that are then combined to make a line. The printer has to exercise reasonable care in butting the slugs so that they don't show on the printed material.

(4) Careful attention must be given to corrections and/or alterations made in Linotype or Intertype composition. Because each line is on one slug, to correct a single error or to make even a minor change, requires resetting the entire line, and sometimes also resetting the line above and below the one in error for rejustification. This means that in correcting one error the operator can

make another. When examining corrected proofs, it is imperative to read the entire corrected line and the one above and below rather than checking only the correction.

When working on composed copy it is wise to make alterations so that a minimum of lines must be reset. Printers charge for resetting lines in which changes from the original copy are made. These are called *author's alterations*, or A A s.

(5) Composition other than straight matter is more expensive, again because of the time factor.

It is difficult to compose tabular matter on these line-casting machines, particularly when some of the columns are very narrow, requiring vertical rules as separators. This is so because slugs have to be sawed into proper widths to be placed between the rules. It is impractical to be dealing with lengths as narrow as 1, 2, or 3 picas.

Sometimes, when it is essential to reproduce such tabular matter and only a Linotype or Intertype is available for composition, type can be composed without the rules. Then a high quality proof is drawn and lines are ruled onto the proof with pen and ink, after which an engraving is made. Printing is then done, of course, from the engraved plate. (For details concerning engraving procedures, the reader is referred to Chapter 6.)

With the exception of some machines with automatic centering, centering on the measure should be avoided whenever possible for it demands special attention from the operator. Irregular line lengths also add to expense. Changing widths (line lengths) calls for several time-consuming machine adjustments.

When an illustration or perhaps a headline "cuts into" text matter and type lines run around it, the composed text is called a *run-around*. (A headline so designed is called a *cut-in head*.) To make a run-around the operator must set the copy to the required length on a slug of column width. Then the slug has to be sawed to required width in order to make room for the illustration or head. Setting the copy short on the original slug requires slow hand spacing.

(6) Spacing between words set on the Linotype and Intertype is often typographically imperfect. Spacebands vary in thicknesses, from thin to jumbo, with sizes between. This means that the operator inserts narrow bands when setting small sizes and wider with large sizes. Most printers and compositors cannot stock spacebands in a full range of sizes because of expense, so they are apt to use perhaps only one or two for a fairly comprehensive number of type sizes.

THE LUDLOW TYPOGRAPH

Commonly referred to as a Ludlow, this machine casts type on a single slug from mats assembled and distributed by hand. Actually, it is not a typesetting machine, as are the Linotype and Intertype. Its primary use is for casting lines of display type; that is, type in sizes above 14-point all the way to 144-point.

As indicated earlier, the Linotype and Intertype can also compose large sizes. However, because of the time required for setting them up, it is often quicker to compose a few display lines on the Ludlow.

The Ludlow is not a straight-matter machine, but is nonetheless often used for setting type as small as 4-point, particularly in job shops when only a few lines are needed; for example, on calling cards or letterheads. It has the advantage in this case of making new type available for each job, since slugs are melted down after use, as in the case of the line-casting machines. Moreover, the slugs are easier to handle than lines of foundry type.

A Ludlow and the storage cabinets where the matrices are kept are shown in Figure 5-3. Mats are assembled by hand from cases and placed in a stick, which is actually a metal frame in which the line of mats is secured. Spacing and justification is a manual process.

This stick is then placed in the casting unit. The slug is usually cast on a 12-point body and faces larger in size than 12-point overhang this body. The overhang is supported by placing blank slugs underneath. To the printer this is known as *underpinning*. The length of the line to be cast presents no problem, since slugs can be butted as necessary.

It is possible to multiple-cast from each stickful—a particular

FIGURE 5-3. The Ludlow with type cabinets. (Courtesy Ludlow Typograph Co.)

FIGURE 5-4. The Monotype keyboard and caster. (Courtesy Lanston Monotype Company.)

advantage when extra slugs are needed. This would occur, for example, when a job can be run two or more up; that is, duplicates are printed on a single sheet, later cut to yield two or more copies. Or again, duplicate slugs could be needed for running heads—that is, regularly repeated headings—in a book.

Printers usually stock faces for casting on the Ludlow that are not duplicated in foundry type or on machines.

THE APL

The All-Purpose Linotype is similar to the Ludlow in that mats are assembled by hand and casting is done by machine. The casting unit is similar to the casting mechanism of the Linotype machine.

THE MONOTYPE

In reality, the Monotype is two separate machines. One is the keyboard machine, which, when operated, perforates a paper tape. This is then fed into the casting machine, the second unit, which casts the type. The keyboard and caster are shown in Figure 5-4.

Perforations in the tape represent the characters and letters of the type font, together with the spacing required for justification. As the operator composes, he puts normal spacing between words. Near the end of the measure, a signal is given, and he records on the tape, according to an automatic scale, the required symbols to divide the remaining space evenly between all the words. The tape is fed into the caster backwards, so that the machine "knows" exactly in advance how much space to put between words.

As the tape moves through the caster it controls blasts of compressed air that move levers to pull a matrix case backward, forward, and side to side. This action brings a different matrix over the mouth of the mold, where hot molten metal is forced against it to form the letter, character, or space. A matrix case is shown in Figure 5-5.

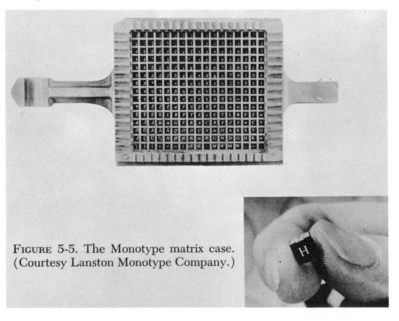

FIGURE 5-5. The Monotype matrix case. (Courtesy Lanston Monotype Company.)

The casting is done at a high rate—one-hundred-fifty casts per minute; as each unit is cast it is pushed into place until a full line is formed. Then another is started.

Faces available for Monotype casting are similar to those on the Linotype and Intertype. The machine sets type in measures up to sixty picas and sizes from 4- to 18-point. A *display attachment* allows the printer to compose type as large as 36-point and specially built casters accommodate faces as large as 72-point. Faces up to and including 18-point may be composed using the keyboard and the regular caster. Faces above 18-point must be hand composed.

A unique feature of the Monotype system allows the addition of a small amount of space to each side of each letter or the removal, in some cases, of a small amount from both sides. This has no effect on the point size but does alter the set width, so that 10-point type might be composed in 10½-set. Thus the face requires 5 percent more space when composed. The 10-point face composed 9½-set would allow a 5 percent savings in space. This flexibility can become very important when composition must be expanded or contracted to fit within a certain area.

The following advantages and limitations of the Monotype are worthy of attention:

(1) The system is well-adapted to intricate composition (for instance, mathematical text) and tabular work. In the latter case, vertical rules can be easily inserted. A special scale on the keyboard machine allows the operator to compose tabular matter with a minimum of difficulty. Adjustments are readily made for setting run-arounds and irregular lengths, and when the composition is finished, blank spaces at either or both ends can be simply removed by hand. The student will recall that composition from line-casting machines requires sawing.

(2) Because of its precision in calculating space between words, the Monotype produces better-spaced composition.

(3) Although the cost of composition on the Monotype is higher on an hourly basis than on the line-casting machines, it can prove less costly, if used for complicated material or for quality book work. Also, composition can be done with a harder metal than that used in the line-casting machines, guaranteeing better and longer-lasting printing opportunities. However, many printers use the same metal for Linotype, Intertype, Ludlow, and Monotype. Figure 5-6 illustrates seven steps in Monotype book composition.

MATERIALS MAKING

Special materials used in printing are available from outside suppliers. Printers and publishers can purchase from founders items such as base, rule, border, ornaments, metal or wood furniture, if they cannot produce their own materials as needed.

This they can often do, however, for the Linotype and Intertype machines can turn out border and rule, and the APL can be set up to produce furniture, rule, border, decorative materials and spacing materials. Furniture, it will be recalled, is a spacing material used for separating pages in a form or for filling in large, blank nonprinting areas, as for example, between the type and the metal chase.

The Standard and the Giant Monotype casting machines can

a

FIGURE 5-6. Seven steps in Monotype book composition. (a-f Courtesy Monotype Composition Company.) (a) Copyholder recording manuscript on tape before composition. (b) Monotype keyboard operator. (c) Checking type on Monotype caster. (d) Pulling galleys on a Vandercook proof press. (e) Proofreader marking galleys while listening to tape recorded by copyholder. (f) Planing type form in preparation for pulling proof. (g) Checking running heads, margins, and pagination against required imposition on a line-up table. (Courtesy Montauk Book Manufacturing Company, Inc.)

d

f

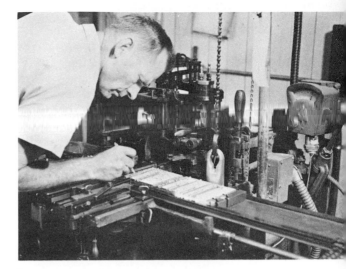

b

c

e

g

supply leads, slugs, rule, border, ornaments, initials, and similar materials, as well as *base metal*. The latter is used for mounting engravings, shell-cast stereotypes (stereos cast less than type-high), and *stripped slugs*. Type slugs can be trimmed to less than type-high and then mounted at any desired angle on this base.

Many printers and publishers use the Monotype Materials Making Machine for producing these various materials. Others use the Elrod Caster, made by the same company that produces the Ludlow, to turn out leads, slugs, rule, and base material.

THE TELETYPESETTER

Before turning attention from the traditional methods of type composition, mention should be made of the Teletypesetter, or, as it is more commonly known, the TTS.

This is not a composing machine but rather an attachment that allows a Linotype or an Intertype to compose automatically, without an operator. A keyboard perforates a tape that is then fed through and activates an operating unit attached to the composing machine. The tape may be prepared locally on a Keyboard Perforator or impulses may be sent into the plant by wire service to an automatic telegraphic perforator. Editing can be done before the tapes are fed to the machines. One man in attendance is able to maintain the operation of four machines. The Teletypesetter finds its greatest use in the newspaper field; as an example, much of the Western Edition of *The New York Times* is teletypeset in New York City and received for printing in Los Angeles.

 cold-type composition

Every printing process requires original composition in some form. Type composed by any of the traditional methods can be printed from directly or be duplicated in stereotype or electrotype form so that printing can be done from the duplicates. Either case is true of letterpress printing.

It is also possible to make a sharp quality print from original type, photograph it and transfer it to an offset or rotogravure printing plate, as already mentioned in this text. The reader may detect an indirection here. Well he may reason that if composition can be made directly onto paper or film, the traditional methods of composition and the need for a reproduction proof can be bypassed.

The various methods of cold-type composition are designed to achieve this end. But it must be remembered that the quality standard applied to all forms of printing is that the final reproduction look "printlike." This is another way of saying that the reproduction must look as if it were printed from raised type.

The various cold-type composing methods can be classified as paste-down, photocomposing machines, and typewriters.

PASTE-DOWN TYPE

Together the three kinds of paste-down type represent one of the most widely used techniques for composition of cold type in display sizes. There are a number of brands, and the variety of sizes and faces literally runs into the hundreds. Paste-down type is available as: (1) alphabet sheets; (2) precut letters; and (3) transfer alphabets.

Alphabet sheets are transparent adhesive acetate sheets affixed to a paper backing. Complete fonts are printed on the back of the acetate, with commonly used letters repeated several times. The letters are cut from the acetate sheet as needed, peeled from the paper backing, and positioned on the art work. Letter alignment is not difficult because a guideline is printed under each character and can be registered to a guideline drawn lightly in blue on the art work. After composition is complete, the printed guideline is cut from the bottom of each letter. The blue remains, but will not record on the film when the type is photographed.

That these alphabets are printed on a transparent medium and can be placed across art work is a unique asset. The art "shows through" for photographing. Alphabets should not be used on photos or other continuous-tone art that will require halftoning for reproduction, since the acetate base may appear in the reproduction.

Alphabets are frequently printed on the acetate in black or white. The latter can be applied to a black area on art work. Thus a reverse can be prepared on the original copy, avoiding the extra charge made by engravers and offset printers for reversing type.

Among the many faces are a large number of hand-lettered alphabets. Some suppliers specialize in the production of these, and their offerings include many distinctive styles. Manufacturers of these sheets also supply symbols, lines, rule, border, numbers, arrows; for Benday or other shading effects screen patterns, tints, tones, and textures are available printed in black or white.

The precut letter system has its characters printed on separate pieces of cardboard. The required letters and spaces (blank pieces of cardboard) must be assembled into a special frame called a stick. A piece of transparent tape is then placed across the type and the composed line is ready to be lifted from the stick and added to the art work.

A font of this type consists of a tray filled with pads of letters and other characters in both positive (black on white) and reverse faces (white on black).

Transfer alphabets are similar to alphabet sheets since they are on transparent acetate sheets. They differ because letters are affixed to it rather than printed on the back. For composition, the sheet is positioned over the art work and pressure is applied to transfer letters to the layout. No cutting apart is needed. These are also made in positive and reverse. They are particularly good for lettering on continuous-tone art work.

PHOTOCOMPOSING MACHINES

The various photo-composing machines operate on a common principle. Basically, they are photographic units in which type characters, either in film positive or negative form, are exposed onto either paper or film. However, they vary widely in complexity and in production capacities.

Complex machines require keyboard operation. Five are in use today: the Fotosetter, the Linofilm, the Monophoto, the Photon, and the Typesetter. All are capable of composing block (straight matter), tabular and display sizes.

THE FOTOSETTER. This adaptation of the Intertype machine not only resembles its hot-metal counterpart but operates on the same basis. As the operator depresses the keys, matrices like the regular Intertype mats are assembled in the same fashion. They differ in one respect: a photographic image of the letter is borne by the mat. After a line is assembled and justified as on the standard machine, the mats are exposed, one at a time, onto film or paper. The exposure unit replaces the casting unit on the standard machine. The mats are then returned to their proper location in the magazine. Of the five keyboard machines, only the Fotosetter operates on the circulating matrix principle.

More than two hundred faces are available for Fotosetter use, including the regular Intertype faces. The photo unit has a series of lenses that allow for eighteen different sizes of type in each font, ranging from 3- to 72-points. Line widths up to 51 ems can be composed.

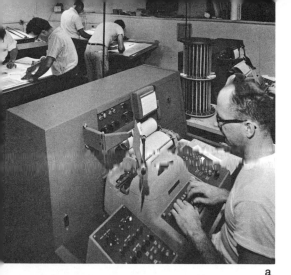
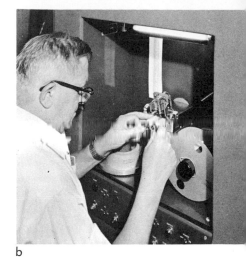

a   b

c

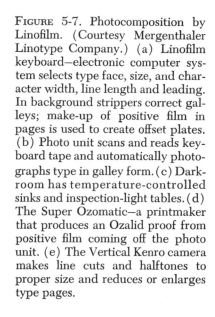

Figure 5-7. Photocomposition by Linofilm. (Courtesy Mergenthaler Linotype Company.) (a) Linofilm keyboard—electronic computer system selects type face, size, and character width, line length and leading. In background strippers correct galleys; make-up of positive film in pages is used to create offset plates. (b) Photo unit scans and reads keyboard tape and automatically photographs type in galley form. (c) Darkroom has temperature-controlled sinks and inspection-light tables. (d) The Super Ozomatic—a printmaker that produces an Ozalid proof from positive film coming off the photo unit. (e) The Vertical Kenro camera makes line cuts and halftones to proper size and reduces or enlarges type pages.

e

d

THE LINOFILM. This machine, counterpart of the Linotype, has two units: a keyboard that perforates a tape to be fed into a photo unit; where composition takes place. (Figure 5-7a-b.)

The Linofilm mixes regular Linotype faces, changing type size, width, and leading as required by the tape. Composition in the photo unit ranges from 4¾-point to 18-point type up to 30 ems wide. An auxiliary unit, the Reproducer, enlarges composition from the photo unit, increasing line-width capacity to 96 picas.

THE MONOPHOTO. This is the Monotype entry in the cold-metal field. The standard Monotype keyboard perforates a tape, which is fed into the casting unit. The latter is an adaptation of the regular Monotype Caster.

The system offers the same versatility as the Monotype. All the faces are available and can be composed 6- to 24-point in lines up to 60 picas wide. Faces can be mixed and type enlarged or reduced as required.

THE PHOTON. The Photon is also operated from a typewriter keyboard contained in one console with the exposure unit. An electronic memory system, rather than a punched tape, relays composition instructions to the exposure unit.

The latter is equipped with a matrix disc containing sixteen type styles. This rotates at ten revolutions per second. A stroboscopic flash, synchronized with the rotating disc, illuminates letters on the matrix to expose them on the light-sensitive material, as dictated by the typed information. The strobe flashes at four-millionths of a second, thereby "stopping" the disc for exposure. Twelve lenses are utilized in composing in order to produce type from 5- to 72-point.

More than one-hundred faces are available, and the machine adapts to straight matter or tabular composition to a maximum width of 54 picas.

Copy can be "paged up" directly on the machine by an indicator that can set pages up to 9 inches wide.

THE ATF TYPESETTER. This tape-operated machine consists of a typewriter keyboard for perforating and a photographic unit. It uses a separate spinning disc for each type style in the exposure unit. Block and tabular matters can be composed in "galley form" or by pages. Faces can be mixed and set in sizes from 3- to 72-point. There are more than two-hundred faces. The ATF Typesetter is marketed by American Type Founders.

Because these five machines operate on a photographic principle, a darkroom is required for processing film and paper immediately after composition. Special equipment capable of precisely inserting corrected lines on film or paper into the proper place is employed.

A number of less complex photocomposing machines without keyboards are available. The operator hand-selects the desired characters to position them over film strips on paper for exposure and development. Since composition is limited to strips, the machines are less practical than others for block or tabular composition. They are generally restricted to composition of display type.

Largest of these is the ATF-Hadego photocompositor, which can set display type in sizes from 4- to 115-point at any size or fraction within this range. It can mix its more than one-hundred faces during composition. The Hadego resembles the Ludlow in appearance and operation.

TYPEWRITERS

The typewriter is made to order for cold-type composition. Acceptable camera copy can be prepared on a regular office machine, which has been carefully cleaned and has a dark ribbon. By reducing size photographically to minimize imperfections and by justifying the right-hand margin, ordinary typing can be dressed up. Of course if typing is done on a paper offset plate with a special grease ribbon, reduction is not possible. The justifying process requires typing the copy twice. In the first typing each line is ended short of the desired measure. In the second typing spaces are added between words as necessary to bring each line to full measure. However, this frequently results in loosely spaced lines.

A second major difficulty, that standard typed copy does not have the desired "printlike" quality, arises because all letters are of the same width, 1/10 inch in the case of pica and 1/12 inch in the case of elite type.

Some special typewriters overcome or at least minimize these shortcomings and are more adaptable to cold composition. They are the IBM Executive, the Remington Rand Statesman, the Varityper, and the Justowriter.

THE EXECUTIVE AND STATESMAN. The Executive and the Statesman are electric typewriters with proportional spacing systems that give each character its own amount of space. Although justification requires a second typing, the typist has greater control over the extra spacing between words than in the case of a standard machine. Spacing can thus present an even appearance, since each unit added in the second typing is narrower even than the letter *i*.

Both of these machines utilize a carbon-coated paper ribbon, capable of producing cleaner, crisper letters that will reproduce better than those inked by conventional fabric ribbon.

The Executive and Statesman come equipped with a choice of type faces, ranging from 8- to 12-point. These faces cannot be changed on the machines.

THE VARITYPER. Perhaps best-known of the various cold-type typewriters, the Varityper's outstanding features are (1) fonts, many closely resembling book types, that can be interchanged quickly; and (2) automatic justification on the second typing.

Several models are available. The Model DSJ (Differential Space Justifying) is the most adaptable to cold-type composition, since it features proportional spacing.

More than 300 fonts, ranging in size from 2- to 12-point, are available for this model.

THE JUSTOWRITER. The Justowriter features semiautomatic composition. It is composed of two units—a Recorder, which perforates tape, and a Reproducer, which reads the tape and composes in one of fourteen different faces at a rate of 100 words per minute. Justification is automatic. Type sizes range from 8- to 14-point, and a different Reproducer is required for each face and size. The Justowriter does not have proportional spacing, and although the Flexowriter, another model produced by the same manufacturer, does, the Justowriter is much more widely used in cold composition.

 the brightype process

Another process that by-passes the drawing of reproduction proof as demanded by hot-type composition is the Brightype system. It is marketed by the Ludlow Typograph Company, which converts letterpress-printing materials—type and engravings—directly into film or paper positives or negatives. This enables type set by the traditional methods to be promptly recorded on film, ready for use in offset, rotogravure, or other processes where photographic exposure is a production requirement. Thus repro proofs are eliminated.

The Brightype process employs a camera to photograph type and secondary elements at the same size; enlargement or reduction are not possible.

The technique treats what would otherwise be the printing surface of the type and illustrative materials to make them light-reflective. At the same time the nonprinting areas are made non-reflective—as, for example, the shoulder of type—by a spray of a special lampblack coating over the entire form.

Photography with special camera and auxiliary equipment follows. The process is unique in two specific respects: (1) the high-fidelity conversion of process-engraving plates to film for use in offset; and (2) the restoration of worn type to near-perfect form on film.

Brightyping is being adapted more and more to bookwork. Forms of several complete pages can be made up and then photographed onto one piece of film.

 ## make-up and lock-up

A discussion of type composition is not complete without reference to *make-up* and *lock-up,* the final composing room functions before type and other elements are taken to a press for letterpress printing.

Make-up merges metal type with illustrative materials, and divides the matter into page lengths, adding running heads and folios (page numbers), and special material (apt to be set in a smaller face than the text) such as captions and footnotes.

The printer's make-up man follows instructions from the author or editor in placing illustrations properly and separating materials into page form. These instructions are in the form of either explicit written information on proofs for uncomplicated make-up or a dummy (blueprint for the make-up man), which will be discussed in detail in Chapter 10.

As soon as make-up of pages is complete, *page proofs* are drawn. These indicate how the complete printed job will appear. After page proofs are O.K.'d and final corrections complete, pages are locked up for printing or for electrotyping or stereotyping.

Lock-up involves placing type and other printing elements in a *chase,* which is a metal frame, and securing it so that the chase can be lifted without fear of printing matter falling out. This is done on an imposing stone by a lock-up man, or stoneman. He puts furniture around the printing form (printing material) to fill in the nonprinting areas, against the sides of the chase, and against the form, with the pieces at the four sides longer than and overlapping the sides of the form.

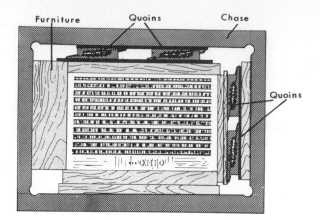

Furniture   Quoins   Chase

Quoins

FIGURE 5-8. Locked-up form.

To secure the form, wedge-shaped *quoins* (pronounced coins) are utilized. They are commonly placed at the top and the right of the chase. As they are expanded (by tightening with a key), they exert pressure against the furniture and toward the form and chase. Figure 5-8 shows a locked-up form with quoins in position.

If the form is to be duplicated—made into electros or stereotypes —type-high slugs are locked up inside the chase to protect the form when pressure is applied.

Foundry proofs, which are drawn from duplicates, carry heavy black borders formed by the bearers. These areas are removed from the duplicates before final printing is done.

If the form is being readied for a printing press and consists entirely of plates—that is, engravings, electros, and/or stereotypes —lock-up may be done by using *patent base*, a metal base consisting of a pattern of holes like a honeycomb or of diagonal grooves (Figure 5-9).

The patent base is placed inside a chase. Then the plates unmounted are secured to the base with special hooks that fasten to the plates and to the grooves or holes. The combined thicknesses of plates and base should be type-high.

FIGURE 5-9. Patent base with plates locked on bed of press.

6 In early chapters, emphasis was placed on the need in letterpress printing for separate metal or plastic plates for illustrations. The original plates are called *engravings, cuts,* or *etchings* and are divided into two basic types depending upon the nature of the copy from which they are made.

Some illustrations, such as cartoons and other pen and ink drawings, contain only solid lines and full whites, and the plates made from them are called *line* plates, engravings, cuts, or etchings. These are also often identified as *zincs,* or *zincos,* because of the metal used. Although this description is generally understood, it is not accurate because other types of plates are also made from zinc.

Other illustrations, such as photographs, paintings, and wash drawings, contain tonal values of all gradations from white to full tone and require plates called *halftones* for their reproduction. If these illustrations are in full (lifelike) color, they can be reproduced with either *three-color* or *four-color process plates.*

These line, halftone, and process plates as described are all *original* plates because they are made from original copy. Much of the high-speed letterpress printing of newspapers and other publications, however, is accomplished by duplicate plates. These can be made of all or any part of a printing form, and are usually either *stereotypes* or *electrotypes,* getting their names from the process by which they are made. Rubber and plastic duplicate plates are also used.

 original letterpress plates

The simplest to make of the original letterpress plates is the line etching; consequently, it often is the cheapest of these plates.

HOW LINE ETCHINGS ARE MADE

The process of making line etchings starts with the photographing of the original copy. This copy, which may be a drawing, type matter, or any other subject with no tonal variations, is mounted on a copy board in front of an engraver's camera. It may be reduced, enlarged or copied the same size.

Light is directed to the copy and reflects back through the camera's lens to the contrasty film used for such work. The film, when developed, is opaque where light-struck and clear where it has received no light. Hence the subject shows up as transparent lines on the negative because light was reflected only from the white areas around it and not from the drawing itself.

It should be understood that not only is the negative a reverse image of the original copy in that what was light on the original is dark on the negative and vice versa, but the subject is in reverse direction also. In other words, a figure facing left is now facing right, and any type matter reads from right to left instead of left to right. This reverse direction must be carried over to the finished plate so that the printed impressions made from it will read correctly. In order to maintain reverse direction on the plate, the negative is turned before the image is transferred to metal.

To get a sheet of zinc ready to receive the image from a negative, the zinc is thoroughly "pummied" (cleaned with water and powdered pumice). It is then made light-sensitive with a coating of a solution of ammonium bichromate, egg albumin, and water. This coating is evenly distributed and dried over the sheet of zinc when the sheet is whirled over low heat.

The dried sheet is placed with its sensitive side next to the line negative in a vacuum printing frame. Light is then directed through the negative to the plate. The light passes through the transparent areas of the negative (these are the image lines) and is held back by the opaque areas of the negative. As it strikes the coating on the zinc plate, the light causes the coating to harden and become insoluble in water. In areas where the light has been held back, the coating remains water-soluble.

After it has been exposed in this fashion, the entire sheet of zinc is covered by roller with a thin layer of black etching ink. The surface is then gently washed with water, shedding the coating—and ink—from all areas not hardened by exposure to the camera lights. The result is an inked print of the original in reverse.

Remember that, in letterpress printing, material must stand out in relief in order to be printed. Producing the image area of a line cut in relief on the zinc is achieved by *etching*, or eating away, the metal from the nonimage areas.

The inked print is prepared for etching with a coat of shellac or other acidproof material on its back. The larger open spaces on its printing surface are roughly covered with liquid asphaltum, another acidproof substance, in order to confine the etching action of the acid to vital areas.

A solution of nitric acid is used in etching the zinc, and the image areas are protected from the acid by a resinous powder called *dragon's blood.* When the zinc is heated, the dragon's blood melts and then dries to form an acidproof layer over the image areas. When the zinc is bathed in acid it "bites" away some of the metal from the nonimage areas. The zinc is then removed and powdered again, this time to protect the sides of the etched lines. This precaution prevents the acid from undercutting and weakening the lines so much that they could not withstand the pressures they get during press operation. The acid baths (or "bites," as they are called) are repeated until the desired depth is obtained.

The number of bites needed varies, but four are usually required. Before each, the dragon's blood must be skillfully applied from four directions; between each application of the powder, the zinc is heated to melt the dragon's blood so it will not be carried away as the brushing is done from another direction.

After it has been etched, the plate is sent to the finishing room where it is cleaned, and any excess metal that escaped the acid baths is routed away, including what had been retained in the large open areas coated with asphaltum.

More than one subject are usually handled at a time. Several negatives, before being printed on the zinc, are mounted on a sheet of plate glass called a *flat.* In the finishing room, each of the subjects is cut from the sheet of zinc, squared, and mounted on a block or base. Each is then ready to be put into place in a printing form.

REVERSE LINE PLATES. When it is desired, the values in a line drawing or other subject can be reversed by the engraver; that is, the black areas in the drawing can be made to print as white and the white areas as black.

OHIO UNIVERSITY   FIGURE 6-1. A reverse line plate.

To make a reverse line plate (Figure 6-1), the engraver first makes a normal line negative. Then, by placing the line negative over another sheet of film and exposing it to light, he creates a negative on which the values are the same as the original copy. The lines that were black on the copy are black (opaque) on the negative; the other areas are clear.

When the second negative is transferred to the metal, and the plate is etched, the areas that were white on the original stand in relief and will carry ink. These plates cost slightly more than standard line plates because of the extra negative. A common use of the device is for signature logotypes in advertisements.

APPLYING SHADING TO ZINC ETCHINGS. Line etchings, as we have said, can be used only for the reproduction of illustrations that contain no middle tones—only the extremes. The *effect* of middle tones can be obtained from zinc etchings, however, through a mechanical process called *Benday* (Figure 6-2).

FIGURE 6-2. A line drawing before and after the application of Benday patterns.

The Benday process, which gets its name from Benjamin Day, its inventor, is a method of applying dots, designs, lines, and other effects to any portion of the surface of a line cut. The pattern may be applied directly to the zinc, to the film, or by the artist onto the original drawing.

In the traditional method, the engraver applies the pattern directly to the plate, using Benday patterns, which come in a wide variety of designs. After a line illustration has been exposed photographically on the sensitized plate in the usual manner, the plate is lightly stained to bring the image into view. All of the areas that are not to receive shading are then painted with a pasty, water-soluble solution. Meanwhile, the Benday pattern sheet, on which the specified pattern stands in relief, is inked. By pressing the sheet against the zinc, the inked pattern is transferred; the water-soluble solution is then washed off. When the surface is dusted with dragon's blood powder, the lines in the Benday not torn as well as those in the original drawing, receive the powder and resist the acid baths to stand in relief.

The term "Benday" originally applied only to the method just described, but today it is used loosely to describe the addition of shading to drawings by other similar means as well. Because of cost savings, it is becoming increasingly common for the artist to apply the shading to the original art work.

It is possible, of course, for an artist to draw dots, screens, or other patterns by hand as he makes his illustration. Although this procedure is sometimes followed, it is usually too time-consuming. Instead, artists ordinarily use any of several shading sheets now offered by a number of manufacturers.[1] Some of these are made of clear acetate with an adhesive backing; patterns may be either of black lines for graying-in light areas, or white lines for lightening dark areas. The artist applies a piece of patterned acetate that is slightly larger than the area to be covered, then cuts away the excess to leave the pattern in the desired area only.

The preprinted acetate sheets described are but one of the types currently available. Some are of special fluid; with others the screen pattern may be scraped off as desired with a sharp blade. The only real problem with any of these arises when the illustration is to be reduced or enlarged; the screen or dot pattern may become too small or too large for good reproduction. The artist must take into account any change in size when he selects a pattern.

Pattern application by any of these devices has become so popular that in general it can be said that when an artist's services are available, the artist is asked to do the work rather than the engraver.

Artists can also use stippled boards containing patterns of raised dots or lines to achieve a shaded effect as they make illustrations for reproduction as line etchings.

---

[1]Shading sheets are referred to by various trade names. Common ones include *Craftint,* a product of Craftint Mfg. Co.; *Zip-A-Tone,* of Para-Tone, Inc.; *Contak* of Transograph Company; and *Tintograph* of The Tintograph Company.

LINE ETCHINGS AND COLOR. Drawings can be reproduced in colors with line etchings, as well as in black and white. Benday shadings can be applied to plates to be printed in color also.

In either case, a separate plate must be made for each color to be printed. For Benday, each of the plates must have the screen applied to it at a different angle so the pattern's dots or lines, when printed, will fall next to, rather than directly upon, those of the other colors.

HALFTONE PHOTOENGRAVINGS

Original printing plates for continuous-tone illustrations are also made by the photoengraving process, and in most respects the procedure is the same as that in the making of line plates.

The biggest difference is in the first step, the photographing of the original copy. To make a halftone negative, the engraver must use a screen in his camera. At first, this screen was made up of two pieces of glass upon which parallel ruled lines were etched and blackened with pigment. The two pieces of glass were then fastened together with a transparent adhesive so that the lines on each ran at right angles to those of the other piece and at a forty-five-degree angle to the border of the screen to make the pattern less conspicuous in finished plates.

These are still in extensive use today, but some engravers now use film screens. The glass screens are placed in the camera in front of the film but at a slight distance from it. Because they are over the film and in direct contact with it, film screens are usually called *contact screens*. These are more commonly used by makers of lithographic plates; their chief advantage is that a dot pattern in white areas can be eliminated much more easily by their use than by glass screens.

IMPORTANCE OF SCREEN "SIZE." Whether contact or glass screens are being used is relatively immaterial to most users of engraving, but the screen size is of great importance. Screens are designated according to the number of parallel lines in each linear inch. Therefore, a 65-line screen has sixty-five lines to the inch, and a 100-line screen has one-hundred lines to the inch. Which screen to use depends on two basic factors: the surface of the paper and the quality of reproduction. Rough papers demand a coarse (few lines to the inch) screen, and the potential quality of reproduction increases as the screen becomes finer. Therefore, for highest quality reproduction of halftones by letterpress, it is necessary to use plates made with a fine screen and to print on smooth-surfaced paper.

Halftone screens in most common use for letterpress printing are 50-, 55-, 65-, 85-, 100-, 110-, 120-, and 133-line. Less used are 150-, 175-, and 200-line screens. For newspaper production, because the paper is soft and coarse, 65-line screens are common. The selection of halftone screens is also limited to the coarser screens (usually 100 lines or less) when printing is to be done from duplicate plates made by stereotyping. Some detail is lost during the stereotyping process, making it difficult to retain the fine dots produced by the finer screens.

Generally speaking, coarse-screen halftones are made with zinc; fine-screen (110 lines or more) are made with copper. However, the greater durability of copper causes it to be preferred for long press runs when zinc might otherwise be used.

How Halftone Photoengravings Are Made. With the specified screen in his camera, the photoengraver places the copy on a copy board in front of the lens, puts the film behind the screen in the camera, and proceeds to make one or more exposures.

Halftone negatives may be made with only one exposure, like line negatives, but cameramen usually take a series of short exposures in order to get greater tone control and to retain detail in the extreme light and dark areas of the copy.

As the light is beamed to the copy, it reflects back through the lens opening and the screen to the film. Because the light that goes through the lens is reflected from the copy, it varies in intensity directly according to the lightness or darkness of the various areas of the copy. A photograph of a man with a white shirt and dark suit, for example, will reflect light strongly from the shirt and weakly from the suit.

When the light pierces the thousands of tiny holes in the screen, it is broken into thousands of small beams. The intense light spreads, as it goes through these apertures, breaking the screen lines into clear dots on the negative. The dots vary in size and shape, and are connected or separated, depending upon the amount of light reflecting from the copy. It is because of this variation in the dot structure that all the tones in a photograph or other such illustration can be captured on film, transferred to a plate, and finally produced in the printing process.

The developed halftone negative looks like a standard photographic negative to the naked eye. With a magnifying glass, however, the thousands of dots created by the lines of the screen can be clearly seen. The image appears composed completely of dots, both clear and opaque. One can readily realize how tiny the dots are by understanding that the number per square inch is always the square of the screen size: a 50-line screen produces 2500, 100-line screen produces 10,000, and so on.

In the finished plate, each of the dots that were clear on the negative stands in relief as a printing surface; the metal surrounding them has been cut away by an acid-etching method similar to that used for making line plates.

One point about halftones must be underscored. *The dot pattern of a standard halftone, though it varies considerably, is present over all portions of the negative and consequently will be present over all portions of the finished plate.* Therefore, even in areas that seem to be pure white in the copy, some dots will stand to carry ink to the paper. For this reason an ordinary halftone will reproduce no absolutely pure whites. Only with special treatment by the artist and/or engraver can pure whites be obtained. Halftone plates containing the pure whites are called *high-light* or *drop-out* halftones and are usually much more expensive than standard plates.[2]

Exposing, Developing, and Etching the Plate. To etch a halftone plate made from zinc, a nitric acid bath is used. Etching of copper plates is generally done with an iron perchloride bath. In either case, the sheet of metal is first coated with a light-sensitive material. The negative is turned, put into position on the plate-glass flat along with other subjects, and is then placed in a photographic printer along with a sheet of sensitized zinc or copper. Intense light is beamed through the negatives in the flat to the sensitized metal. As the light hits each negative, it penetrates to the plate through only the clear dots of the negative, hardening the emulsion at these points.

When the metal is etched, the acid eats away from around these dots, leaving each of them standing in relief as a tiny printing surface. Areas that were dark in the original subject will have many relatively large and closely grouped dots standing in relief to carry ink to paper. Consequently, as the plate is printed, most of the paper will be covered with ink in these areas, and the areas will be dark to the eye. Light areas of the subject will contain relatively small dots widely spaced and will be light when printed.

[2]Figure 12-9 of Chapter 12 shows a high-light halftone.

Figure 6-3. On the right, portion of the silhouette halftone of the cogwheel (left) has been enlarged to show how the dot structure produces shades of tone. (Courtesy S. D. Warren Company.)

The Magic of the Dots. This is how the dot structure recreates all the tones of the original photograph, within certain limitations. Because the dot pattern exists in all parts of the plate, there can be no absolute blacks or whites in the standard halftone. Coarseness of screen and paper have a bearing on the fidelity of reproduction, too. But to the viewer, unaided by a magnifying glass, the dots blend with the background to form a faithful reproduction of the original (Figure 6-3).

The principle of blending dots with the background can be easily illustrated by any student. By holding a newspaper at normal reading distance, all the letters and characters can be seen clearly. These represent the dots of a halftone. By pinning the newspaper to a wall and stepping back several paces, the letters and characters appear as masses of gray; the difference in tone created by columns of standard type matter as compared with areas of boldface type is the best illustration of how tones vary in halftones depending upon the size and spacing of dots.

Tint (Tone) Blocks. It is possible, because of the dot magic of the halftone process, to reproduce areas of any given size in a uniform tint, or tone, of the color being used in a printing job. These tints can be produced according to any percentage of the full density of the color.

For example, when black is being used, a 50 percent gray (just half the density of solid black) can be printed from an engraving made to that specification. Other desired percentages, such as 20, 30, or 80 can also be obtained (Figure 6-4).

FIGURE 6-4. Screen tints. Top, left to right: 10, 20, 30, 40, 50 percent tone values; bottom, left to right: 60, 70, 80, 90, 100 percent tone values.

The term "tint block" is apt to designate both the engravings made for this effect and the printed areas themselves. They can be made by the methods described under Benday shadings, but the engraver normally employs the halftone process. Instead of photographing an illustration, he puts a white board in front of the camera, obtaining the desired tone by controlling the amount of light going through the screen to the film. The plate is etched and processed like a halftone. Any screen, 50-line, 133-line, and so on, can be used.

Solid tints (100 percent of the tone) are made on unetched plates simply cut from the sheet of zinc or copper and mounted type-high.

The impression that an additional color was used in printing is often created by screened tint blocks. When red ink is being used, a tint appears as pink; when brown is used, tan results, and so on.

Tint blocks behind type matter of another color are effective in drawing attention to areas that would be otherwise weak in display.

SPECIAL TYPES OF PHOTOENGRAVINGS. The discussion of original plates has been limited up to now to standard line etchings and square-finish halftones. It has been pointed out that ordinary square-finish halftones have a dot pattern covering the full surface of the engraving. But even the casual reader of letterpress-printed material will have noticed that many reproductions show a figure fully outlined against a field of white, and also perhaps that line and halftone seem to be present in the same plate. These and other special effects are attained through the use of special types of original plates.

Combination Plates. As the name implies, combination

plates are made by combining one or more line negatives with one or more halftone negatives. Any case where line copy has to be included on the face of a halftone or adjacent to and touching the halftone, demands a combination plate.

An engraver produces combination plates by making separate negatives of the line and halftone copy in the usual manner. These negatives are then stripped together on one glass flat. If the line work is to merely touch the halftone, the two negatives are first overlapped slightly and then cut. Because both negatives are cut with the same stroke, they will abut each other perfectly. From such plates, the line work on finished printed copies appears as it did on the original copy; that is, lines that were black on the copy against a field of white show the same way when printed.

If line work is to appear on top of the halftone, an additional step is required. Either a reverse line negative must be made, or the two negatives must be burned (exposed) on the plate in two separate operations.

If a reverse line negative is made, the result is a *reverse-combination* plate. The line and halftone negatives can be exposed on the plate at the same time in this case because the line negative, as a reverse, will be clear in all nonimage areas. It therefore permits passage of light through the halftone negative.

When the line and halftone negatives are burned on the plate in separate operations, the result is a *surprint,* sometimes called a *double print* because of the two exposure operations. The separate printings are required because the line negative is opaque in the nonimage area; consequently the light could not go through a halftone negative exposed at the same time.

Silhouette, or Outline, Halftones. A halftone subject silhouetted against a clear background is produced in letterpress printing from a special plate called *silhouette* or *outline.*

These are made in the same way that standard halftones are plus some additional work. After the plate has been etched, the engraver outlines the subject by tooling a fine line around it. The area outside that line is then routed away.

If the outlining is especially intricate, the work may be done on the negative before the plate is burned. In these cases, the engraver paints away the dot pattern from around the subject.

Vignettes. A vignette plate is similar to a silhouette, but the edge of the subject area is softened, so that it seems to fade away (Figure 6-5). These plates also start out as regular halftones, although the engraver is helped if the soft-edge effect has been retouched on the copy before processing.

FIGURE 6-5. Special plate finishes. Left, a square-finish surprint; right, a reverse combination outlined at the top and vignetted at the bottom.

The engraver first outlines the extreme outside edge of the fade-out area, much as he outlines for a silhouette plate. Then, by re-etching, he reduces the dot pattern gradually toward the edge until the effect of fade-out is obtained. The excess metal from beyond the original outline is then routed out.

Special Shapes. Ovals, circles, and other special geometric shapes are attained for photoengravings through methods similar to those used for outline plates. The shapes may be hand-cut, but often a line negative of the desired shape is stripped over the halftone negative for making the plate. Masking the shape in this fashion means better results with less costly handwork.

Duographs. A two-color effect from original copy in only one color is achieved with a pair of duograph plates. Two halftone plates are made from the same original copy. One is etched for detail, the other is only flat-etched. The two-tone effect results when the flat plate is printed in a second color.

Snow scenes, with the key plate in black and the flat plate in blue, can be attractively reproduced as duographs. Forest scenes in black and green, sea or lake scenes in black and blue, and fall scenes in black and brown represent typical uses for duographs.

Sometimes, especially when cost is of special importance, an editor will use a screened tint in a second color to get an effect similar to that created with duograph plates. In such cases the engraver makes a standard halftone plate and a tint block of the same size. In making the tint block, he changes the screen angle to avoid creating a disturbing screen pattern, called a *moiré*. The use of a tint block over a halftone produces a uniform tint over the whole subject, whereas duographs reproduce tints in the tones of the original subject.

Either of these devices are often erroneously referred to as *duotones,* but true duotones are made with color-separation negatives from original copy that is in two colors. The same method is used to reproduce copy that is in full color.

PROCESS PLATES FOR FULL-COLOR REPRODUCTION[3]

Originals for color reproduction include: all copy in which the subject is rendered in full continuous tone color, such as oil, water-color, or tempera painting; the color transparency; and the photoprint in full color, such as carbo, chromotone, dye transfer, imbibition, and wash-off relief.

Under discussion here are full-color originals where facsimile reproduction can only be achieved through the blending of the three primary colors plus black. Where an original is to be reproduced in one color only, the line etching or halftone is printed in that color; when a two-color original is to be reproduced, duotone halftones are employed; but, for full, four-color reproduction, it is necessary to make process color plates, one for each of the primary colors and one for black. Should the black plate be eliminated, the reproduction becomes a three-color process, still achieving the full blending of the primary colors but lacking the emphasis of black and its shades.

All full-color originals drawn or painted upon a material such as paper or canvas are reproduced by the light reflected from the original, whereas color transparencies are reproduced by transmitting light through the transparency. The color transparency

[3]The section on full-color reproduction which follows is reprinted from "Line, Halftone & Color—An Introduction to Modern Photoengraving," a publication of the American Photoengravers Association. Reprinted with permission granted 8/6/62 by the American Photoengravers Association.

is preferred over color photoprints because some loss of detail and color value occurs in prints or copies made from transparencies. Hand-colored photographs are inferior in reproduction because the underlying photographic image is recorded in the negatives and interferes with correct color separation.

THE COLOR PROCESS. In pigment, such as printing inks, the primary colors are yellow, red, and blue. By mixing these colors in correct proportions, any desired color can be obtained. In the same manner, superimposed printing of the process color plates in precise register causes a color-blended image with all the colors and values of the original. An artist can paint a picture using pigments of a score of different colors and hues, and a perfect reproduction can be achieved on the printing press using three halftone plates, each printing one of the three primary colors. In four-color process, a black plate is added to obtain strength in detail and to produce neutral shades of grays, which are difficult to make with the primary colors. The addition of the black plate also makes possible the use of red and blue printing inks in purer tones than those used in straight three-color process.

COLOR SEPARATION NEGATIVES. While it is true that the color principle of light differs from that of pigments, it is not essential to consider this distinction here. Photographic color separation takes a simple knowledge of the pigment primary colors and their complementary relationships.

In photographing a color original, the photengraver first analyzes it for yellow, red, and blue color content. He then separates and records each of these colors on film. A color separation is accomplished by photographing through a color filter that absorbs or "quenches" those colors of which it is composed and permits the remaining color to be recorded.

To separate the yellow color in the original, a violet filter prevents the photography of its component colors, red and blue, and permits the yellow to be recorded; similarly, to separate the red, a green filter deters yellow and blue and permits the red to be recorded; to separate the blue, an orange filter blots out the yellow and red and permits the blue to be recorded. To make the "black" separation, a specially modified filter is employed that limits color absorption and produces the required negative, eliminating the primary colors.

In the indirect method of color photography, the resultant negatives are in continuous tone (no halftone screen) and are called continuous-tone separation negatives. They are an accurate record of each of the primary colors in all their gradations of tones, plus black.

Color correction—that is, improvement of color rendition—is usually done at the time separation negatives are made, by a process of introducing photographic masks in the camera.

The separation negatives are then placed before the camera and rephotographed to produce positives; or they are placed in contact with a photographic plate, and a photoprint (positive) is made. It is necessary to make these positives so that they can again be photographed through a halftone screen.

It is also possible to employ a direct method of color photography, to separate the primary colors and produce halftone negatives in one photographic operation by placing the halftone screen in the camera at the time of color separation. The indirect method, however, permits greater photographic control of color separation, which would otherwise be performed manually by the etcher and finisher.

THE ELECTRONIC SCANNER. One of the newest and most promising devices for color correction should be mentioned before proceeding to halftone negatives. The scanner produces negatives or positives that are electronically color-corrected for color errors due to inherent characteristics of ink and color filters; it computes correct values for the black plate, removes the correct amount of undercolor, and carries out tone correction to compensate for gray-scale distortions. Mechanically, the time involved in color correction is reduced both in the camera work and in the attention given the plate by the etcher and finisher.

COLOR HALFTONE NEGATIVES. In order to print continuous-tone color, the metal plate must have printing surfaces capable of reproducing color gradations. This is accomplished with the halftone screen, which breaks up the image into minute dots varying in size, shape, and proximity.

In making halftone color negatives, each color positive is photographed through the same desired screen, but, for each color, the screen is placed at an angle thirty degrees apart from the other colors. This is so that in the printing no color dots will interfere with proper blending. Experience has determined that this thirty-degree angle will also keep a moiré pattern from forming.

This is the standard procedure for three-color process negatives.

With the introduction of the fourth color, black, the screens for the black, red, and blue negatives are placed thirty degrees apart, and the screen for the yellow negative is placed between the black and red positions at an angle of fifteen degrees from each. The yellow dot being the least visible, the moiré is not offensive.

ETCHING, FINISHING, AND PROOFING COLOR HALFTONES. After the color halftone negatives are made, a photoprint of each is made on metal, as with standard halftones, and the resulting plates are etched, finished, and proofed.

For various reasons, photographic color separations are not exact. The task of final color corrections falls to the etcher and finisher—a task that, in addition to mechanical skill and artistic technique, requires a thorough knowledge of color composition. The color etcher must estimate the amounts of each color required and then etch the plates to produce that amount. Not until all four colors are combined on one proof can he see the results of his efforts.

Modern power proof presses simulate pressroom conditions, with specified inks and paper. Usually the yellow is printed first, followed by the red, blue, and black, in that order, although it is feasible to change this sequence if desired. The first proofing invariably shows that more etching, correcting, and reproofing are necessary.

 duplicate letterpress plates

Duplicate plates are of great importance in letterpress printing for a number of reasons:

(1) They permit doubling up or "gang running" of small jobs. For example, when press size permits, a printer might make four duplicate plates of the form for a small booklet. With all four plates on the press, each impression delivers four copies of the booklet that can be cut from the sheet or web and folded. Thus, with duplicate plates the letterpress printer achieves what the lithographer does with his step-and-repeat machines.

(2) The high-speed rotary presses used by newspapers became possible because of stereotyping. By duplicating the printing forms for full newspaper pages as one curved metal plate, the stereotyping process increased the rate of production of newspapers tremendously.

(3) Production of national advertising and syndicated material

has been simplified. An advertiser wishing to place the same ad in a number of publications can provide each of them with a duplicate plate of the ad. Or, as is also common, he may supply the publication with a matrix (the sheet of a special paper material that serves as a mold for stereotypes), thus keeping shipping costs to a minimum because of the matrix's light weight. Syndicates can provide publications with comic strips, cartoons, crossword puzzles, and similar features in the same fashion.

(4) Publicity and promotion men also make effective use of matrices or duplicate plates. It is much easier to get the photograph of a client published in a small newspaper if a matrix is provided instead of the original photograph. Instead of being forced to pay for an original halftone plate, the newspaper can quickly make a cast from the mat at virtually no cost.

(5) Duplicate plates also provide insurance against damage to costly original plates and type matter. Printing can be done from the duplicate, and if it is damaged another plate can be made quickly from the first. Otherwise, type would have to be set again and expensive photoengravings would have to be made, starting back with edited copy and art work.

(6) Duplicate plates eliminate the wearing out of type in extremely long runs. One can readily realize the disadvantage of resetting a complete book because the type did not last for a full press run; with duplicate plates this cannot happen.

HOW DUPLICATE LETTERPRESS PLATES ARE MADE

Because stereotyping is a cheaper method, it is more commonly used by newspapers than electrotyping. Other media that demand greater fidelity of reproduction often use electrotypes in spite of added cost. The newer plastic and rubber duplicate plates are being adopted for an increasing number of special purposes.

THE STEREOTYPING PROCESS. Stereotyping is a simple, easy-to-understand process. Basically, only two steps are involved: (1) pressing a *mold,* or "mat" as it is called; and (2) casting the plate from molten metal.

Making the Mat. In the beginning stereotype mats were of *papier mâché,* which had to be made by pasting sheets of paper together. The papier mâché was placed over the type form on a steam table where the mat was formed by the application of pressure and heat at the same time. The mat then had to be dried before a casting could be made.

Dry mats, because of features that save both time and labor, have replaced wet mats. Dry mats consist of a single layer of tough, cardboardlike paper, specially composed and treated to resist heat and bought in large sheets to be stored for instant use as needed.

Steam tables are not needed in dry-mat stereotyping; instead rolling machines or hydraulic impression presses are used to make the mats. When rolling machines are used, the type form is placed on a flat bed and covered by a mat and a blanket of a soft material such as felt or cork. The bed then moves automatically under a heavy roller that exerts sufficient pressure to emboss the surface of the type and plates into the mat. Because of the wear on type and plates caused by the rolling action, hydraulic presses have gained wide acceptance in mat making. These machines operate on the principle of the platen press: pressure is exerted directly to the mat and backing with no rolling.

Casting the Plate. Stereotype plates are in either flat or semicylindrical form. To illustrate the differences in making the two different forms, it is helpful to trace the casting process for both.

One type of flat casting is a mat received in a publications office from a public relations firm. Typical examples of these are a mat pressed from a photoengraving of a head-and-shoulders photograph of one of the firm's clients, an illustration in an advertisement, a complete advertisement, a comic strip, or any other subject to be part of a printing form—no matter the content, the procedure is the same.

The mat, in most instances, is taped together with other mats so that several may be cast at one time. Each is backed with cardboard in the open areas. The mats are then placed in a flat-casting box, made up of two smooth iron plates hinged together so that one can be dropped to a horizontal position. They are placed against the horizontal plate and held in position by three bars, one at the end and one at each side. The plate is then raised to a vertical position against the other plate. The bars holding the mats in position also perform the function of keeping the two plates apart with an opening at the top. Molten metal is poured or injected into the opening until the mats are covered. When the metal has hardened, the casting box plates are separated and the stereotype casting—a duplicate engraving—is removed, cut, and trimmed.

Depending upon the thickness of the bars used to hold the mat in position, the stereotype plates produced in a flat-casting box may be type-high or much thinner. If they are type-high, they may be put into position in a printing form, which can then be locked on a flat-bed or platen press for printing to commence. If the stereotypes are thin-cast, they must be put on bases thick enough to make them type-high. Thin casts are used when semicylindrical plates for a rotary press are to be made. Because the only impression to be made from them is the rolling of a mat, thin-cast plates under these circumstances can be quickly taped into position on the base with a tape that is adhesive on both sides.

Thus, in a small-newspaper operation, a stereotype cut takes its place in a printing form along with original engravings, headlines, body type, and other stereotypes, and printing is done directly from the form. In a large-newspaper operation, semicylindrical stereotype plates of the whole page form are made, and printing is done from this duplicate plate.

The casting of semicylindrical plates is quite similar to the casting of flat plates, although the process is ordinarily more automatic.

For example, the mat is first backed up with cardboard or gummed felt in the open spaces, just as for flat casting. In both cases, the backing helps the mat withstand the force of the metal during casting, for its large open spaces might otherwise give way.

Next the mat is put into an ovenlike device called a *scorcher*. This forms the mat into the curved shape of the press cylinder to which the plate will eventually be fastened. Next, the mat is put in the casting machine. Today these are mainly semiautomatic or completely automatic, although hand-operated machines are still to be found. The casting operation can be as simple as putting the mat in the machine, pressing a button, and watching the curved plate come out.

Finishing operations are often automatic, too. Undesired raised spots on plates must be routed away, the plate must be trimmed to proper size, the inside surface must be shaved to a desired smoothness, and the edges must be beveled so the plate can be clamped to the press.

The speed with which semicylindrical plates can be cast allows large metropolitan newspapers to make several castings of each page in a matter of minutes. Each plate can then be put on a press unit, and the multiple unit presses can then turn out several copies of a newspaper simultaneously. Stereotyping can truly be described as a pillar of modern mass production of publications.

THE ELECTROTYPING PROCESS. Except for newspaper work, the most commonly used duplicate plate is the electrotype, or *electro* as it is commonly called. Electros are preferred because they duplicate the original more faithfully and last through much longer press runs. Like stereotypes, they can be of full page forms or of single halftones or other matter, either flat or curved.

Electros are made by depositing copper or nickel on the face of a mold electrolytically. Nickel is usually used if the plate will turn out especially long runs or color work.

Material to be duplicated is locked into a chase in a manner similar to that in printing directly from the form. A mold, called the *case*, is made by pressing either wax, lead, or other substance against the form. It will be used to receive the metal coating.

If wax is the mold substance used, the case must be sprayed with graphite. This serves as a conductor of electricity when the case is connected to a cathode rod and hung in a bath of copper sulphate and sulphuric acid. As electric current and the acid eat away copper from copper anodes suspended in the bath opposite the case, the graphite attracts the copper particles to the case. When these particles form a shell of sufficient thickness, the electrical current is stopped and the case is removed from the bath. The shell is then taken from the case and backed with metal. The plate thus formed is ready for finishing—whatever routing, beveling, and mounting required to make it ready for use.

If lead is the mold substance, procedure is the same except that graphiting is not needed because lead itself conducts electricity. Electro molds are also made from plastics and from Tenaplate, a patented molding material.

PLASTIC DUPLICATE PLATES. Duplicate plates made of plastic have been in fairly common use since World War II when the Government Printing Office tried them with considerable success. Many advertisers find them especially useful for newspaper ads. Unlike stereotype mats, they do not shrink, and newspapers can make the curved stereos for cylinder presses directly instead of first casting a flat stereotype. They are less expensive than electrotypes and are light in weight, thus reducing mailing costs.

Plastic plates are made in almost the same manner as stereotypes. Instead of using a paper mat for a mold, however, sheets of plastic are used. In casting, another plastic compound is used instead of molten metal.

RUBBER DUPLICATE PLATES. Rubber plates are also made similarly to stereotypes, and they have gained increasing acceptance in recent years, particularly for book and job printing. They are made in flat or curved form for either flat-bed or rotary presses. Great durability is one of their chief assets for they can outlast the other kinds of duplicate plates. They also are especially useful in printing on rough surfaces.

recent developments in platemaking

Improved materials and methods are always being devised for making letterpress plates, both original and duplicate. The competition from other processes constantly acts as a catalyst to bring about changes. Typical is the introduction of magnesium plates and methods for their use.

MAGNESIUM PLATES

As a metal for plates, magnesium has several advantages. It is light, etches quickly, and has great durability. Although it serves to make photoengravings, the metal and its plates are more important as the basis for introducing lithographic principles to letterpress printing.

For example, magnesium plates are now being used to permit cold-type composition for letterpress printing while skipping the time-consuming and costly duplicate plates for rotary presses. Cold type and illustrations are combined on a thin, light magnesium *original* plate, which can be put around a rotary cylinder and printed from directly. These plates therefore have advantages over original plates or stereotypes because: (1) they are much lighter; (2) no duplicate plates need to be made for a rotary press; (3) the plates can be etched much more quickly; (4) they wear longer (when chrome-plated they can last indefinitely); and (5) cost is low.

Many printers believe that magnesium plates will rescue jobs for letterpress from absorption by offset lithography.

ELECTRONICALLY ENGRAVED PLATES

The Fairchild Scan-A-Sizer and other electronic engraving machines are gaining increasing acceptance for the making of letterpress plates. Some, such as the Scan-A-Sizer, produce plastic plates while others turn out metal.

Generally speaking, these machines electronically scan original copy and transmit impulses to a stylus that cuts, in a dot or line pattern, the image in relief on plastic or other material. The plates thus made can be used directly for printing or for molding duplicate plates. Their most widespread use has been by small newspapers.

DYCRIL PLATES

A light-sensitive plastic coating over metal is used in a system developed by the du Pont Company to produce letterpress plates much more quickly than traditional methods can.

Exposure of the plate by ultraviolet light through a negative hardens and renders the plastic coating insoluble where struck by light. The unexposed plastic washes away leaving the hardened plastic in relief as the printing surface.

These Dycril photopolymer plates are prepared exceptionally fast (only about fifteen minutes from negative to plate as compared to several hours for metal plates) and are gaining wide acceptance, especially for high-speed rotary presses using "wraparound" plates.

POWDERLESS ETCHING MACHINE

The four-way powdering used during the making of zinc etchings is time-consuming but necessary when the plates are etched as described earlier in this chapter. A new machine now etches plates with only one bite and eliminates powdering between bites to prevent undercutting of dots or lines.

7

The pressroom is the heart of the publishing or printing plant. Here the end product—the printed sheet—is produced; and the planning of how printing materials should look reaches fruition when type and auxiliary elements are reproduced in ink on paper. The press is the vital link between planning and the actual printed piece, whether it be newspaper, magazine, book, folder, leaflet, booklet, package, or bread wrapper.

Many kinds of presses exist, and they vary widely in terms of speed, size, and principle of operation. It is probably true, as reported by Melcher and Larrick, "There is a perfect or near-perfect press for every job."[1]

Therefore it behooves the person devising printed literature to know about the kinds of presses, their capacities and limitations. Only in this way can he (1) select a printer with the right press for his specific job; or (2) tailor the job to the press equipment available to achieve his desired results.

 types of presses

Presses will be discussed on the following pages in terms of the three principles of operation: (1) platen; (2) flat-bed cylinder; and (3) rotary.

These are shown in schematic form in Figure 7-1. Note that in the case of the first two printing is done from type; these are therefore restricted to letterpress printing.

The rotary press, on the other hand, involves the use of curved plates made from type. They may have a raised printing surface (letterpress printing), a flat surface (lithography), or an indented surface (gravure).

THE PLATEN PRESS

In this simplest printing press, the form of type is placed in a vertical position. Paper is positioned against the platen, which closes in clamshell fashion to press it against the inked form. When the platen swings open to receive another sheet of paper, the form is inked.

Platen presses are limited in size and are, consequently, used

[1]Daniel Melcher and Nancy Larrick, *Printing and Promotion Handbook* (New York: McGraw-Hill Book Company), 1956, p. 249.

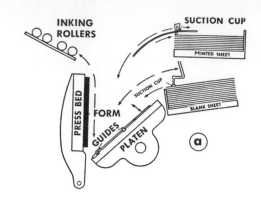

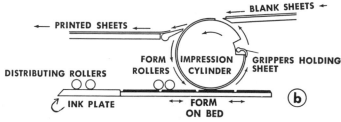

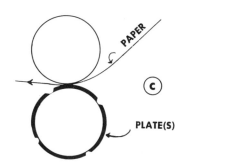

FIGURE 7-1. The three principles of press operation, top to bottom: (a) the platen press; (b) the cylinder press; and (c) the rotary press. The printing surface (form) in (a) and (b) must be raised. The surface (plate or plates) in (c) can be raised, flat, or intaglio. (a and b reprinted from *Production in Advertising and the Graphic Arts* by David Hymes, by permission of the publishers, Holt, Rinehart and Winston, Inc.)

primarily for printing letterheads, cards, business forms, and other small jobs.

Hand-fed platen presses, in which paper is positioned by hand and removed in the same manner, run at speeds of 1000 to 1800 pieces an hour. Those equipped with automatic feeders are capable of approximately 3000 pieces an hour.

Printing in more than one color is entirely feasible. If a job calls for two colors—for example, black and red—the paper is fed to receive the impression of one of the two colors. Then the press is cleaned and the other color ink is put on the press. The form for the second color replaces the first form, and the paper is run through a second time. Platen presses are capable of fine *register;* that is, placing the additional color in exact alignment.

THE FLAT-BED CYLINDER PRESS

Like platen presses, flat-bed cylinder presses print from raised surface materials. Among those in general use are: the one-color cylinder press, the drum-cylinder press, the two color cylinder press, and the newspaper flat-bed web-perfecting press. The first two are sheet-fed presses, the latter roll-fed.

ONE-COLOR CYLINDER PRESS. The operating principle of the cylinder press (also known as a *two-revolution press*) is shown in Figure 7-1. The form is locked on the bed of the press. Blank sheets fed into the press are held to the impression cylinder by the grippers. This cylinder rotates and as it does so it presses the sheet against the type form. It revolves twice for each impression that is drawn. In the first revolution impression is made; in the second the cylinder rises to allow the paper to be removed. At the same time the form moves back to be inked and then returns to its position under the impression cylinder. Paper is usually fed automatically. After sheets have been printed they are carried by moving delivery tapes to be stacked on the delivery platform of the press.

Printing two or more colors on the two-revolution one-color cylinder press is possible by changing forms and ink and running the paper through the press for each additional color.

The presses range widely in size from 9 by 12 inches up to 50 by 73½ inches. Press size is always stated in terms of the printed sheet accommodated. They are usually horizontal, as in Figure 7-1 but vertical cylinder presses (Figure 7-2) are available. A pro-

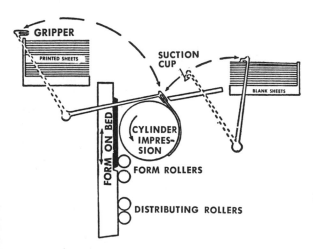

FIGURE 7-2. A vertical cylinder press.

duction rate of 3500 to 4000 impressions an hour is considered typical.

Two-revolution cylinder presses are widely used for bookwork, folders, pamphlets, catalogues, booklets, and similar jobs; and for printing many weekly or semiweekly newspapers in sizes large enough to accommodate four full-size newspaper pages in one form.

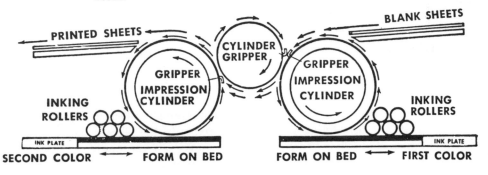

FIGURE 7-3. A two-color cylinder press.

TWO-COLOR CYLINDER PRESS. This press consists of two units, each similar to the unit in the two-revolution one-color cylinder press, as shown in Figure 7-3. Between the two units is located a transfer cylinder that takes the sheet from the first impression cylinder to the second for printing the second color.

Thus the sheet is printed in two colors one time through the press. Sheet sizes are comparable to those of the one-color cylinder presses. The two-color presses offer substantial time-saving advantages in color printing.

DOUBLE-CYLINDER PERFECTING PRESS. A perfecting press can print on both sides of a single sheet one time through the press. Like the two-color cylinder press, it has two similar units. However, it does not have the transfer cylinder. The impression cylinders rotate inwardly in opposite directions. The sheet is passed directly from the first to the second impression cylinder. Thus the direction of the sheet is reversed, enabling it to be printed on the back side in the second unit. These presses are particularly useful in book printing and often are roll-fed.

NEWSPAPER FLAT-BED PERFECTING PRESS. This press is especially designed for newspaper printing direct from type on a web (paper fed from a roll) that is perfected (printed on the opposite side) then folded on an integrated folder to be delivered as complete newspapers. Capacity is approximately 3500 papers an hour, delivered either as eight full-size pages or sixteen tabloid pages.

Its greatest application is in the large weekly or semiweekly field, although many small dailies are also printed on such presses.

Figure 7-4 shows the general principle on which the press oper-

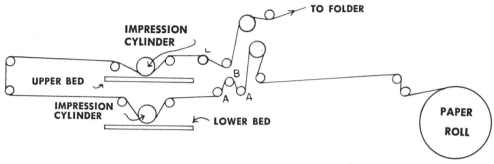

FIGURE 7-4. A flat-bed, web-perfecting newspaper press.

ates. There are two beds, upper and lower. One side of the web is printed by impression against a four-page form (eight-page form if a tabloid is being printed) on the lower bed. The web is perfected on the upper bed.

Paper is fed into the press at a uniform speed. However, while impression is being made, the web must stop at the two points where it receives impression from the type forms, which are stationary. The impression cylinders move back and forth constantly.

Since the paper feeds into the press from the roll and feeds out to the folder at a constant speed, a device called an *equalizing mechanism* is required to take up the slack that could accumulate between the infeed cylinder A and the lower bed and between the outfeed cylinder D and the upper bed, as shown in Figure 7-4.

Printing of an additional color is generally not possible, although a so-called *fudge attachment* may be utilized to add limited color to one side of the web after it passes the upper form and before it enters the folder.

THE ROTARY PRESS

Rotary presses do not print direct from flat forms as in the case of flat-bed presses. Not only is the impression cylinder curved but so is the cylinder that carries the printing elements. In other words, printing in this operation is done from a curved surface.

This principle of operation offers certain advantages. Since each revolution of the impression cylinder prints, greater speed is possible. At the same time such presses are engineered to facilitate more efficient color printing.

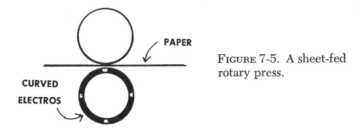

FIGURE 7-5. A sheet-fed rotary press.

LETTERPRESS: SHEET-FED ROTARY. Used primarily in commercial printing for medium to long runs of magazines, catalogues, books, and the like, sheet-fed rotary presses receive and deliver single sheets, print one or several colors, at speeds up to 6000 or 7000 an hour. Sheets range from 23 by 30 inches up to 52 by 76 inches.

The presses have a dual construction. Their *unit system* involves two cylinders for each unit, one cylinder carrying inked plates against which another cylinder presses the sheet. The latter is called the impression cylinder; the former, the plate cylinder (Figure 7-5).

The number of colors that can be printed is governed by the number of units. The sheet moves from one to the next to receive additional color. Large presses may be made up of six units.

The plate cylinder is comparable to the flat bed of a cylinder press, and printing materials for a number of pages may be locked on to it.

The *common-impression cylinder system* makes use of a single impression cylinder, against which as many as five plate cylinders can operate (Figure 7-6). The sheet travels around the impression cylinder and receives an image from each of the plate cylinders in rapid succession. This method is often referred to as wet printing. The individual plate cylinders carry different colors.

The unit system is advantageous because each color has a separate impression cylinder, and it is possible to pack the cylinders in much the same way as is done on flat-bed presses for control of impression.

The Wrap-Around Press. This small sheet-fed rotary press was introduced to the printing industry about 1960. Two sizes are

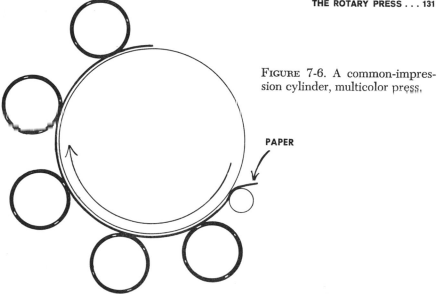

Figure 7-6. A common-impression cylinder, multicolor press.

PAPER

currently available, 23 by 30 inches and 25 by 38 inches.

Printing is done from a thin, shallow-etched letterpress or relief plate of press size, containing both line and halftone elements. The press plate is produced like an offset plate. That is, line and halftone negatives are stripped together in a flat, which is then burned into the metal or plastic wrap-around plate.

The presses have a running speed of 7000 impressions an hour, and since all printing elements are on one plate, make-ready for getting an even impression is reduced. Moreover, the offset technique of step-and-repeat—that is, repetition of a single image a number of times on one plate for gang running—is adaptable to wrap-around.

LETTERPRESS: WEB-PERFECTING ROTARY. For the high-speed printing of newspapers, magazines, and catalogues these presses place one or more colors on both sides of a web of paper as it passes through the press. Usually a folder is an integral part of the press, making possible the delivery of a folded product. Newspapers are complete as they come from such a press; magazines and catalogues require binding.

Both the unit principle and the common-impression cylinder principle are utilized. A typical arrangement in multicolor magazine printing calls for a unit similar to that shown in Figure 7-6 for printing on one side. The web is then led to drying units before

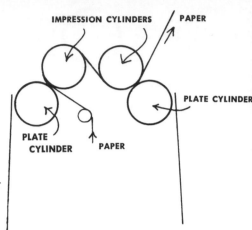

IMPRESSION CYLINDERS / PAPER

PLATE CYLINDER

PLATE CYLINDER   PAPER

FIGURE 7-7. A newspaper
rotary-press unit.

entering another printing unit for perfecting; from here it is again
taken to drying units, after which it enters the folder. Magazines
are usually printed from electrotypes. Stereotypes are sometimes
used, particularly for late-closing pages as in news magazines,
since they can be made more rapidly than electros.

The Newspaper Rotary. As shown in Figure 7-7 these
presses are built in units, each unit consisting of two plate cylinders
and two impression cylinders. Printing is done from stereotype
plates locked on the plate cylinder. Each plate represents a newspaper page, or two, if tabloid.

The web is led through the pair of cylinders, plate and impression, on the left, to be printed on one side. It then moves to the
pair on the right for perfecting. Each pair of cylinders is referred
to as a *printing couple;* a unit, therefore, consists of two couples.

Newspaper rotary presses are classified as either *semicylinder*
or *tubular.* The printing plates of the latter type are circular and
are sometimes called *stovepipes.* Those of the former are half-
cylinder; the plate cylinder of a semicylinder press can accommodate two of these diametrically opposite each other. A tubular
press-plate cylinder can accept only one plate.

There are two semicylinder presses: (1) the single width, which
means that the plate cylinders are two-plates-wide; that is, they
print on webs as much as two full-size newspapers wide, and
(2) the double width, with cylinders four-plates-wide. Tubular
presses are single width only.

Newspaper rotary presses deliver a maximum of 60,000 newspapers per hour.

Folders have page-capacity limitations. Generally, a ninety-six-
page paper (full-page size) in eight sections is maximum, although

one manufacturer offers a one-hundred-twenty-eight-page, eight-section unit.

Color in Newspaper Rotary Presses. Built in units or pairs of couples, rotary newspaper presses are particularly adaptable to color printing.

Before reviewing the various techniques for adding color, one must bear in mind the basic fact, which must be kept in mind in connection with color printing: for each color, in addition to black, that is printed on a side of the web, a separate printing plate is required; further, a blanket or impression cylinder is needed to press the web against the plate, which is inked with the desired color. Color may be added in the following ways:

(1) Through use of a color-plate cylinder, complete with its own inking rollers, printing against the blanket cylinder of a regular unit (Figure 7-8). This arrangement can be built into a press on either blanket cylinder of a unit, allowing for an additional color to be printed across the width of one of the sides of the web perfected in black. Thus three impressions are made.

(2) Either couple of a unit normally used for black printing can be adapted to run reverse, or the entire unit (both couples) may also be reversed. Reversing is done when the web is not fed directly into the unit but is led from another printing unit. Making use in this way of a normal black unit for color printing reduces the black-and-white page capacity of the press but increases the color capacity.

Figure 7-9 shows two adjacent units in a press. The left-side couple of unit B is shown reversed to receive the web, led over

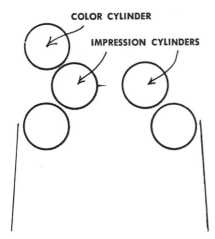

COLOR CYLINDER

IMPRESSION CYLINDERS

FIGURE 7-8. A color-plate cylinder addition to a rotary unit.

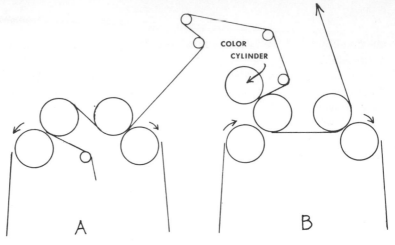

FIGURE 7-9. A web led from one unit to another in a newspaper press for color printing.

from unit A. Thus the web might receive black in unit A and additional colors in unit B. By tracing the web, one finds that four colors can be printed on one side and one color on the other.

(3) One or more printing couples may be superimposed over the standard units; that is, placed on a deck above to make, as it were, a "two-story" press.

These second-story couples can be reversing where necessary, and when used together with the regular black-printing units below, which are also reversible as required, spot color or four-color process can be placed in a maximum number of locations in the paper. With a sufficient number of superimposed couples, color printing can be done without reducing the black-page capacity of the press.

These additional considerations should be mentioned in connection with color. More than one color can be printed in any one couple at a time. By use of *split fountains* and split inking rollers, different colors can be fed to the different plates across the plate cylinder. Normally the fountain contains one color—black, for example—and this is fed to all plates. But if the fountain is divided into sections, each to contain a different color, and if the rollers are also divided or split into sections so the various colors cannot blend as the rollers oscillate, each color can be fed directly to the required plate.

Manufacturers can supply portable ink fountains, one or two pages wide, for use on standard black couples. They eliminate flushing and cleaning the fountains when a color other than black is to be run, since they can be fitted into position so that inking rollers can be fed from them in an efficient time-saving procedure.

Angle bars in large presses offer added possibilities for the location of color-bearing pages in the paper. After slitting the web, a portion can be turned if desired and inserted either side out in various positions in the paper. A large newspaper pressroom is shown in Figure 7-10.

The Flying Paster. An important adjunct for large metropolitan rotary presses is the so-called *flying paster.* This is a splicing mechanism that automatically attaches the exhausted roll of newsprint to a fresh roll, without slowing the running speed. Incidentally, such presses can be fed from the end or from below.

The greater the speed of a press and the larger the number of rolls fed into the units of the press, the more often rolls must be changed. The average roll runs about twelve minutes at a folder speed of 36,000 papers an hour.

If four rolls are being fed into a press, a stop is required every three minutes of running time to change a roll without the automatic paster. Manual changing of rolls requires at least one to two minutes. Starting and stopping the press under such conditions increases the hazard of web breaks, which mean at least five minutes spent rethreading paper through the press from one unit to the next.

Counting two minutes for roll changing by hand, but excluding time for repairing possible web breaks, ninety-six minutes are required for a 36,000 run that can be done in sixty minutes with the paster. This is a 37½ percent saving of time.

OFFSET: SHEET-FED. Most offset presses today are sheet-fed, range in size from 14 by 20 feet to 54 by 77 inches, and operate at speeds that are generally about 7500 impressions an hour.

Short-to-medium run work is usually done on a single-color press, illustrated in Figure 7-11. Even color work is handled on such presses, with sheets being fed through the press the necessary number of times, once for each color.

Two-color and multicolor presses (up to six) are available for longer runs. These are of the unit type, and are essentially a number of individual presses similar to the single-color, set in a line, with provision made for transferring the sheet in register from one to the next.

The Sheet-Fed Perfecting Press. This press, which delivers a single sheet printed on both sides once through the press, is available in sizes from 17 by 22 inches to 53 by 76 inches and is single-color only. Its speed is comparable to that of other sheet-fed presses.

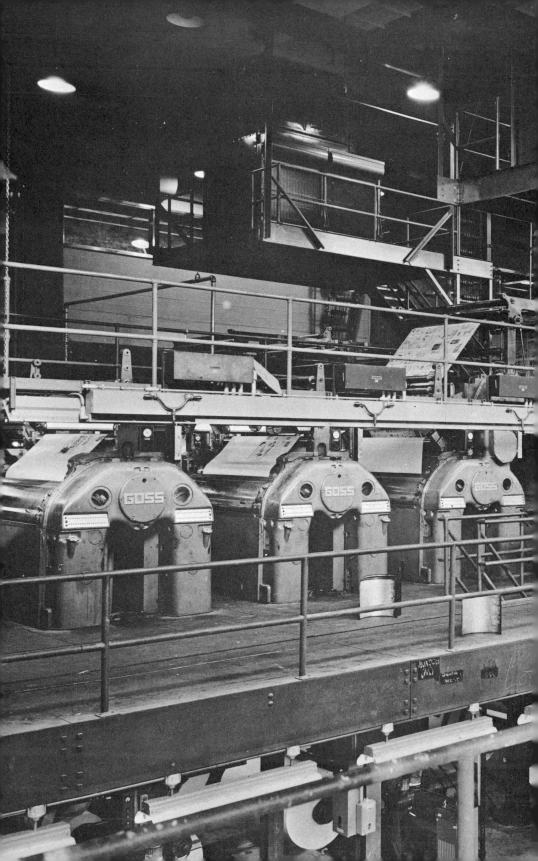

FIGURE 7-10. A newspaper press-room. (Courtesy the Goss Company.)

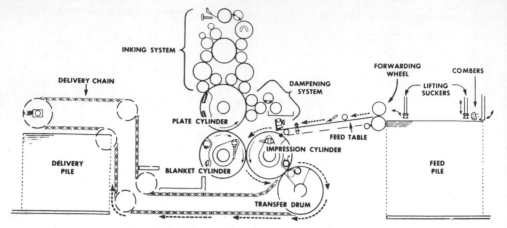

FIGURE 7-11. A single-color, sheet-fed offset press. (Courtesy Lithographic Technical Foundation.)

Perfecting the sheet is accomplished by the *blanket-to-blanket* principle of construction. The press is arranged with one unit above another, the blanket cylinders together. When the paper passes between them, it is printed on both sides, one blanket cylinder acting as the impression for the other.

OFFSET: WEB-PERFECTING. Since 1950 the demands for increased production from offset presses have brought about the rapid growth in the number of web-perfecting presses. These produce magazines, catalogues, books, and similar materials, ready for binding. They deliver cut sheets or rewound rolls. More and more publishers in the medium-size newspaper field—particularly in suburban areas—are adapting them to their needs.

The vast majority of web offset presses operate on the blanket-to-blanket principle. Figure 7-12 shows a four-unit press plus its folder, which is at the extreme right. As the press is shown, it is printing one color on each side of four webs. One web could be fed straight through all four units to print four colors on each side.

FIGURE 7-12. A four-unit web-fed offset press.

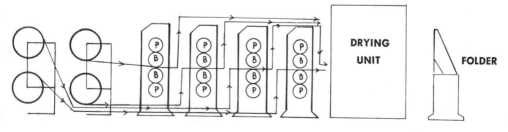

On many, particularly those other than newspaper presses, special drying ovens are located between the last unit and the folder. Here the inks are dried and then chilled to harden before the web passes into the folder.

Most of the newspaper presses print a maximum of sixteen to twenty-four full size pages (or double, if tabloid) at speeds as great as 30,000 an hour. However, one available version can deliver up to sixty-four full-size pages (one-hundred-twenty-eight tabloid) at speeds of 30,000. A newspaper web offset unit is shown in Figure 7-13. Some large presses produce 50,000 sixteen-page magazine-size signatures an hour.

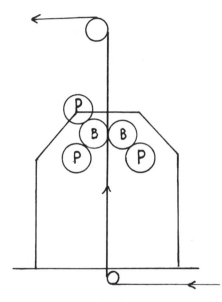

Figure 7-13. A newspaper web-fed offset-press unit.

Rotogravure Presses. Rotogravure presses are either sheet-fed or web-fed, perfecting. Figure 7-14 illustrates a web-fed press and shows four units, each being used for a separate color. The web would next be turned over and fed through additional units for perfecting.

The large cylinder, shown rotating clockwise, is the plate cylinder. Directly above it is the impression cylinder, which presses the paper against the printing area.

The sheet-fed press works on the same principle but prints a sheet up to 29 by 43 inches at a rate of 6000 to 7000 impressions an hour. The web presses, on the other hand, operate at speeds comparable to those of large rotary letterpress equipment.

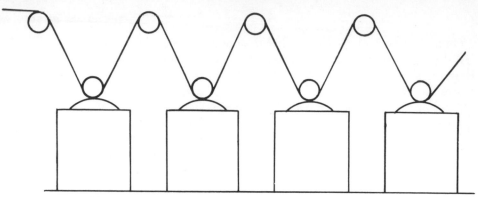

FIGURE 7-14. A rotogravure press of four units.

Web-fed is widely used in the production of Sunday newspaper magazine supplements, catalogues, magazines, books, and other advertising literature. Sheet-fed is also used in the printing of advertising literature in shorter runs. It is particularly capable of the high fidelity reproduction of works of art.

The web-fed rotogravure presses, like those in the letterpress and offset fields, make use of the flying paster.

make-ready

A discussion of presses and presswork would be incomplete without reference to *make-ready*. It is significant because of its effect upon the cost of presswork, for it can be a lengthy process often consuming hours. In the broadest sense, it refers to adjusting the press to produce the job exactly as required. This involves placing the proper ink in the press and adjusting the feeding and delivery mechanisms to accommodate the paper size.

When the form is on the press, a few sheets are printed and then checked for positioning of the printing elements. This is referred to as checking the *line-up* and is done on a line-up table, which has a glass top illuminated from below. It is equipped with sliding rulers set at right angles, used to measure the positioning, margins, bleeds, and trim of all pages in the form.

The first few sheets printed may also reveal that impression is not even over the entire form. Theoretically, all type elements are exactly type-high. Practically, this is not always the case, and as a result the pressman must make necessary adjustments. He does so by adding tissue-thin paper under the type elements—termed *underlaying,* or by building-up low spots under the *tympan,* or outer cover, on the impression cylinder—termed *overlaying.* Some of the packing under the tympan may have to be removed in areas where impression is heavy. A check of the line-up may reveal that repositioning of certain elements is also necessary.

Make-ready is particularly important in letterpress printing and most especially when printing is being done from flat forms on platen or cylinder presses. It is vital to process color printing, where inks must be laid evenly in order to effect quality reproduction. These adjustments in impression can be made in rotary letterpress by altering cylinder packing.

Many printers using cylinder presses make use of a make-ready machine which "reads" a press proof and electronically produces an overlay of proper build-ups to effect an even impression over the entire form.

In offset and roto, line-up is carefully checked before the printing plates are made. Any line-up change once the plate is on the press requires remaking the entire plate.

Uneven impression is less likely in offset and roto. If it occurs in offset it may be due to a depression in the blanket, which the pressman is often able to adjust by underlaying the localized spot with tissue.

relationship of press to the job

Noted earlier, a near-perfect press exists for every job.

This has special meaning for the person who is contracting to have printing done and to the publisher who contemplates owning his own press equipment.

ECONOMIC CONSIDERATIONS OF THE PURCHASER OF PRINTING

The purchaser of printing may be the publisher of a medium—a newspaper or magazine—who contracts with a printer to produce his publication. Or he may be a businessman in search of a printer to handle production of advertising and similar literature. In either case, a knowledge of presses and their capacities is a benefit in locating the printer who can most effectively meet the needs and in deciding the best printing process.

Most printing jobs can be handled efficiently and quickly in a number of ways. For example, an annual report or a magazine might be printed by letterpress on a large cylinder press or by offset on a press large enough to produce a multipage signature.

If the publication is printed in two or more colors, either process may still be feasible. And if the run is long enough to justify the use of faster equipment, web-fed presses are available, both letterpress and offset. Because of this, the buyer might profitably consider bids from printers other than those whose equipment would seem to meet the exact requirements of his work.

There are three general classes of printing plants:

(1) The large publication, catalogue, and book printer. His equipment may include both letterpress and offset, primarily the larger units. Some have web-fed rotaries and/or web-fed offset for high volume work. In addition, presses may be available 38 by 50 inches or larger, sheet-fed, single- and multi-color. They may have medium-size presses (25 by 38 inches) for process color work and smaller (12 by 18 inches) automatics for producing covers and for smaller job work, which they will often accept. Rotogravure printers fall into this category.

(2) The medium-size printer, often referred to as a general commercial printer. His major equipment includes medium-size presses, both one- and two-color, offset and letterpress, and also the small automatics and possibly small job presses for limited short-run jobs.

(3) The small job printer who specializes in letterheads, announcements, and occasionally on jobs as large as four-page 8½- by 11-inch folders of relatively short run. He may offer offset and/or letterpress.

The purchaser's primary interest in presses is concerned with capacity. This, in turn, involves the following:

(1) Maximum size sheet the press will handle.
(2) Largest area of printing that can be placed on a sheet.
(3) Number of colors that can be printed in a single run.
(4) Speed of delivery.

A small sheet of paper can be run through a large press but under many circumstances this is uneconomical, since the cost for press time is the same as for a large sheet.

Yet there are conditions under which such a run might pay; for example in a case involving one of the largest rotary letterpresses or offset presses. Each can handle a 52- by 76-inch sheet maximum, or a 28- by 42-inch minimum. Each can produce from one to five colors.

If the desired sheet is of minimum size but requires five-color printing, the printer with such equipment might be considered, particularly if the quantity desired were large enough to justify the expense of using such a press and if speed of delivery were important.

On the other hand, if a single color is desired, or even two or three, printers with single-color and two-color presses capable of handling a maximum sheet of 28 by 42 inches might better be consulted.

In either case, it should be remembered that rotary letterpress entails the additional cost of electrotypes.

Let us consider another example in which size of the printed area becomes significant. A sheet 17 by 22 inches with color bleeding off all sides (running beyond the trim, or three cutting edges, and into the gutter, or binding) is desired. A press 17½ by 22½ inches is available. Maximum area of printing on the sheet in the case of this press is 17½ by 22. Since the grippers on the press require ½ inch of the short dimension, color can only be printed, under perfect conditions, to exact dimensions of 17 by 22.

It would be wiser to print the job on a 19 by 25 press with an image of approximately 17¼ by 22¼ on a 19 by 25 sheet. When ⅛ th inch is trimmed from each side of the color, a 17 by 22 finished sheet remains, with color running off, or bleeding.

Of course the buyer might be willing to accept a slightly undercut sheet from the 17½ by 22½ press—in other words, a 16¾ by 21¾ sheet. Thus, by fitting the job to the press, he could effect a savings on paper stock and make use of a smaller press at lower cost.

ECONOMIC CONSIDERATIONS OF THE PUBLISHER OWNING HIS OWN PRESSES

The majority of magazine and business and industrial publishers contract for outside printing of their publications. Those who do not are likely to publish several periodicals of medium-length runs and can thereby justify the expenditures for printing equipment by spreading costs over the several publications. A number of industrial publications are produced in company printing plants, which are also used to produce other company literature.

Newspaper publishers are more likely to invest in printing equipment, although in the small-newspaper field outside contracting is not uncommon. More efficient use of equipment is effected in the metropolitan- and small-newspaper fields by producing two or more publications in a single plant.

Many papers with a small market are printed on two-revolution cylinder presses, direct from type. The typical press is capable of printing four full-size newspaper pages at one time. If operated at 2000 impressions an hour, 1000 completed eight-page papers can be delivered an hour, not counting the time required for press make-ready between the two runs, one each for each side of the sheet.

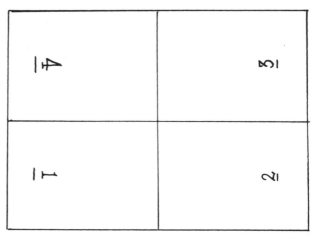

FIGURE 7-15. Four newspaper pages on one side of sheet, to be backed up with same pages on rerun through a cylinder press.

If four pages are required—for example, as part of a twelve-page paper—the four pages can be printed at one time, as shown in Figure 7-15. Then the delivered sheets are turned endwise, and on the second impression page 2 backs page 1, and page 3 backs page 4. Completed sheets are then cut in the middle and folded, each half making a complete four pages. Printing is speeded by elimination of the changing of forms and make-ready between the two runs.

For printing 4000 twelve-page papers, a total of approximately six hours press time is required, four hours for the eight pages and two hours for the four pages.

Because of the attendant problems between runs (changing the printing forms and making-ready the press for proper impression on the succeeding run, preparing the paper, and so on), press runs are often scheduled for separate days.

For color printing, sheets must be rerun after the press has been cleaned completely and the inks changed. The additional time for folding must be considered after printing is completed.

The other type of direct-from-type press, the flat-bed web-perfecting, offers the small-market publisher certain advantages and is used by many weeklies and some dailies. These advantages include the following:

(1) Time saved on presswork and folding. Up to eight pages may be printed simultaneously and papers are delivered from the press folded.

(2) Time saved on make-ready. A considerable portion of the time spent in printing on the cylinder press is consumed in make-ready. Much of this is spent changing impression-cylinder packing. The flat-bed perfecting press requires less frequent changing of cylinder packing.

(3) Increased flexibility in the number of pages. In little more than twice the running time for an eight-page paper, another section can be printed and the two sections "stuffed" together. It is also possible to "twin" two such presses for a maximum capacity of sixteen pages printed and delivered.

(4) Greater editorial balance. Because of the shorter time for the press run, later and more carefully edited news can be printed. And the paper can be better departmentalized and stories placed with greater consideration of their news value.

(5) Savings in newsprint costs. Paper in rolls is at least 10 percent less in cost than sheet stock.

The publisher whose needs extend beyond the capacity of the direct-from-type presses, must consider a rotary-press installation, either a stereotype or a web offset. Among his more important reasons for using rotary equipment are the following: (1) desire for greater speed of delivery; (2) increased number of pages; (3) earlier release of page forms, since they are not used directly in the printing; and (4) increased color capacity.

Such presses are expensive, and acquisition of rotary equipment may increase the capitalization of a paper in the 5000 to 10,000 circulation range as much as 50 percent to 100 percent because stereotyping equipment needs are expanded in the case of letterpress, and camera and platemaking equipment must also be acquired for offset. Moreover, personnel must have special training in both cases.

Offset has an advantage for it can be combined with cold-metal composition, thereby effecting a savings in total publishing costs. It is likely that in the years ahead publishers in increasing numbers will turn to web offset.

8 By now it should be obvious that successful graphic communication is possible only when the desires of the user of any printing process are closely co-ordinated with the mechanics of the process. Obvious, too, the fact that although the user may wish to think only in terms of the esthetic values and/or utilitarian properties of printed material, these qualities cannot be separated from mechanics and cost.

The interrelationship of mechanics and desired effects come into still sharper focus with a study of paper selection and imposition —the preliminary steps in printing; and folding, binding, and finishing—the final production stages.

A discussion of these also serves to stress the need for comprehensive advance planning that takes into account all phases of printing production. For, as will be shown, paper selection is affected by folding, binding is affected by paper, and so on. None of the steps in production can be separated from any of the others.

 paper selection

There are several important factors to consider when selecting paper. Some are the immediate concern of the user; others mainly of interest to the printer.

Paper shares full responsibility with type and illustrations in giving personality to any printed piece. It, too, contributes to the "voice" of printed material. It can say quality or cheapness and speak loudly or softly. From the user's standpoint, this may be the most vital role of paper. But, although color, weight, and smoothness must be judged according to their esthetic contributions, these and other paper characteristics must be analyzed in other ways, too.

Practical properties such as the ability to withstand age are very important. Printed matter supposed to last for years may disintegrate long before its intended life span has expired if proper paper was not chosen. Or, faulty paper selection can cause printed pieces to fall apart at the folds before the material has completed its usefulness.

Cost, of course, is always a determinant. Paper is priced by the pound, with the rate according to the type and amount of processing needed to give it the desired qualities. Thus weight, or thickness, becomes significant, increasingly so if the finished product

. . . 147

is to be mailed. A small difference in weight per piece can multipy postage costs by thousands of dollars if great numbers are to be distributed by mail.

Thus the user of printing is apt to be most concerned about these characteristics of paper: (1) the esthetic or psychological effect of its appearance and "feel"; (2) its permanence; (3) its durability; and (4) its cost and weight.

The printer must, of course, share his customers' concern. But, because he is charged with the mechanics of production, he sees these characteristics from a slightly different angle, regarding the many other technical properties with special meaning to him.

He must be aware of the opacity of paper, for example, because he knows that appearance can be ruined if the inked impression on one side shows through to the other. He tries to insure that a printed piece is planned to fit a standard size sheet of paper that matches his press capacity. By so doing, he can minimize the unnecessary costs that increase through wastage from trimming.

A letterpress printer knows that only with a smooth-finish paper can he reproduce fine-screen engravings to a customer's satisfaction. The offset lithographer or gravure printer requires other special papers for good reproduction.

Chemical and physical properties such as acidity, porosity, and surface-bonding strength must be checked. Papers with high acid content are fine for some work, but are not permanent enough for many uses. Ink spreads after contact with paper according to the porosity of the paper; surface-bonding strength determines paper's resistance to "picking," the undesirable release of small bits of paper surface during a press run. If picking is excessive, press time can be lengthened because of the need for frequent clean-ups.

Printers must always be conscious of the grain of paper. As paper is manufactured, the watery pulp is carried over fine wire cloth and the pulp fibers tend to lie in the same direction. In this way, the fibers give paper a grain, much like that in wood. Grain direction is important because it affects (1) the ease with which paper will run through a press; and (2) folding and binding. In a magazine or booklet, for example, the grain should run parallel to the binding in order for sheets to lie flat when open. The bindery must always be consulted to be sure the grain is in the right direction for folding and binding.

The printer, then, in addition to the end-use properties of paper that may be apparent to his customer must also consider: (1) opacity; (2) sheet size; (3) special properties for particular printing processes; (4) capability of reproducing illustrations; (5)

chemical and physical properties that affect presswork, folding, and binding; and (6) grain direction.

It is therefore essential that the user of printing work closely with the printer in selecting paper for any job. Although the buying of paper is a highly specialized task that should ordinarily be left to the printer, a basic knowledge of kinds, weights, sizes and finishes is important to the user so that he can regulate his requirements to those of the printer.

BASIC KINDS OF PAPER

Paper can be classified in many ways; for example, *wood* papers and *rag* papers. Most paper is made of wood pulp, but some is made of rags or a combination of both.

The cheapest paper is made by grinding bark-free logs into a pulp that is formed into sheets without benefit of any chemical action to remove impurities. This *groundwood* paper is commonly used for newspapers and disintegrates quickly because of its imperfections.

Wood-pulp papers of more permanence are treated to be rid of substances that cause fast deterioration. Called *sulphate, soda,* and *sulphite* papers, they are used for all kinds of printing.

A 100 percent rag content paper is virtually imperishable, but is so expensive that its use is limited.

To order paper, one must know its four basic classifications named by appearance and proposed use: *bond, book, cover,* and *cardboard.*

Aside from its use for bonds and stock certificates, bond paper is standard for office use. Because its primary application is for letterheads and typewriter paper, it has a semihard finish ideal for typing or handwriting.

As the name implies, book paper is used for books, but it also is the vehicle for virtually every mass-printed medium of communications. It comes in textures ranging from rough to a smooth gloss.

Heavy and durable, cover paper has been formulated to withstand the extra wear on booklet and magazine covers. It is available in many colors and finishes. Publications are often "self-cover"; that is, the cover is printed of the same stock and at the same time as the inside pages, but when special bulk or durability is desired, cover stock is specified.

Posters, stand-up advertising displays, and direct-mail promotion pieces are frequently printed on a stiff, heavy paper composed of several plies, or layers. Cardboard stock may also be referred to as *Bristol board* or by a number of suppliers as *postcard.*

In addition to the basic classes, there are special papers for special uses. *Offset* papers have properties designed to compensate for the moisture and other problems unique in offset printing. *Gravure* or *roto* paper is especially made to absorb the large amount of ink applied in rotogravure printing. There are other types of paper, but most are variations of those already described. Much of the variety in paper is acquired by giving standard types different finishes or surfaces.

PAPER SURFACES

Paper sheets are formed during manufacture when pulp is passed between rollers. This is called *calendering,* and the amount of calendering depends upon the desired degree of surface smoothness.

Paper with a minimum of calendering is called *antique* or *egg-shell* and is widely used for books and brochures. It has substantial bulk and is rough in texture. Although it is not suitable for reproducing letterpress halftone illustrations, its nonglare surface makes it serviceable for lengthy reading matter. The bulk of antique papers is often reduced by additional calendering gentle enough not to eliminate the rough texture.

Fairly extensive calendering produces a smoother surface for paper called *machine finish.* Many magazines use it because of its good printing surface; *English finish* is very similar (slightly more calendering) and provides only slightly better letterpress halftone reproduction.

Supercalendered paper has been processed until its surface is slick enough to take all but the finest-screened letterpress halftone engravings. It also is popular for magazines.

Paper manufacturers, when confronted with the problem of finding a suitable surface for fine-screened halftones, developed *coated* papers. Originally these were brush-coated with a clay substance, and some still are, but most coating is now applied by machine as the paper is being made. Coated papers are expensive but essential for the finest quality of photographic reproduction.

PAPER WEIGHT AND SHEET SIZES

Paper is priced by the pound but is sold in lots of a given number of sheets as well as pounds. Standard lots are a *ream* (five-hundred sheets), a *case* (about five-hundred pounds), and a *skid* (about 3000 pounds). A *quire* is one twentieth of a ream and a *carton* is one quarter of a case.

It would be impossible, of course, to identify paper's weight in terms of a single sheet. Instead, this vital element of paper, usually called *substance*, is expressed in terms of the number of pounds in a ream of sheets of a basic size. Hence, paper would be labeled "100-pound" if five-hundred sheets of the basic size weighed one-hundred pounds.

Unfortunately, the *basic* size is not the same for all types of paper. Generally, the basic is the size most suitable and efficient for the most common uses of the type of paper. The basic size for bond paper, for example, is 17 by 22 inches because it will fit most presses and will cut into four 8½ by 11-inch sheets.

Basic sheet sizes in inches are:

Bond: 17 by 22
Book: 25 by 38
Cover: 20 by 26
Card: 22½ by 28½

These must be kept in mind when ordering paper. Obviously, five-hundred sheets 25 by 38 inches will weigh more than five-hundred sheets 17 by 22 inches of the same paper. The user of twenty-pound bond who orders a thirty-pound book paper expecting to get a sheet of more thickness will be shocked to find that it is, in fact, much thinner.

In addition to the basic size, paper is available in many sizes said to be *standard* because they match press sizes, will cut or fold into standard-size booklets that, in turn, fit standard-size mailing envelopes.

Of course, the printer can use practically any size sheet of paper and cut it to fit a particular job. But when he does, waste results and, more importantly, a loss of efficiency in each of the printing, folding, binding, and finishing steps that follow.

 imposition, binding, and folding

IMPOSITION AND SIGNATURES

As he produces booklets, magazines, books, or other such publications, a printer ordinarily prints several pages on a single sheet of paper. All of the type pages that are to print on one side of the sheet must be positioned so that, when printed, the sheet can be folded and bound with the pages in proper sequence. This arranging or arrangement of type pages is called *imposition.*

Each printed and folded sheet is called a *signature* and makes up one or more sections of the publication. Any section of a publication in which all pages were printed on one sheet is a signature, but some impositions have more than one signature printed on one sheet.

The simplest of signatures can be two pages (one leaf printed on both sides), but ordinarily they range from four to sixty-four pages, in multiples of four. For booklets, books, or magazines, the most common signatures are eight, sixteen, or thirty-two pages.

There are numerous types of impositions, especially for the great variety of intricately folded pamphlets and folders that are produced. In any case, the imposition a printer will use is dictated by the folding and binding that are to follow. It can likewise be said much of the planning of the printed piece is dictated by the imposition the printer will use.

The problems of the editor of a sixteen-page publication, whether it be a newspaper, a magazine, or a public relations booklet, constitute a good case in point. Whatever the type of publication, both its deadlines and any use of a color in addition to black are directly affected by imposition.

If, as is typical, the printer plans to print half the pages on one side of a sheet and half on the other, the editor must know which pages go on which side of the sheet. He can then set separate deadlines for each unit of eight pages that must go on the press at the same time. Only when all eight pages are complete right down to the last plate and the last line of type is the form ready.

If he plans to use a color in addition to black on less than eight pages, the editor, knowing the imposition, can assign color only to those pages that fall on one side of the sheet. By so doing he gets the color with only one additional press run; if one or more pages of color were to be assigned to each side of the sheet, two additional press runs would be required.

Imposition, therefore, is of great importance because press delays, missed publication dates, and unnecessary color costs can be avoided by a planner informed of what method the printer will use.

TYPES OF IMPOSITION. For most purposes there are two basic kinds of imposition. One of these is shown in the example above: half the pages in a signature are printed on one side of the sheet and the other half back up the sheet. This method is

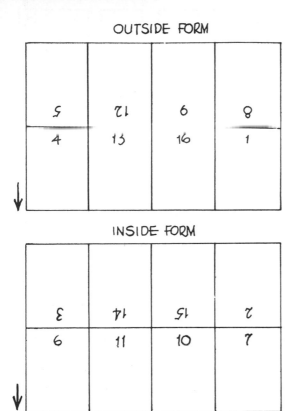

OUTSIDE FORM

| 5 | 12 | 9 | 8 |
| 4 | 13 | 16 | 1 |

INSIDE FORM

| 3 | 14 | 15 | 2 |
| 6 | 11 | 10 | 7 |

FIGURE 8-1. A sheetwise imposition for a sixteen-page signature.

called *sheetwise,* and is preferred by most printers for most jobs. Figure 8-1 shows each side of a sheet printed sheetwise.

In the other kind, all pages of a signature are printed on one side of a sheet for half the press run, and the sheet is then turned over for the same pages to print on the opposite side during the final half run. The sheet is then cut apart to form two signatures. Depending upon how the sheet is turned before it is backed up, this imposition has three variations—*work-and-turn,* which is most common; *work-and-tumble;* and *work-and-twist.*

In work-and-turn, the sheet is turned so that the left edge becomes the right edge, but the front (gripper) edge remains the same. In work-and-tumble, the sheet is tumbled so the back edge becomes the gripper edge when the sheet is being printed on the second side. In work-and-twist all edges are reversed. Because work-and-turn employs the same gripper edge for printing both sides, it is used much more than the other two. Figure 8-2 shows a sheet that has been printed with this imposition.

Figure 8-2 also shows a rather specialized printing technique

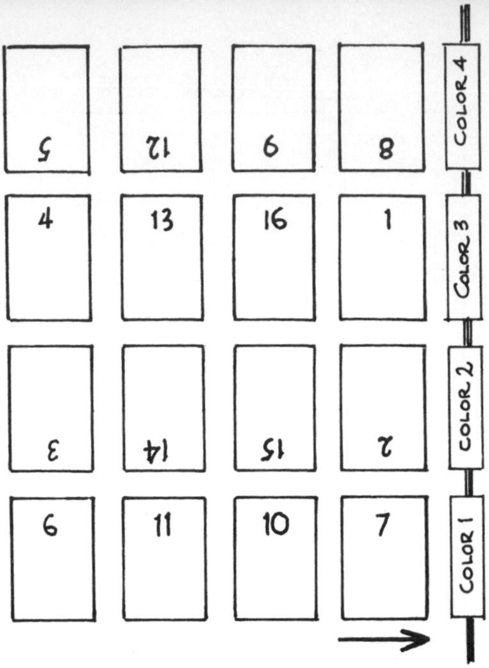

FIGURE 8-2. A work-and-turn imposition for a sixteen-page signature also showing how fountain and rollers might be split to put four different colors on a signature in one press run.

for which imposition has an even greater importance. This is *split-fountain* or *split-color* and applies several colors to a sheet during one press run. Once a sheet has been printed in black, several colors can be added with one impression if they are planned to fall in "channels."

Although procedure varies, the ink fountain and the inking rollers are usually divided so that, as the roller gathers ink from the fountain, it gets a different color from each compartment. Any pages in line with one section of the roller can then receive the color on that section; as many colors can be printed simultaneously as there are sections of the roller.

This technique is used quite extensively by magazines to satisfy the color requirements of advertisers at minimum cost. Roller splitting for a one-time-only job may be too costly, but for magazines that can use cut rollers repeatedly it can offer substantial cost advantages.

To plan color according to the channels covered by each roller section requires the user of the technique to know the location of each page in a form.

WRAPS AND TIP-INS

Although good planning dictates a consideration of imposition and signatures, it is not always possible to produce a publication that will adhere to standard sections of pages.

An advertiser, for example, will frequently insist that his magazine ad be on a special paper or other material. The ad must then be specially handled and inserted into the publication. In bookwork it is not unusual for the publisher to want a special glossy paper for reproducing the few illustrations to be used, and under the rest of the book printed on a cheaper stock.

In these and other cases where standard signatures cannot be used, the printer will most likely take care of the problem with a *wrap* or a *tip-in*. The former is a four-page insert placed around a signature before it is bound. Because they can be stitched into the binding with their signatures, wraps are as durably bound as the rest of the magazine or book. They represent a problem to the editor, however, in that he must plan their location carefully if he is to get the desired continuity of subject matter.

It is possible, but more time-consuming, to place four pages within a signature rather than around it. In that case the pages are simply called an *insert,* if they are in the center of the signature, or an *inside wrap* if they are put somewhere between the center and the outside.

A tip-in is a pasted-in two- or four-page section. Most tip-ins are of two pages—a single sheet. They are given a coating of paste in a narrow strip along the inner edge that is used to "tip" the sheet into position. Tip-ins are not so durable as wraps or inserts because they are not stitched during binding, but they are frequently used.

Although these inserting methods are common, their use is restricted to situations demanding such treatment. Only when substantial costs are avoided or imperative special effects are obtained should the use of units other than standard signatures be considered.

FOLDING, BINDING, AND TRIMMING

When the printed sheets come off the press, the work of the printer, as such, is completed. He may or may not process the work further, but basically the remaining work is that of the bindery, or finishing specialists.

In most cases, bindery operations begin with folding, an often underrated step in publication production. Sheets sometimes must be cut before folding, but this step is avoided whenever possible. Even with the best cutting, the knife "draws" the paper as it goes through a stack, and a variation in page sizes results. Unbound circulars using bleed illustrations, however, must be cut before folding.

Figure 8-3. Common folds for printed matter: (a) single-fold four-page folder: (b) eight-page accordion: (c) eight-page folder with two parallel folds: (d) six-page accordion: (e) eight-page booklet or folder with two right-angle folds, also called French fold if printed one side and not trimmed: (f) six-page standard fold: (g) eight-page right-angle fold with first fold short: (h) eight-page accordion: (i) eight-page parallel, three-fold over and over: (j) eight-page parallel map: (k) eight-page reverse map: (l) ten-page accordion: (m) twelve-page letter fold: (n) twelve-page broadside, first fold short: (o) sixteen-page broadside: and (p) sixteen-page parallel booklet.

TYPE OF FOLDS. The most common fold, because it is used for books, booklets, and magazines, is the *right-angle* fold. Thus, a single sheet folded once becomes a four-page signature; folded again at a right angle it becomes an eight-page signature, and so on. An eight-page signature folded in this manner must be trimmed before the pages are free to be turned so that pages 2, 3, 6, and 7 can be read.

A *French-fold* is an eight-page unit made with right-angle folds and not trimmed. French-fold leaflets are often used in advertising and promotion work.

Parallel folds may be either *accordion,* where each succeeding fold is parallel but turned in the opposite direction, or *over-and-over,* where each fold is in the same direction. Like the French-fold, these require no trimming. See Figure 8-3 for examples of the common folds.

TYPES OF BINDING. Binding may be either a minor or major contributor to the cost of any printing job. With simple leaflets it can be skipped entirely; for an elaborate sales presentation book it may be the major cost element. This influence on cost makes binding an important part of production planning. Binding also has a direct bearing on planning in signature units. This point can be more clearly seen with a comparison of two common binding types.

Saddle-Wire Binding. The most used type of binding, because it is inexpensive and adequate for many magazines and booklets, is *saddle-wire binding.* Signatures to be bound by this method are inserted one into the other, and wire staples are driven into the fold through to the center of the publication. As they are bound, the signatures resemble a saddle, hence the name.

Saddle-wire binding has some special advantages. Because there is no backbone, only a fold, pages will lie flat. Inside margins can be small, because the binding does not infringe upon the page. Separate covers can be used but are not necessary. Saddle-wire binding is limited, however, as to the number of pages it can accommodate. Generally speaking, it is usable only for publications up to about one-quarter-inch in thickness.

Side-Wire Binding. Thicker magazines or booklets (up to about one-half-inch in thickness) may be *side-wire* bound. In this type of binding, signatures are stacked atop each other and staples are driven through from the top through the bottom. Because these staples are inserted about one-eighth-inch from the backbone, they prevent side-wire publications from lying flat when open. A separate cover is usually wrapped around and glued to the backbone of side-wire publications. Figure 8-4 illustrates these two binding systems.

Once again, the effect of the mechanical operation on editorial planning should be emphasized. In this case, the pages that fall into each signature can vary according to the type of binding. Except for the center signature, half the pages in each signature of a saddle-wire booklet come from the front of the booklet and the other half from the back. Thus, in a thirty-two-page booklet of two signatures, the outside or wrap signature contains pages

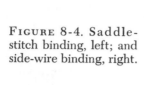

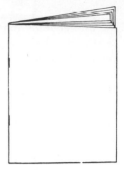

FIGURE 8-4. Saddle-stitch binding, left; and side-wire binding, right.

1 through 8 and 25 through 32. The center signature contains pages 9 through 24. On the other hand, all signatures in side-wire booklets have pages with consecutive numbering. The editor, therefore, must know which binding system is to be used as he completes signatures to meet press deadlines.

The planner of a side-wire bound booklet or magazine must also allow a larger inside margin to compensate for the eighth-inch or more taken up by the binding.

Perfect Binding. The development of durable and pliable plastic glues has brought so-called *perfect* binding into increased use. It is a much cheaper method than traditional book binding, yet it can be used for large volumes such as municipal telephone books.

No sewing or stitching is used in perfect binding. Instead, the backbone area is roughened by grinding, the pliable adhesive is applied to it, and lining cloth is then glued to the backbone. Paper covers are usually used with perfect binding.

Traditional Book Binding. Several steps are involved in traditional book binding. Regular hard-cover books are said to be *sewed and case bound.*

After signatures have been gathered, end sheets are tipped (pasted) to the first and last signatures. Signatures are then sewed together (Smyth sewing), and the book is "smashed," or compressed before the three sides are trimmed. In Smyth sewing, the signatures are saddle-sewed and sewed to each other at the same time.

Books are often *rounded* and *backed* after trimming. They are said to be backed when the backbone has been widened enough to compensate for the thickness of the covers to be added. When rounded, the backbone is made to form a slight arc.

The backbone is then reinforced with mesh and paper, which are glued to it, and the *case* (cover) is attached by gluing the end sheets to it.

Loose-leaf and Mechanical Bindings. There are scores of

loose-leaf and mechanical binding systems being used today. Their uses range all the way from student notebooks to elaborate catalogues and price books.

The chief advantage of these binding types are that pages open flat, may be of different paper stock and even different sizes, and there is no need to be concerned about signatures.

All the mechanical binding systems use more or less the same principle. Sheets are punched with holes along the binding edge and are then bound together by plastic or metal rings or coils that are slipped through the holes.

SOME SPECIAL FINISHING OPERATIONS. Some of the so-called finishing operations may be carried out by the printer, but many of them are the responsibility of a binder or a firm specializing in the particular technique. In many cases, finishing techniques are used to increase the utility of the printed piece, but they are often also employed simply to enhance visual appeal.

The following list is by no means all-inclusive, but it does present the more commonly used techniques.

(1) *Die Cutting*. Some printed pieces are much more effective if they are cut to special shapes. Any special shape—a company's product, a question mark, the outline of a state—can be acquired through die cutting. Several sheets of paper or cardboard can be cut at one time when *high dies*, very similar to rugged cookie cutters, are used. Some *steel-rule* cutting is done, however, on standard printing presses with only one or two sheets being cut at a time.

For steel-rule cutting, the desired shape is cut into three-quarter-inch plywood with a jigsaw, and steel rules are cut and bent to fit the shape. The rules, when put into the cutout, are sharp enough and high enough to make the desired cut with each press impression.

(2) *Easeling*. Finishers have stock sizes of easels, which are applied to display cards and other printed pieces so they can stand on counters, desks, and table tops. Either single or double wing easels are used, depending upon weight of the board or width of the base.

(3) *Embossing*. Initials, seals, medallions, and other designs can be raised in relief on paper or other material by running the material in a press between a relief die (below) and an engraved die (above). Embossing may be either blind (no color applied) or printed. Inks or paints are applied before embossing. The major expense is in the making of the dies, but careful make-ready is also required.

a

b

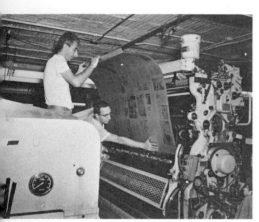

c

d

e

f

g

h

FIGURE 8-5. Steps from imposition to sewing of signatures. (a) Stripper lining up negatives on a goldenrod flat according to binder's imposition (offset process, see p. 227). Light table enables him to follow ruled-up master form underneath. (b) Exposed plate ready for developing and fixing. (c) Putting finished plate on press. (d) Taking printed sheet out of delivery end of press. (e) Banding skid of printed sheets for delivery to bindery. (f) Cutting printed sheets according to specifications. (g) Skids of printed sheets ready to be placed on Dexter quad folding machines in background. Note skid in left foreground has stacks of sheets cut and prefolded in half, each half containing a 64-page signature (32 pages on each side of sheet). Folded signatures may be seen at right. (h) Signatures being Smyth sewn before binding. Note spools of thread upper left and stack of signatures in front of each operator. (Photographs a-e courtesy New York Lithographing Corporation; f-h courtesy Monk Book Manufacturing Company, Inc.)

(4) *Gumming*. Labels and other stickers may be gummed by hand or by machine either before or after printing. Machines can apply gum in strips of any number and in any direction. Many printing problems are avoided if gumming follows presswork.

(5) *Indexing*. Indexing is a die-cutting process for providing the tabs needed on such items as index cards, address books, telephone pads, and so on.

(6) *Numbering*. Most letterpress printers can easily and cheaply provide numbering because numbering machines can be locked in a chase with or without other plates and type matter. These machines can number consecutively or repeat.

Other printing processes require the use of special press attachments.

(7) *Pebbling*. Any texture can be added to paper following printing by running the paper through rollers embossed with the desired design. Paper manufacturers offer a *pebble* stock, a paper with a textured surface, as well as other uneven finishes, but as a finishing term pebbling means the addition of *any* texture after printing. Linen and other clothlike surfaces are included.

By applying texture to paper as a finishing process instead of during paper manufacture eliminates the problems connected with running rough stock on letterpress machines.

(8) *Perforating*. Either the printer or finisher can do perforating. If it is done by the printer, ink is carried to the paper at the perforating line because the sharp rule used is slightly more than type-high. A perforating wheel is attached to the cylinder if the technique is to be done on a cylinder press.

The type of perforating found on postage stamps is the work of a finisher who uses a rotary machine that punches rows of tiny holes. Perforating, of course, is simply to make tearing easy.

(9) *Punching*. Standard male and female dies are used to punch holes for the various styles of loose-leaf or mechanical binding.

(10) *Scoring*. Scoring, like perforating, is done to make tearing easier or to aid folding. A sharp steel rule is used to slightly cut the outer fibers of the paper; if heavy stock or cardboard is being used, the rule may have to cut partially through the board.

Scoring should not be confused with *creasing*, a similar operation in which a dull, rather than sharp, rule is used. Creasing is also an aid to folding, but its other purpose is to make tearing more difficult, not easier. The blunt rule merely compresses the fibers, making the stock more durable at the fold.

To avoid confusion, it is wise to tell the finisher *why* the technique is being requested.

9 People spend good money to have type set and printed because they want it to be read. So much else competes for readers' attention that a major portion of the typographer's job consists of choosing type and other printing elements attractive and legible enough to beguile the public from television and to the client's message.

During the past one-hundred years scientists, primarily psychologists, have worked long to learn about the business of communicating to the reader via the printed page. Their findings have tended to confirm the empirical standards—rules developed by typographers through experience—especially in the areas of selecting and using type. Thus, this chapter moves into the area of psychology and the problems involved in measuring motivations, for while the conclusions of the psychologist can be viewed as provisional,[1] they have much value either as suggestions for procedures or as a recall to empirical standards.

 the factors affecting legibility of type

There are two aspects to studying the use of type: (1) legibility; and (2) appropriateness. The factors that affect legibility are face, size, boldness, leading, length of line, margins, ink, paper, presswork, lighting, and the interest of the content for the reader.

The last factor is controlled by the selection of ideas, not type, but it is nonetheless cogent to the typographer. Tests indicate that reader interests are related to legibility and bear an effect on use of type.

TESTING LEGIBILITY

Legibility factors have been reported in association journals and in two books. The text by Burt[2] has already been mentioned; the other will be referred to later.

Observations about the mechanics of reading are helpful to a discussion of legibility. Reading is done while the eyes make short jumps along a line. At each stop, called a fixation, words are

---

[1]Sir Cyril Burt, *A Psychological Study of Typography* (Cambridge: Cambridge University Press, 1959), p. 31.

[2]*Ibid.*

absorbed. Enough letters or words are perceived to fill in the gap between one fixation and the next.

Readers vary in proficiency. One who is skilled takes few fixations along a line, exercises great rhythm in eye movement, and rarely has to retrace to a previous point in the line to pick up something missed.

Second, legibility of words or idea groups is more significant than that of individual letters. Effective reading requires recognition of a whole word, sometimes more than one.[3]

Third, tests have clearly established that interest in subject matter, clarity of expression, and absence of unfamiliar words are aids to more rapid reading.

The following are the major tests utilized in legibility testing:

(1) Tachistoscope tests. The tachistoscope measures reading accuracy of letters and words by presenting them in brief exposures to the reader.

(2) Measuring the ease of distinguishing letters and reading words and sentences at varying distances.

(3) Studies of eye movements, blinking, and indications of reading fatigue. The specially designed "eye camera" is used to record movements over a printed area on film. Observations through one-way glass allowing an undetected observer to study readers are also utilized.

(4) Time tests of prose reading followed by a questionnaire to determine the extent that content was retained.

Paterson and Tinker[4] and Sir Cyril Burt, recognized authorities in the field of legibility testing, have used as their principal means the time-comprehension tests.

Results from various types of tests often disagree, for a face may be found more legible by one procedure than by another. But in general findings have validated the soundness of the standards established through experience.

The student of typography should be on guard against confusing the terms "legibility testing" and "readability testing." The latter was developed by readability experts, most notably Rudolph Flesch, John McElroy, and Robert Gunning. They measure relative difficulty of reading in terms of clarity of writing, ease of reading, and human interest. Briefly stated, they have found

[3]*Ibid.*, p. 2.
[4]D. G. Paterson and M. A. Tinker, *How To Make Type Readable* (New York: Harper & Row, Publishers, Inc., 1940).

that a message is most readable when sentences are short and words are familiar and personal. Inasmuch as these factors bear an influence on reading efficiency, legibility and readability tests can be easily mistaken one for the other.

THE TYPE FACE

Typographers have long contended that legibility is maximized by use of the standard Roman faces. Tests to date have neither confirmed nor refuted the contention, although researchers have inclined to conclude that it is valid. Typographers feel that familiarity and design factors render legibility to such faces. They point out that we learn to read from books printed in Roman faces and that so is the majority of what we read thereafter in books, magazines, newspapers, and other literature. Further, the more irregular design features of Roman faces help the reader grasp word forms more rapidly in the reading process because the contrasting strokes give a rhythmic structure to words and serifs assist horizontal eye movement.

On the other hand, the monotonous sameness of Gothic faces, they feel, impairs reading. Gothic is often used for text material, especially when the number of words is not great; its use for display is well-established. Advertisers in the large national magazines, who seek the best possible typographical advice, prefer Roman faces for text matter, a fact the student can readily verify by browsing through the pages of the well-known publications.

Burt has offered evidence that among the Roman faces the modern designs seem less legible than the old, especially for children and older persons.[5] He concluded that legibility is reduced in modern faces because the designs place emphasis on the similar parts of the letter; old designs accentuate dissimilar characteristics.

Typographers generally agree that regardless of type face caps and lower case are preferred to material set all caps. Tests by Paterson and Tinker have shown that text matter set all caps caused a 12 percent loss in reading time.[6] Of course this does not negate the use of all caps in display matter.

Italic type is better in restricted use as a contrast to roman type in placing emphasis on certain words.

[5]Burt, op. cit., p. 7.
[6]Paterson and Tinker, op. cit., p. 23.

BOLDNESS

Like italics, the boldface variation of a type face serves well for emphasis. The families designed to give a heavier appearance when compared to others have been suggested by Burt as useful for the very young and the very elderly.[7]

SIZE

Typographers recommend 10-, 11-, and 12-point types for text matter for the average reader, and tests have borne out their contention. Burt, however, believes type may be too large or too small in terms of individual readers.[8] He asserts that larger sizes are often preferable for both younger and older-than-average readers.

Logically, text matter presented in very large sizes—as is occasionally done in promotional literature—risks a decline in legibility. It is apt to call attention to itself at the expense of the material it should be transmitting. Moreover, since few words fall within the eye span, more frequent fixations are required of the reader with possibly the additional result of increased reading fatigue.

LEADING

Printers and typographers use leading primarily to enhance legibility. These are the rules they follow:

(1) For ordinary text sizes, one or two points of leading are adequate.

(2) For faces that are small on the body, 1-point leading is sufficient.

(3) As length of the measure is increased, the need for leading becomes greater for any face.

Burt reported, "Little seems to be gained by 3-point leading; 4-point leading usually diminishes legibility; like excessive letter-size, it tends to increase the number of eye movements and fixation pauses."[9]

[7]Burt, *op. cit.*, p. 10.
[8]Burt, *op. cit.*, p. 12.
[9]*Ibid.*, p. 13.

LENGTH OF LINE

That length of measure influences legibility has been substantiated by research.[10] Short measures in a large type face require more frequent fixations, since the reader has more difficulty absorbing longer phrases. The number of hyphenated words at the ends of lines increases. Both decrease reading comfort and increase time taken for perception.

Long lines, particularly in a small type, also impair legibility, since the reader is slowed in picking up the succeeding line after swinging back from the end of the long line.

For many years charts expressing the limits for length of line relative to size of type have been available to printers and typographers. The limits have generally been expressed in picas or inch equivalents.

Burt has suggested that since set of type (width of individual letters) varies from face to face, limits of measure might better be expressed in terms of lengths of alphabet. He has proposed that limits of two to three lower-case alphabets encompass maximum legibility[11] and that alphabet length should correspond to body size. That is to say, if the type face is set 10 on 12, or 10-point leaded two points, the alphabet size of 12-point type should be used.

The usual book faces are not considered satisfactory for newspaper editorial straight matter, partly due to the narrow column width of generally eleven and one-half to thirteen picas. Because of the short measure, small size faces are often used, 7-, 7½-, and 8-point being common. Special newspaper faces are masterfully designed to hold maximum legibility despite the major handicaps of small size and short measure. They have an x-height (body height) as large as possible and are at the same time condensed enough to allow a reasonable number of characters per line. Although the number of alphabets per measure falls below Burt's minimum, his studies were primarily concerned with book printing. Moreover, one need but give a hasty check to realize there are not an unreasonable number of hyphenations in the typical newspaper column of straight matter.

Many typographers find these rules of thumb for length of line useful: (1) minimum line length: one alphabet; optimum line length: one and one-half alphabets; maximum line length: two

[10]*Ibid.*, p. 14.
[11]*Burt, op. cit.*, p. 14.

alphabets; (2) length of line in picas should not exceed twice the type point size. Thus 10-point type should not be set on a measure exceeding twenty picas.

MARGINS

Research findings vary widely regarding the effect of book-page margins on legibility. Burt reported, "There can be little doubt that books with excessively narrow margins are more apt to produce visual fatigue." Paterson and Tinker, on the other hand, found that reduction of normal margins had no effect on reading speed.[12]

Practitioners have long contended that ample margins invite reading, a fact Burt seems to substantiate by suggesting that reader preferences for margins are mostly a matter of esthetics.[13] Considered ample are margins comprising about 50 percent of the page.

In bookwork *progressive margins* are used: the narrowest margin is at the fold (*inner margin*), the next width at the top of the page (*head margin*), next at the outside (*outside margin*), and the greatest at the bottom (*foot margin*). These margins move clockwise on odd-number pages and counterclockwise on even-number pages. Thus they are held together by the narrow margins at the center.

The purpose of margins in all printing is to frame the type and other elements within a border of white space. Thus the amount of white space between elements within the printed area should be less than that of the margins in order to provide unity and coherence.

OTHER FACTORS

Little research has been published regarding the effects of paper on legibility. Typographers follow the general rule in letterpress that type faces with delicate hairlines print better on a coarse paper stock for it makes the hairlines spread. On a hard-surface stock as used, for example, in letterpress printing when fine screen halftones are being reproduced, the type selected must print with sufficient strength on the paper. Other than fine hairline faces are better for these purposes.

[12]Paterson and Tinker, *op. cit.*, p. 109.
[13]Burt, *op. cit.*, pp. 14–15.

There is, of course, no pressure into paper in offset printing. Thus a greater latitude is allowed in selecting the face to appear on offset paper. Repro proofs of hairline faces can be pulled on soft stocks and then reproduced by offset on any stock, soft or hard, and get the full effect of the face.

The faces used in rotogravure printing must be able to withstand the screening process. Typographers recommend avoiding hairline types for use in gravure, regardless of the nature of the paper stock.

The density of ink and quality of presswork are less under the control of the typographer than most of the previous factors. Their influence on legibility is obvious. Overinking, as well as underinking, reduces visibility, and improper press make-ready has the same effect if some parts of the printed area are heavy and some light.

The typographer has no control over the lighting conditions under which the message is read, but he *can* control the background against which type is printed, a factor closely related to lighting.

Tests have shown that type printed against a screen tint of the same color reduces legibility; for example, black type on a gray background or dark blue type on a light blue background. Also reverse printing seems to impair legibility as does one color printed against the background of another. Black on white has proved to be of the highest legibility. The effects of various color combinations will be discussed further in Chapter 13.

APPLYING THE PRINCIPLES

There are three major reasons why the typographer must exercise considerable judgment in applying the rules or principles of legibility:

(1) Since legibility testing has been limited primarily to book printing, adapting the principles to other areas requires care.

(2) Researchers have observed a definite dependency of one legibility factor upon another. As Burt pointed out, "assessments obtained by varying just one characteristic in isolation may at times be highly misleading."[14]

(3) Considerations other than legibility should enter the selection of type and its arrangement. If legibility were the sole

[14]Burt, *op. cit.*, p. 30.

criterion, all printed matter would tend toward a monotonous uniformity.

What value, then, should the typographer place upon the principles? He should look upon them as flexible aids to judgment rather than as an end in themselves, realizing that no one combination of the individual factors gives an absolute, maximum legibility.

THE USE OF DISPLAY

The body, or text type, is of little significance in terms of impact value. As a consequence, the typographer can concentrate his efforts on making it as legible as possible. However, he has to pay special attention to the treatment of type used for display purposes. While legibility is also desirable for display, it is not so imperative because it has a primary function before that of reading speed. It is often used to get attention. Although much literature is not illustrated, almost all of it has headlines, the most common display device. A number of techniques for the imaginative use of display type are suggested in following chapters, particularly 15.

Although legibility is sometimes secondary in display, it must not be overlooked. For example, heads in all-cap Script or Cursive

FIGURE 9-1. Head in all-cap Cursive is difficult to read.

HARD TO READ

(Figure 9-1) or set vertically and diagonally (Figure 9-2) become

FIGURE 9-2. Heads set vertically and diagonally are difficult to read.

very difficult to read. Legibility of display is affected by the same principles as straight type.

appropriateness of type

Appropriateness, or fitness, is the second fundamental to be observed in the use of type. In the process of communication the message from source to receiver should fall within a field of experience, or knowledge, common to both. In other words, the message must be in terms that can simultaneously express the ideas the sender wishes to deliver and be comprehensible to the receiver.

The reader's response is conditioned by the over-all effect of the complete printed message. The subject matter is embodied, of course, in the words. How they appear plays an important part in their delivery. Selection and arrangement of elements should combine into a unified communication, appropriate to the message.

"Appropriateness" in this context has three meanings: it can be (1) the selection of faces in terms of the psychological impressions they bear; (2) the adaptation of legibility rules to fit the education and age levels of the reader; (3) the use of faces harmonious with the other elements and the over-all design of the printed communication.

PSYCHOLOGICAL IMPLICATIONS OF TYPE

The individual letters that comprise the upper and lower case alphabets of a given type case were designed to work together. The entire font is seen in infinite combinations within a block of type. From this comes a total visual impression that can be termed the "feel" of the face. It can suggest definite physical qualities in blocks of composition as for example, strength is conveyed by Bodoni in the paragraph following, a touch of delicacy is created by Caslon in the last paragraph. Both specimens are machine set the same size and leaded equally.

A block of copy set in Bodoni presents a "rough" texture somewhat like a corded material. This is due to vertical emphasis in the design of the face. Textural effect is due not only to the thickness of line but also to the amount of spacing between lines.

Copy composed in Caslon presents a "smooth" texture. The contrast between the vertical and the horizontal strokes is less pronounced than in Bodoni. The skilled typographer seeks a textural effect that is compatible with the nature of the message.

Some faces remain neutral and arouse no feelings in terms of physical qualities. Studies indicate many people have esthetic preferences for different type faces. While Burt warned that his findings should be considered provisional, he reported that most readers are not in any degree typographically conscious, many even stating, "All kinds of type look much the same to me."[15] Those with preferences frequently mentioned abstract qualities.

Other writers have suggested that the various faces by reason of their design can suggest different moods and feelings. Lists have been drawn up giving a "personality" to each face, but they are no more than subjective evaluations. It will be far safer to depend upon research to uncover the psychological associations held by the readers when more investigation has been done.

APPROPRIATE USE
OF THE LEGIBILITY "RULES"

The typographer can temper the application of legibility fundamentals to fit specific types of readers. Large bold faces seem desirable for the very young and the very old. Generous leading helps beginning readers move from line to line.

Where the degree of reader interest is high, great flexibility is possible, since reading will be done despite reduced legibility.

HARMONY

For the total printed piece to present a unified communication, type and other elements must be in harmony. Type should blend, in terms of its tonal feeling, with border, illustrations, and other printing elements, and should be applicable to the paper and printing process used.

 check list

To summarize this chapter, the real heart of a communication is in its body copy. Its headlines and illustrations serve to grasp attention; then, once the reader is caught, the body must be inviting to the eye and easy to stay with. Sound typography accomplishes this.

[15]Burt, *op. cit.*, p. 23.

A check list of typographical rules follows. The student must remember that they have to be applied with judgment in every individual case.

(1) Long copy should be broken for easy reading. There are several techniques, include paragraphs, or, if they begin flush left, add extra space between paragraphs. Use subheads in contrasting type or in the bold face of the body copy. Consider leaders and dashes, especially in advertisements. Relieve monotony by occasional italics and boldface at points of textual significance. Set some paragraphs on a narrower-than-text measure, centered in the column, especially in ads. Do not kill all widows (short line or single word at the close of a paragraph) for they let in white space.

(2) Headlines, too, should be broken sometimes, and long heads can be more effective in a different type style. Headlines set in two or three lines must be broken between lines at a point where neither a thought nor a grammatical construction will be broken. For instance, "Three Youths Are/Sent to Detention" is incorrect. Better breaks occur in "Three Youths Are Sent/To Detention" or "Three Youths/Are Sent/To Detention."

(3) Set copy on the proper measure. One-and-a-half to two alphabets make a sound line length.

(4) Do not use too many different faces in one body. Harmony and unity result with a single face, with its italic and boldface, for body and display.

(5) Avoid reverses for body copy, especially in newspapers where the ink tends to fill in letters because of low-grade paper quality.

(6) Avoid text over illustrations or tint areas. If used, be sure there is strong contrast.

(7) Consider carefully before setting headlines all caps. They slow reading.

(8) In general, irregular margins hamper easy reading. If they must be used, try to avoid breaking a thought between two lines, and place the ragged edge on the right rather than on the left because the eye is accustomed to returning to a common point after reaching the end of a line.

(9) Roman type is generally preferred for body copy, for readers are used to it.

(10) Stay with the 10-, 11-, and 12-point types for body copy. They are easier to read, especially for anyone with sight impairment.

(11) Consider leading as line length increases or if the x-height is large. Do not overdo—3- and 4-point leading is seldom justified in text matter.

(12) Margins should approximate 50 percent of the page area and be progressive in book matter.

10

The graphic elements of printed communication consist of the art work including photographs, the decorative elements, and display type. Within a given space these must be arranged with the verbal elements for strictly functional reasons—to attract attention, arouse interest, and aid in conveying the message to the reader.

Planning this vital arrangement starts with a drawing representing how the message will look. If the finished work is to be an advertisement, the drawing is called a *layout;* if it will be a page in a newspaper, magazine, or the like, the drawing is a *dummy.*

In dealing with layouts alone in this chapter, basic principles of design will be discussed. They are applicable to all forms of printed matter. Layouts, rather than dummies, take the fore here because advertisers have been more active in researching design principles involved in printing than have printers or other users. This is probably because of the high cost charged for advertising space and the rugged competition from other advertisers and from the editorial content of the media in which ads appear.

From the information that follows the beginner should become acquainted with the fundamental principles of design and receive a starting point from which he can develop basic skills by applying them.

 kinds of layouts

The laying-out process puts elements into a composition that pleases and also accomplishes a purpose. Therefore it must be carefully planned. The first step, *visualization,* is a thinking process from which come decisions about:
 (1) The ideas the words will represent.
 (2) The elements to be used.
 (3) The relative importance of the ideas and elements.
 (4) The order of presentation.
These decisions are influenced by the type of product being advertised, the type of consumer, and the degree of his interest in the product. The person who is to do the layout must be aware of these for they affect his composition.

There are three kinds of layout, each classified according to the care with which it is produced, and this in turn is influenced by the purpose for which it is made. They are: the *miniature,* or *thumb-*

nail sketch, often made to help visualization; the *rough;* and the *comprehensive.*

THE MINIATURE LAYOUT

The miniature can be any size, but it is usually proportioned to the full-size layout it precedes. Thumbnails have three advantages:

(1) They are an economical means of testing various layout plans.

(2) Because they can be done quickly, the designer is free to discard unsuccessful attempts. Working full-scale expends precious time and energy and results in a hesitation to discard a bad try.

(3) The execution of thumbnails begets further ideas. Though the first and second sketch may miss the mark, they warm up the creative process and stimulate a flow of more productive ideas.

In Figure 10-1 are three miniatures in which headline, illustration, body type, and logotype (sometimes also called a *signature* or *nameplate*) are shown in different arrangements.

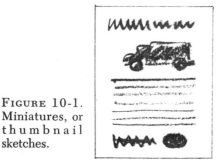

Figure 10-1. Miniatures, or thumbnail sketches.

There are definite means of indicating the various elements. Body type may be shown as in Figure 10-2. The varying weights of line

Figure 10-2. Technique for indicating body type.

roughly give the weight of the body face. Indications of illustrations are shown in Figure 10-3 where one is square finish and the other of irregular shape like an outline halftone. These too can be weighted according to their relative darkness of tone. An italic or

FIGURE 10-3. Technique for indicating illustrations.

hand-lettered headline is sketched as in Figure 10-4. Again, light

FIGURE 10-4. Headline and logotype indications.

or heavy strokes delineate boldness of type. Ornamentation, such as border, can be pictured as in Figure 10-5.

FIGURE 10-5. Technique for indicating ornamentation.

Miniatures can be prepared with a great degree of finish (Figure 10-6). In either case the layout should be done carefully so that the elements assume reasonably accurate shape and weight.

FIGURE 10-6. Carefully drawn miniatures.

THE ROUGH LAYOUT

The best of the miniatures is enlarged into a rough, full-size layout (Figure 10-7). This is more utilitarian than experimental. Several drafts may be called for to take care of revisions and changes. The final rough bears a resemblance to the finished ad. Headlines are lettered in to approximate their finished type. Illustrations are often hastily sketched as shown but can be depicted as in miniatures. The locations of elements are so precise that the printer can work from the rough in composing and making up the ad.

FIGURE 10-7.
The rough lay-
out.

Designing layouts is simplified by the proper equipment. The best paper is a transparent bond known as layout paper. A drawing board is a desirable work surface; a T square and a triangle facilitate accuracy. Also needed are soft graphite, charcoal, and chisel-point pencils, and a ruler graduated in inches, picas, and agate lines.

Color areas are blocked in with pastel chalks available in a wide range of colors, black, white, and grays. They are applied to the paper and rubbed in with the finger tips.

The chisel-point pencil is excellent for lettering, and its technique can be easily learned. The beginner should use a 3-B or 4-B.

The pencil has a rectangular rather than round lead. Sharpening thus requires cutting *down to* but *not into* the lead, never in a pencil sharpener but rather with a knife. The lead should be shaped to a keen chisellike point.

The basic strokes of various styles of letters are shown in a text on Speedball pen lettering.[1] The Speedball C-style pen is used for shaping Roman letters, and with practice the typographer can learn to use the comparable chisel-point pencil in the same manner.

The pencil can form sans-serif letters. The technique is more difficult, however, since the pencil does not resemble the B-style Speedball used for this purpose. Since Gothic letters are of full-width strokes, the pencil must be frequently shifted in the fingers to shape the letters properly.

THE COMPREHENSIVE LAYOUT

The comprehensive is a very exact layout, rendered to show how the finished reproduction will look. Illustrations imitate their finished appearance and headlines are precisely inked in. Body type is usually indicated by ruled lines. A *type comprehensive* is prepared with proofs of composed type pasted in position for clients who prefer a closer representation than is afforded by a rough.

principles of design

Design occurs in space. For a layout man to make effective use of space, he must understand something of man's relation ·to it. From birth the human being is in a constant effort to

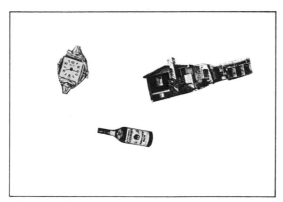

FIGURE 10-8. Unrelated items in space.

[1]Ross F. George, *Speedball Textbook for Pen & Brush Lettering, 18th Edition,* (Camden, N. J.: Hunt Pen Co., 1960).

project himself into space, to understand it, to conquer it. The baby reaches out from his crib, learns to crawl, then to walk. The grown man contemplates the day he may set foot on other planets.

It is inherent in man to seek order in space. The isolated, unrelated elements in space in Figure 10-8 are disturbing because they defy orderly arrangement. They cry for readjustment like a picture hanging crooked on the wall.

A good composition is orderly. Consider the message presented in Figure 10-9. The reader cannot grasp its communication until he has grouped logical elements together. Figure 10-10 is an improvement.

FIGURE 10-9. Poor organization.   FIGURE 10-10. Weak organization improved by proper grouping.

To understand space man must be able to manipulate distances between units placed in it. Thus, in designing printed matter, some elements must be made larger than others, or elements may be overlapped. In Figure 10-11 the sketch on the left suggests that type is in front of the box. The reverse is true in the sketch on the right.

Man also tends to connect points in space. Our delineation of

FIGURE 10-11. Combination of elements to create impressions of distance.

constellations in the sky evidences this trait. It is a sound practice in layout to place elements in relationship to each other so the eye can move from one point to the next, as in Figure 10-12. The movement must, however, be kept within the bounds of the space designated as the layout area. Thus three strong points should never establish a movement tendency out of the layout as in Figure 10-13.

FIGURE 10-12. Placement of element to direct eye movement.

FIGURE 10-13. Improper movement tendency created by poor placement.

As the typographer arranges elements to form the layout, he observes six design principles closely related to the observations above: proportion, balance, contrast, rhythm, unity, and harmony.

PROPORTION

Proportion refers to (1) the relationship of one element to another or to the whole layout with respect to size or area; and (2) the dimensions of the layout and the dimensions of the component parts. Proportion also infers a harmonious relationship among the elements and pleasing dimensions of layout and the individual parts. The end result is the pleasing and effective appearance of the whole.

The first task in layout is to select the size of the advertisement or its dimensions. A similar task exists in book work, of course, except that page or sheet size is determined.

Pleasing dimensions are those in which relationship of height to width is not obvious to the eye. Thus a square layout, with dimensions of 1 to 1, is very uninteresting. Proportions of 1 to 2 are also easily detected and to be avoided. Proportions close to 1 to 1 or 1 to 2 are weak because of their proximity to the above dimensions. Because they are less obvious, approximate width to height relationships of 1 to 3, 2 to 3, 3 to 5, or 5 to 7 are better. What applies to pleasing dimensions of the layout can be applied equally to dimensions of elements in the layout.

Although a clue to proportion of one element to another or to the whole layout can be found in mathematics, the most pleasing proportions are not attained mathematically. They are, rather, more a matter of taste and subtlety, and neither of these can be reduced to rigid standards. For instance, in Figure 10-14 four ele-

FIGURE 10-14. The layout with unequal division of space is more interesting.

ments are shown—headline, illustration, copy, and signature—that divide the layout area into four unequal and consequently interesting amounts because of their tastefully differentiated sizes.

BALANCE

Balance exists when the elements in an ad are placed with a sense of equipoise or equilibrium. That is, the weights of the elements counteract so that they seem settled where they are placed.

Weights are effected by size, shape, lightness or darkness, and color. Large elements appear heavier than small elements, assuming the other factors are constant. Circular shapes bear greater weight than rectangular, and irregular shapes exert greater weight than either of these. Dark elements outweigh light ones, though a small dark element can outweigh a larger but lighter mass.

What, then, determines a placement that achieves the comfortable look of stability?

The reader no doubt recalls the seesaw or teeter-totter. To hold the board in balance, the heavier of two children must sit nearer the fulcrum than the lighter child. This illustrates the principle that weight times distance on one side must equal weight times distance on the other to achieve balance.

Although the same principle is at work in layouts, it cannot be applied by mathematical calculation. It is a practiced and experienced eye that places elements properly for optical balance.

There is a fulcrum in an ad, too, in relation to which the elements are placed. It is at the position of the **X** in Figure 10-15, called the *optical center*—a spot in any space that appears central to the eye. It is somewhat above the mathematical center, which is indicated by the intersecting diagonals. A mass located at the exact center appears to be too low and consequently out of balance (Figure 10-16). The same mass, located at the optical center, appears stable.

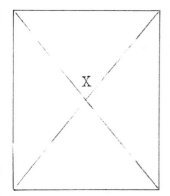

FIGURE 10-15. The optical center is above the mathematical center.

FIGURE 10-16. A mass located at exact center appears low.

FIGURE 10-17. A mass located at the optical center appears stable.

That mathematics offers a clue to the proportion of one area to another can be seen in Figure 10-17 where the mass divides the layout space into two equal areas, the weak proportion of 1 to 1.

In Figure 10-18 are two units in balance. In the left-hand sketch two masses similar in size, shape, and weight are balanced by their locations at equal distances from the optical center. In the other, two dissimilar masses are placed with the heavier closer to the fulcrum. Measurement of the distance is from the center of gravity of an element.

Placement of more than two elements is shown in Figure 10-19.

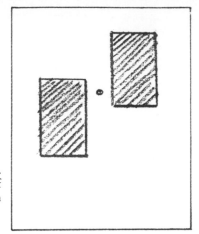
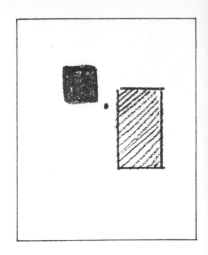

FIGURE 10-18. Placement of two units in balance.

Three elements are on the left. Two are paired off and placed in balance against the third. On the right are four elements in pairs balancing each other. Five or more masses may be handled in similar manner by first separating elements into groups and then balancing the groups.

Working in thumbnail-size areas similar to the illustrations used here, the beginner can experiment by varying the weights of elements and arranging and rearranging the locations of masses to achieve balance. One should begin with two elements and expand to several as the sense of visual balance develops.

A good test of balance, proportion, and other principles of design in printed matter can be made by looking with squinted eyes at the piece placed several feet away. Details are then deleted and only general shapes and weights come into focus. Likewise, the advan-

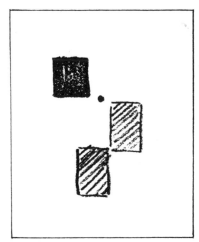
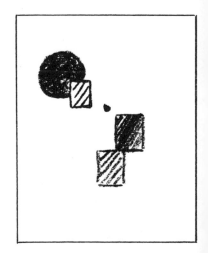

FIGURE 10-19. Proper placement of more than two elements.

tage to working first with thumbnails before developing full-size layouts is that the elements are in terms of approximate size, shape, and tone rather than in detail.

FORMAL AND INFORMAL BALANCE. How elements are positioned determines their balance. There are two types. *Formal*, or *symmetrical*, balance has identical elements on both sides of a vertical line running through the center of the space. *Informal*, or *asymmetrical*, balance has elements of varying weights in balance around the optical center. Figure 10-20 shows both; formal on the left, informal on the right.

The formal layout presents a restrained appearance with a feeling of conservatism. The informal is more exciting since it carries

FIGURE 10-20. Formal balance, left; and informal balance, right.

overtones of change and contrast due to the different weights of various elements. When an advertiser—for example, a bank, insurance company, or funeral home—wants to impart dignity and dependability, the formal balance is advantageous. The informal balance, though more interesting, is not necessarily more forceful for all ads. With a compelling main headline and eye-catching illustration, a simple and direct formal presentation is quite effective.

CONTRAST

In any form of communication some materials or ideas must be stressed more than others. Selecting these is, of course, a part of planning the communication.

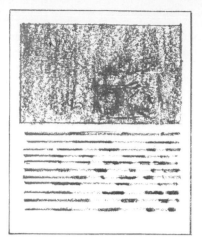 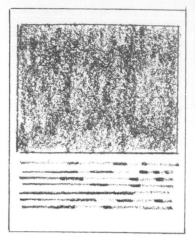

FIGURE 10-21. Illustration and text of equal size, left, is less pleasing to the eye than when the illustration dominates, right.

A speaker expressing his ideas in a deadly monotone bores the listener and fosters inattention. Naturally the retention of the message is low. On the other hand, a capable speaker manipulates his voice, employs gestures and perhaps visual aids to implement his presentation, and stresses the ideas he wishes to emphasize.

In a similar fashion, contrast is the source in print for the power of expression. It is the means of bringing to the fore the various elements that convey the message. Contrast can be achieved by altering size, shape, tone, and direction.

CONTRAST OF SIZE. On the left of Figure 10-21 is a layout showing illustration and text of approximately equal size. On the right, the presentation is livelier because a dominant illustration supplies contrast.

CONTRAST OF SHAPE. Although sizes contrast satisfactorily in Figure 10-22, a monotonous set of shapes appear on the left. Interest is enhanced on the right by an irregularly shaped illustration. To achieve this end in an actual working situation a halftone might be given an outline, or silhouette, treatment.

CONTRAST OF TONE. The dullness in the left of Figure 10-23 is brightened by tonal accents on the right.

CONTRAST OF DIRECTION. The major aim in contrasting direction is to lead the reader's eyes so that all the units of the message are absorbed one after the other. This is obviously *not*

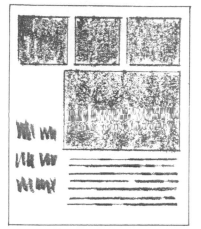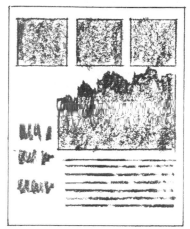

FIGURE 10-22. Monotony of shapes, left, is relieved by a different treatment of the large illustration, right.

FIGURE 10-23. Contrast of tone, missing on the left, "sparks" the layout on the right.

accomplished in Figure 10-24 with its repetition of direction.

In Figure 10-25 the eye moves from element to element because of the placement of shapes. The headline takes the eye to the right where it is met by the diagonal and is led to the copy block. The curved element at the end of the block carries the eye downward and to the left where the signature appears.

In our everyday life, we are constantly surrounded by contrasts of horizontal and vertical—for example, buildings and the horizon. The printed page, a rectangle, acts as a perfect frame for using the familiar directional contrasts to maintain interest and provide emphasis.

FIGURE 10-24. Monotony of directional tendencies.

FIGURE 10-25. Eye movement facilitated by direction.

RHYTHM

Rhythm in a layout is achieved in two ways. It can be developed through the orderly repetition of some feature in the design, such as a shape, tone, or color. In the left of Figure 10-26 it results from a series of rectangular illustrations. The variations in the forms are not so great that they prevent the reader from discerning their similarity at once. Their likeness insures that the eye will follow a course established by the pattern of their positions. Too much dissimilarity and the course would be broken.

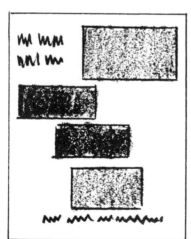

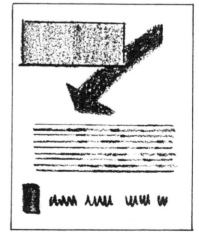

FIGURE 10-26. Rhythm developed through the repetition of shapes, left, and through the use of rhythmic line, right.

Less subtle than rhythm through repetition is the second means —that of a rhythmic line. An example is shown in the right of Figure 10-26 by the sweeping arrow that carries the eye to the copy block.

To be successful in a layout rhythm must be a purposeful movement from element to element in order of their significance to the message

UNITY

The individual elements that together constitute an ad must relate to each other and to the total design so that they effect coherence. Without this unity an ad cannot register a single impression with the reader.

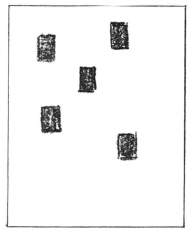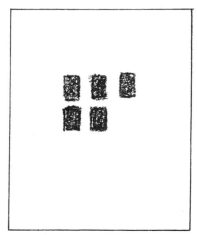

Figure 10-27. Lack of unity, left, improved through a proper grouping of elements, right.

In the left of Figure 10-27 five rectangles are placed at random. In sharp contrast to this confusion is the orderliness in the right-hand sketch where the same five rectangles have been divided into two groups, one of three units, the other of two.

Unity develops from chaos in a layout by the grouping of related elements. Figure 10-28 illustrates several of the techniques, which include background tints, overlapping elements, rules and border, that produce grouping.

A beginner's layout is likely to "fly apart" if he neglects unity. This can be avoided by relegating white space to the outside rather than allowing liberal amounts to fall among the elements of the ad.

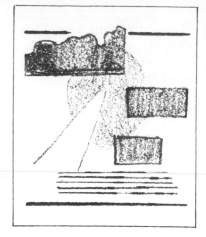

Figure 10-28. Several techniques for achieving unity.

HARMONY

Our discussion of the principles involved in typographic design would be incomplete without a reference to harmony and its relationship to contrast. As the designer arranges the elements in a printed message he must meet two forceful requirements: (1) the layout has to present a strong visual impact; (2) at the same time the total composition must produce a unity of effect.

Although these concepts may seem mutually exclusive, close examination reveals their interdependence.

Harmony is found in the mutual characteristics of the elements' tone and shape and of the type faces. A book page printed in one face—with variations in sizes, the use of italic for folios and head-lines, and borders and decorative devices matching the weight of the type—is a good example.

Quiescence is a characteristic. Complete harmony is passive and makes no demand on the reader. Contrast, on the other hand, is active and vigorous. It calls for variations in tone and shape to effect emphasis and action and to relieve monotony. With con-trast a sound tool for building a stimulating presentation to seize a reader's attention, what then is the value of harmony? To act as a safety factor. A layout made up of many elements of different sizes and tones could be spotty and hodge-podge without harmony.

Harmony occurs in Figure 10-29, although the composition contains two balanced groups of several elements, because the elements are related in size and tone.

In Figure 10-30, two similar shapes are widely separated yet demonstrate an attraction for each other. Their harmony is strong enough to be marked despite the elements between them.

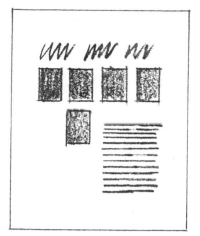

FIGURE 10-29. Grouped elements should be similar in size and tone.

FIGURE 10-30. Two similar elements may be placed widely apart under some conditions.

LAYOUT SHAPE

Why is the left-hand shape in Figure 10-31 less interesting than the right-hand one? Because it is prosaic. The unusual contour intrigues the eye.

The content of a layout presents such shapes. In Figure 10-32, the contour on the right is that of the ad reproduced on the left. All good layouts have forceful silhouettes in common. Their creation is facilitated by having one point, and only one, touch each of the four sides of an ad.

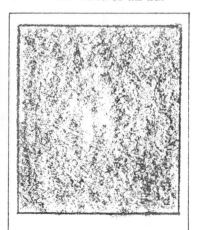

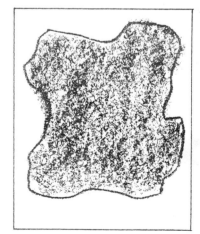

FIGURE 10-31. Unusual contour, right, proves more interesting than the rectangle, left.

 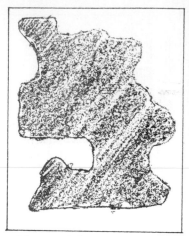

FIGURE 10-32. Contour, right, for the ad layout, left.

 conclusion

Beginner and professional alike should never forget this basic fact: the art of layout is *functional design.* It is not art for art's sake. The designer does not create layouts to satisfy his own creative urges or to prove to the world what a fine original artistic touch he has.

The arrangement of elements has a single job to do—to inform, persuade, entertain, or educate the reader. Very often an unsuccessful layout falls short simply because the designer did not keep this primary purpose uppermost in mind.

Copy preparation is a primary factor in implementing effective printed material. It is the last line of defense against error, against misunderstanding by the printer and the readers, and against sloppy appearance.

When the printer receives copy, it must be accurate in every detail, or errors will certainly mar the final result. Furthermore, without specific and detailed instructions, its appearance in type may not even resemble what was desired. And, as every novice who has been sent in search of a "type squeezer" knows, copy must fit prescribed areas: lead type slugs cannot be compressed.

Therefore, three important aspects of copy preparation are the concern of this chapter: *copy correction, typesetting instructions,* and *copy fitting.*

 copy correction

Fortunately for the student, the basic techniques of copy correction are the same for all media—whether copy is being prepared for newspapers, magazines, books, promotion pieces, or advertising. A universally accepted set of symbols makes this task relatively fast and efficient. These symbols are easy to learn because they are functional and are based on common sense.

Copy to be set should be typed double- or triple-spaced. All corrections can then be made at the spot of error, either on the line or above the line. Figure 11-1 shows the symbols for correcting errors in typewritten copy and those used for typesetting instructions. This latter facet of copy marking is discussed in more detail later.

The correcting process does not end with typewritten copy, of course. When the copy has been set into type, galley proofs are read to detect and eliminate errors made by the typesetter. There is seldom enough space between the lines on a galley proof to enable a proofreader to use any of the symbols shown in Figure 11-1 at the point of error. Even with enough room to do so, the typesetter would have to read through complete proofs to find the symbols, instead of being able to see each correction at a glance. Therefore special *proofreading* symbols are used *in the margin* to correct material that has been set in type. A mark may also be made at the point of error. Many proofreaders for newspapers and magazines draw a line from the point of error to the

COPYREADING SYMBOLS

<u>Correction Desired</u>   Symbol

1. Change form:

        3 to three. . . . . ③

        three to 3. . . . . (three)

        St. to Street. . . . . (St.)

        Street to St. . . . . (Street)

2. Change capital to small letter . . . . ℓ

3. Change small letter to capital . . . . d̳

4. To put space between words. . . . . the time

5. To remove the space. . . . . .news‿paper

6. To delete a letter and close up . . . . .jud̸gment

7. To delete several letters or words . . . . .shall ~~always~~ be

8. To delete several letters and close up . . . . . . .super͡intendent

9. To delete one letter and substitute another. . . . .recei̷ve

10. To insert words or several letters. . . . . .of ∧the time

11. To transpose letters or words, if adjacent. . . . .recie̷ve

12. To insert punctuation, print correct mark
    in proper place:

    comma   ）   parentheses ❨

    period   X   opening quote ᵛ⟩

    question   ?   closing quote ⟨ⁱ

    semicolon ⸴   dash ——

    colon   ⸱⸴   apostrophe ⱽ⟩

    exclamation !   hyphen =

13. To start a new paragraph. . . . . ¶ or [It has been

14. To center material. . . . .]Announcements[

15. To indent material. . . . .[The first

                                    day's work]

16. Set in boldface type . . . . The art of

17. Set in italic type . . . . The art of

18. To delete substantial amounts of copy, draw
    an X over the area and box it in.

19. To set several lines in boldface type, bracket
    the lines and mark <u>bf</u> in the margin.
                      (bf) ⟨The first / day's work

correction in the margin; most readers for book publishing firms
do not. When guidelines are drawn, care must be taken to avoid
obliterating the remainder of the line to be corrected. The symbols for marginal marks (Figure 11-2) are basically the same for
either system.

PROOFREADING MARKS

∧ Make correction indicated in margin.

𝒮𝓉𝑒𝓉 Retain crossed-out word or letter; let it stand.

· · · · Retain words under which dots appear; write "Stet" in margin.

X Appears battered; examine.

☰ Straighten lines.

√√√ Unevenly spaced; correct spacing.

∥ Line up; i.e., make lines even with other matter.

𝓇𝓊𝓃 𝒾𝓃 Make no break in the reading; no ¶

𝓃𝑜-¶ No paragraph; sometimes written "run in."

¶ Make a paragraph here.

𝓉𝓇 Transpose words or letters as indicated.

𝒮 Take out matter indicated; delete.

𝒮 Take out character indicated and close up.

¢ Line drawn through a cap means lower case.

9 Upside down; reverse.

⊃ Close up; no space.

Insert a space here.

□ Indent line one em.

⊏ Move this to the left.

⊐ Move this to the right.

𝓈𝓅 Spell out.

⌐ Raise to proper position.

�_⌐ Lower to proper position.

𝓌.𝒻. Wrong font; change to proper font.

𝒬𝓊? Is this right?

𝓁.𝒸. Put in lower case (small letters).

𝓈.𝒸. Put in small capitals.

𝒸𝒶𝓅𝓈 Put in capitals.

𝒸.𝓉𝓈𝒸. Put in caps and small caps.

𝓇𝑜𝓂. Change to Roman.

𝒾𝓉𝒶𝓁. Change to Italic.

☰ Under letter or word means caps.

═ Under letter or word, small caps.

— Under letter or word means Italic.

〰 Under letter or word, boldface.

⌄ Insert comma.

;/ Insert semicolon.

:/ Insert colon.

⊙ Insert period.

/?/ Insert interrogation mark.

(!) Insert exclamation mark.

/=/ Insert hyphen.

∨' Insert apostrophe.

❝ ❞ Insert quotation marks.

𝑒 Insert superior letter or figure.

⁷/ Insert inferior letter or figure.

[/] Insert brackets.

(/) Insert parenthesis.

⊤/M One-em dash.

2/M Two-em parallel dash.

𝒷𝒻 Boldface type.

𝓈 Set s as subscript.

𝓈 Set s as exponent.

FIGURE 11-1. (Left). Symbols used to correct and mark typewritten copy for the compositor. FIGURE 11-2. (Above). Symbols used to correct printed copy.

Many errors creep into printed material because someone fails to follow through after galleys have been corrected. If errors are detected at the first reading, revised proofs with corrections should be checked for a compositor can err as he sets a correction in a line, or as he substitutes corrected lines. Instead of pulling the line containing an error, he may take out another one and replace it with the one he has corrected. The result is double talk that can destroy all meaning for the material.

It is true that there is usually another opportunity for corrections to be made even if revised galley proofs are not called for, but this final reading should not be used for detecting errors in typesetting. These last proofs are made in the form of pages or, in the case of advertising, of the completed ad. They provide a chance to check if material is positioned properly, headlines are with the right story, captions are with the correct picture, and so on. To delay typesetting corrections to this point is wasteful for it takes more time to unlock a form and exchange lines than it does to make the change when type is still in galleys.

Printers accept responsibility for the errors of their compositors, but charge for the time spent correcting errors that were not detected in original copy or remaking lines for an editor or author who has merely changed his mind. These revisions become more expensive as material moves into the advanced production stages.

Publications with their own mechanical departments can hide the cost of author's alterations or other laxities because there is no bill that must be paid by the editorial department. But the cost remains nevertheless.

Some publications require duplicate sets of galley proofs, one for marking corrections and one to be cut apart and pasted on layout sheets. The set to be corrected is usually on white paper; the other is often on colored stock. Proofs for paste-up bear markings across the type area to identify the storage location of the type. This helps the printer's make-up man find the type as he puts pages together.

Press proofs are also obtainable, and in some cases this additional safeguard may be warranted. But if the person who must check the proofs is not on hand when the material first goes on the press, expensive press time can be wasted, since the time the job is on press must be paid for whether the press runs or not.

Regardless of precautions, errors occur. Absolute vigilance from the beginning of the typed copy to the final production steps keeps them to a minimum. Nothing can be taken for granted; it is amazing how easily errors seem to occur in such obvious places as headlines and titles in large display type.

marking printer's instructions

Before a printer can set a single line of type he must have
at least eight basic points of information:

(1) Type size (expressed in points).
(2) Type family (Century, Cheltenham, . . .).
(3) Family branch (bold, condensed, extended, . . .).
(4) Letter posture (italic or roman).
(5) Letter composition (caps, lower case, . . .).
(6) Leading.
(7) Appointment of space (flush, centered, . . .).
(8) Line length (expressed in picas).

Theoretically, then, the instructions for setting a line of type
would read like this: "*8-point Bodoni Bold Italic caps and lower
case, leaded 2 points, centered on 21 picas.*" However, much of
this information does not have to be written on every piece of
copy. Depending upon the circumstance, it can be taken for
granted that some of the instructions are understood by the printer.

In body copy, for example, it is assumed that the appointment
of space is to be flush left and right. Only exceptions must be
marked. Letter composition is considered to be as shown in the
copy; that is, typed capitals are to be set as capitals, lower case
letters are to be set as lower case. Printers also set copy with roman
letter posture unless there are indications to the contrary.

The marking of copy for titles and headlines is also simplified
because of the following assumptions mutual to editor and printer:
that (1) posture is roman unless marked; (2) machine leading
is not needed unless marked; (3) line length is to be "line for line"
and (4) letter composition is to be as shown in the copy.

But whether by mutual understanding or by specific copy marking, a line of type cannot be set unless the printer has the eight
points of information. This is especially true of "transient" material, as distinguished from periodical copy. Procedure for periodicals differs because the regularity of issue permits considerable
uniformity.

NEWSPAPER PROCEDURE

Marking copy for the mechanical department of a newspaper is simplified by several factors. Selection of type sizes, style,

and leading is a decision of management and is seldom subject to change. Column widths (line lengths) are standard, although there may be some variation on the editorial page for by-line columns or special features. Speed in processing copy is essential and time is at a premium. Because headlines have such a direct effect on the character of a newspaper, they are standardized as much as possible.

Copy is channeled through one central (universal) copy desk and/or a number of departmental desks, directed by men who are expert in the English language and versed in the newspaper's style and its composing and pressroom procedures. It is their job to prepare copy quickly and efficiently for the mechanical department.

Because body type specifications do not change, much of the copy is sent to the composing room with no marked instructions other than those for exceptions (multicolumn leads, special treatment for editorials or columns, and so on). Standardization applies to headlines too. A comprehensive schedule that visualizes all possible headlines and gives all the information a headline writer may need is prepared by the editorial department for the composing room. Each headline is keyed by a number or letter; to give the composing room all necessary information about the final appearance of a headline, the writer simply labels the headline with any agreed-upon designation, such as "#1" or "AA," and this immediately refers the compositor to the type size, face, and so on, similarly marked on the comprehensive schedule.

Body and headline copy are usually sent to the composing room on separate sheets. For the most part, the display sizes of type are composed on the Ludlow or Linotypes and Intertypes reserved for display, and the body sizes are set on Linotype or Intertype straight-matter machines. If body copy and headlines were on the same sheet, men would not be able to set both at the same time.

To place a headline over the proper story when pages are made up, a "slugging" system is used. The body copy is slugged with a word or two to identify the story—most newspapers use the first two words of the headline. As the text type is put in place, the slug line is replaced by the headline it identifies.

Other special problems for the newspaper are handled with equal efficiency. Continuing stories (which are set in type in intervals as they develop during the day), stories that must be changed slightly between editions, and stories that must be set before a headline has been written require special markings. These vary from newspaper to newspaper, but are always conveyed by tech-

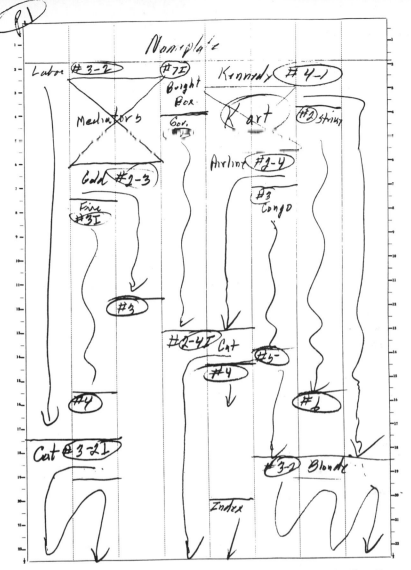

FIGURE 11-3. Typical newspaper page dummy. A slug, the headline designation, and the direction that the text is to run are indicated for most stories.

niques that simplify the communication of instructions from the editorial department to the composing room.

NEWSPAPER MAKE-UP INSTRUCTIONS. A newspaper must be put together in a hurry. Virtually every step of the make-up process is based on approximation, rather than exact calculation. As stories are processed, their length is estimated and each is recorded with pertinent data on an inventory sheet usually called a *copy schedule.*

This information is used for page dummies. As the make-up man prepares the dummy, he writes the slug for each story in the position on the page that he believes the story merits. He indicates the probable length of the story with an arrow, and shows the placement of illustrations by drawing an X through the space. The dummy then serves as a pattern as the stories and headlines are put in a form prior to stereotyping or printing. Figure 11-3 shows a typical newspaper page dummy.

ADVERTISING AND BROCHURE PROCEDURE

The marking of copy for advertisements is quite different. In most cases a full *mark-up* (Figure 11-4) is used for communicating instructions about typesetting and make-up to the printer. It is best described as a drawing of how the ad is to look when printed. All display lines are lettered in exact position, illustrations are sketched in, and body type areas are indicated by drawn lines. Instructions for type size and style are written with colored pencil and circled next to each bit of display type or in the margin. The body type areas are identified by letter—A, B, C, and so on.

Body copy is provided in typewritten form, is marked with typesetting instructions, and is slugged with the corresponding letter from the mark-up. By following these instructions and checking with the mark-up, the mechanical department or printer can create an exact replica of the ad as designed by the advertiser or his agency. The same procedure is followed for flyers, handbills, direct mailing pieces, and other brochures.

MAGAZINE PROCEDURE

The preparation of magazine material is usually a cross between those used for newspapers and for advertisements. Sometimes articles are prepared with full mark-ups by an art department; or the editor may follow a fast course like his newspaper counterpart. But in most cases a middle ground is followed.

There is apt to be no headline schedule; titles follow no set typographical pattern. They are lettered in position on a dummy, with typesetting instructions entered as in advertising mark-ups. The relative stability of column measure and other aspects of body copy permits the use of minimum marking for such material.

Because there is usually sufficient time between issues, a magazine dummy is made by pasting galley proofs of text material or

FIGURE 11-4. An ad layout fully marked. Display type is specified on the mark-up; body copy is keyed only.

specimen copy of body and caption type in position, with the titles lettered in by hand (Figure 11-5). Rough layout sketches in miniature or full-size often precede the paste-up dummy.

copy fitting

The planner of any kind of graphic communication is vitally concerned with copy fitting. It is important to the editors of newspapers and magazines, the advertising designer, and the public relations man who puts together booklets and brochures for without it, unnecessary costs are incurred and/or attractive

Women Make The News

The compression set values are also highest in the 76/24 isomer area with the lowest values obtained in the TDI with 2,4 isomer content of 80-85%.

Tear values for this machine-made foam were highest for the low 2,4 TDI isomer content and lowest at the 76/24 and 90/10 ratios. The tear data shows the 80/85% 2,4 foams are somewhat intermediate in value.

The highest percent elongation results are provided by foams made up from TDI containing 75-80% of the 2,4 isomer. The area around 83% 2,4 isomer provides us with foams of the lowest elongation.

Tensile strengths are highest for the foams made with the low 2,4 TDI contents and progressively decrease reaching a low value at the 75-80% 2,4 TDI range. Another high point for tensile value again is the 86/14 TDI foam.

The stiffest foams were prepared when the low 2,4 TDI was used. The softest ones were those made from TDI containing 76 to 81% of the 2,4 isomer. Intermediate deflection values were obtained in foams from TDI having an 83 to 88% 2,4 isomer content.

The top surface and cell structure of the foams prepared with the previous formulation were generally good

In the isomer ratios covered in this series, only about half of the foams produced were free of fissures enabling us to obtain density and compression deflection data. Density and compression deflection information was obtained on 2 inch thick samples cut out from the original container wherever suitable samples could be obtained.

The lowest densities obtained with the Multron R-18 polyester ranged from 2.6 to 2.5 lbs. per cubic foot with TDI ratios starting at 88/12 and going up to 100% 2,4.

The lowest 25% compression deflection (or lowest stiffness) data for this polyester also follows the same TDI isomer ratios.

On the other hand, the highest density and highest deflection (stiffness) values are obtained at the 88/12 TDI isomer ratio using the Fomrez 50 polyester. The lowest density (2.73 lbs./cu. ft.) and deflection values for this polyester are obtained with TDI isomer ratio of 93.5/6.5 and 96/4.

These differences in density and stiffness occurring at the 88/12 isomer ratio are not readily explainable. We are familiar with the structure of the Multron R-18 polyester, and other than physical properties, we have

In place of the Injection Molders duce a new feature devoted to the pri ing with the February issue.

still Ben Morse called his shots as he column which was probably the most Morse—for six years of hard work—th

Since January 1951 the Injection M the 63 issues of SPE Journal. The s ends with this issue. Though an occa

16

FIGURE 11-5a. Magazine dummies are often combination paste-ups and mark-ups. Here, the title has been lettered by hand and size and face of display type specified; sized proof of art, and sample body and caption type have been pasted on.

layouts are destroyed. If more type than needed is set, the payment for the *overset* is wasted cost. Titles that cannot fit a given space must be rewritten and reset with unnecessary loss of time and money. Areas of text type that fail to fill their allotted space can jeopardize the effect of a good design.

Depending upon the circumstance, copy fitting may be rough or extremely accurate. There are several methods each suitable to its purpose. For body-type sizes, these include an estimation based on number of words per column inch, a *word-count* system, a *square-inch* method, and a *character-count* system. For display sizes, a *unit count* is used.

FIGURE 11-5b. Preparation of dummy. Use of a T-square, triangle, and metal pica ruler produce speed and accuracy in this operation. (Courtesy New York Lithographing Corporation.)

COPY FITTING FOR NEWSPAPERS

The fast pace of newspaper production allows no time for complicated copy fitting methods. Stories are written so they can be cut from the bottom without destroying meaning. When they do not fill a space, filler material is supplied.

Consequently, estimation based on the number of words in a column inch is sufficiently accurate. Depending upon point size, column width, and leading, this figure usually ranges from thirty to forty words per column inch. When reporters use a uniform setting for line lengths on their typewriters, this figure can be converted to lines; that is, four typewritten lines equal a column inch.

It only takes a second, for example, for an experienced copy editor to gauge a story's length to be twenty typewritten lines (four lines equalling a column inch) or five column inches. Other systems take more time, but offer greater accuracy when called for.

WORD-COUNT COPY FITTING

The *word-count* system of copy fitting is reasonably accurate and is useful for estimating space requirements during preliminary stages of production. It is also useful in determining which type size will squeeze a prescribed amount of copy into an allotted space. (Any copy-fitting problem can be solved by this method, but it is ordinarily not used when a type face and size have already been selected; a more accurate result can then be obtained by considering the space characteristics of the selected face.)

A knowledge of printing measurement is mandatory for an understanding of the word-count method. The following must be committed to memory:

(1) A point is one-seventy-second of an inch (72 points equal an inch).

(2) A pica is 12 points (one-sixth of an inch).

(3) An em is the square of the type size (an 8-point em is 8-points wide, a 10-point em is 10-points wide, . . .).

The system also depends on the following estimations:

(1) For type sizes 10-point or smaller, three ems equal one word.

(2) For type sizes 11-point or larger, two and one-half ems equal one word.

Because the word-count system is based on *averages* for word length, spacing between words, and type-design characteristics, it is accurate only to a limited degree. It should not be used for computations involving condensed or extended faces.

How to Use the Word-Count System in Typical Situations. *To find the space needed for a given amount of copy when the type size and length of line is known,* first determine:

(1) The number of words in the copy.

(2) The number of ems in each line, and subsequently the number of words that will fit in each line.

(3) The number of lines of type necessary for the copy.

(4) How much vertical space these lines will occupy.

As a typical situation, follow these steps to determine the amount of space needed for the body copy of a direct-mail promotion piece. Once the space requirements are known for all of the copy, an appropriate size can be selected for the folder. Assume that the lines are to be 18-picas-long, and the type is to be either 8-point solid or 8-point leaded 2 points.

Step 1. Estimate the number of words in the copy quickly by counting the words in five or six lines and dividing the total by the number of lines. Multiply the average number of words in these lines by the number of lines to find the number of words in the copy:

Total number of words in six lines: 72

Average number of words in one line: 12

Total lines (150) times average number of words in line (12): 1800 words in the copy.

All typewritten lines are counted as full lines, including those that begin and end paragraphs because there will be an equivalent number of short lines when the type is set.

Step 2. To find the number of words in a line, first divide the length of the line (in points) by the type size. This gives the number of ems in the line; divide the number of ems by 3 (if type size is 10-point or smaller) or 2.5 (if type size is 11-point or larger) to get the number of words.

18-pica line times 12 points per pica: 216 points per line

216 points divided by 8 (point size of type): 27 ems per line

27 ems divided by 3 (number of ems in word): 9 words per line

Step 3. The number of lines required for the copy is computed by dividing the number of words in a line into the number of words in the copy.

1800 words of copy divided by 9 words per line: 200 lines

Step 4. Amount of vertical space needed for these lines can be found by multiplying the thickness of each line times the number of lines. Remember to be concerned with the thickness of the body of the type; if the type is leaded, leading must be taken into consideration. For example, if 8-point type is leaded 2 points, the line thickness is 10 points.

For 8-point solid: 200 lines times 8: 1600 points

For 8 on 10: 200 lines times 10: 2000 points

The measurement of type areas is usually expressed in picas, so the answer is converted:

1600 points divided by 12 points per pica: 133⅓ picas.

or

2000 points divided by 12 points per pica: 166⅔ picas

Knowing that the body type area must be 18-picas-wide and either 133⅓- or 166⅔-picas-deep with leading, the sheet size for the mailing piece can be decided. Copy can be broken into any number of columns, and space must be allowed for illustrations and display type also; these factors, in addition to standard paper sizes and other elements discussed in other chapters, result in a sound decision.

To find the number of words to be written when an ad, brochure, or booklet has already been designed and space has been designated, determine:

(1) The number of lines of type that will fit into the designated area.

(2) The number of ems and subsequently the number of words that will fit into each of these lines.

(3) The total number of words.

For this example, assume that an ad has been designed with a copy area 21-picas-wide and 28-picas-deep. The copy is to be set in 12-point type leaded 2 points.

Step 1. Find the number of lines by dividing the line thickness into the depth (in points).

14 points divided into 336 points (28 picas times 12 points per pica): 24 lines

Step 2. Figure the number of ems in the line by dividing the point size of the type into the length of the line in points.

12 points divided into 252 points (21 picas times 12): 21 ems

(Note: In this example, because the type is pica size, it was not necessary to have completed this step)

Find the number of words by dividing the average number of

ems per word into the total number of ems in a complete line.

2.5 into 21 ems: 8⅖ words per line

Step 3. Find the number of words to be written by multiplying the number of words in a line times the number of lines.

24 times 8⅖: 201.6, or 201 words needed to fill the space

In writing to fill, it is wise in most cases to write a few lines less rather than more. It is usually easier to expand copy with a little extra leading between lines than it is to shorten it by editing after it has been set.

To find the size of type to use when the space and number of words are known, follow the same procedure with one exception. First decide a feasible type size, with or without leading, and then work the problem as if to discover the number of words to be written. If the answer is smaller than the number of words already written, the type size is too large or some leading must be eliminated. If the answer is considerably larger, the size selected is too small or some leading can be used. Through trial and error, a solution is reached.

SQUARE-INCH METHOD OF COPY FITTING

Although it is somewhat less accurate than a word count, the *square-inch method* is useful for the preliminary planning of all printed matter. Its chief advantage is simplicity; answers can be found quickly. It is based on the following table showing the average number of words per square inch in each common body type size, solid or leaded:

SQUARE-INCH TABLE

Type Size in Points	Number of words per square inch if set solid	Number of words per square inch if leaded 2 points
6	47	34
7	38	27
8	32	23
9	27	20
10	21	16
11	17	14
12	14	11

The ease with which common copy-fitting problems can be solved by using this table is shown by these examples:

Example 1. Finding the number of words to write to fill a given space. Designed is an eight-page booklet, plus cover, with type to occupy an area 5 by 7 inches on every page. There are 35 square inches of type on each page (found by multiplying 5 by 7); multiplying 35 by 8 (the number of pages) yields that the booklet will accommodate 280 square inches of type. Assuming the type to be 10-point, leaded 2 points, a check of the table reveals that 16 words will fit into each square inch. Multiplying the number of words per square inch (16) by the number of square inches (280) tells that approximately 4480 words must be written to fill the booklet.

Example 2. Finding the size of type to use. On hand is an area 4 by 7 inches into which must be put 560 words. Dividing the square inches in the area (28) into the number of words (560) gives 20 words in each square inch. The table indicates that 9-point type leaded 2 points will render 560 words into the space.

CHARACTER-COUNT METHOD

For maximum accuracy, the *character-count method* of copy fitting is used. It is the only practicable system for the precise work of preparing copy in the final stages of production for magazines, advertisements, and most promotion pieces.

It is the most accurate system because the unit of measurement is the character instead of the word and because it takes into account the widths in type designs. Words vary greatly in length, and any copy fitting that depends on an average for word length can achieve only limited accuracy. Type designs—even those considered standard, not labeled as condensed or extended—vary considerably in the number of characters that will fit into a line. If specific information about type design were not necessary for this method, there would be no need for any other system. But, before the character-count method can be put to use, the number of characters that will fit in each line must be known.

The manufacturers of type-casting machines provide such data in accurately compiled tables. Printers relay the information to customers, either with type-specimen catalogues or upon request. Sometimes the number is expressed only as "characters per pica," in which case it must be multiplied by the measure of picas in a line to get the total characters for each line. Usually, however, this bit of computation has already been done, and character counts for pica measures ranging from one to thirty are given, as in the table below. Using this information, some representative character-count problems that follow can be worked out.

SAMPLE CHARACTER COUNT SCALE§

10-POINT KENNERLY										
Line length in picas	12	14	16	18	20	22	24	26	28	30
Character count	27	34	39	45	51	57	62	68	74	79

10-POINT VOGUE										
Line length in picas	12	14	16	18	20	22	24	26	28	30
Character count	28	34	40	46	52	57	62	68	73	79

§ Courtesy Lawhead Press, Inc., Athens, Ohio

FINDING AMOUNT OF SPACE NEEDED. When the type face and size have been selected and line length is known, the amount of space needed can be found by:

(1) Computing the number of characters in the copy.
(2) Finding the number of characters that will fit into each line from the table.
(3) Dividing the number of characters per line into the total number of characters to find the number of lines needed.
(4) Convert the number of lines to any desired unit of measure.

Example: A magazine article is to be set in 10-point solid Kennerly. The columns are 20-picas-wide. How much space should be allowed in these 20-pica columns for the article?

1. Find the number of characters in the copy by counting the characters in a few lines and deciding an average. Multiply that figure by the number of lines to get the total. For this example, assume that there are 100 lines of 70 characters, or a total of 7000 characters.

2. A check of the table shows that 51 characters will fit into a 20-pica line.

3. Dividing 51 into 7000 yields 137 and 13/51 lines. Since there is no such thing as a fraction of a line of type, space must be allowed for 138 lines.

4. The depth of 138 lines can be converted to any unit of measurement. Each line is 10-points-thick, so the depth is 1380 points. If a line gauge is used in preparing the dummy pages for the article, the answer may be needed in picas. By dividing the 12 points per pica into 1380 points it is found that 115 picas of space must be left in the 20-pica columns of the magazine.

FINDING THE AMOUNT OF COPY TO WRITE TO FILL A GIVEN SPACE. When space for copy has been prescribed, the amount of copy that will fill the space can be found by:

(1) Checking the table to find the number of characters per line.
(2) Dividing the point size of each line into the depth of the area (in points) to find the number of lines to be written.

Example: An advertisement has a copy area 18-picas-wide and 22-picas-deep. The type to be used is 10-point Vogue leaded 2 points. To know how much to write for the message to fill the desired space:

1. Check the table. Forty-six characters will fit into each line.

2. Because each line is 12-points-thick (10-point type plus 2 points of leading), 22 lines will fit into the 22 picas of depth. If each line were not 1 pica in thickness, the number of lines would be found first by multiplying 22 picas by 12 points to get the depth in points, and then by dividing by the line thickness (12 points) into the area. The writer can set the marginal stops on the typewriter so that each line written contains 46 characters and equals a line of type.

If there were a need to find the total number of characters, a third step of multiplying the number of lines (22) by the number of characters in a line (46) would suffice. There is seldom a use for this information.

SOME COPY-FITTING SHORT CUTS

Some of the work of copy fitting can be reduced by cooperation between writers, editors, and layout men. The time to determine the number of characters contained in articles is cut by writers using consistent typewriter settings so that the person doing the copy fitting knows in advance that typed lines always average a certain number of characters.

The copy paper used by a magazine can be ruled to show line lengths of typewritten copy that correspond to lines of type in the publication's columns. By typing within these lines, the writer helps the copy fitter find the space needed for the material almost instantly.

fitting display type to space

Even the most accurate copy-fitting method described is inadequate for computing the space requirements of headlines, titles, or other lines of display type.

The character-count system, sufficient for type sizes as large as 12-point, requires some modification before use with larger sizes. For body copy, the character-count method depends upon averages for the width of characters, an allowance being made in the scales for wide letters (*m* and *w*), narrow letters (*f, l, i, t*), and capitals according to their normal frequency in text material.

But the large size and limited application of display types create a possibility of intolerable error unless specific attention is paid as each individual letter in a title or headline is fitted to space.

UNIT COUNT FOR DISPLAY TYPE

For near-perfect copy fitting of newspaper headlines, magazine titles, and the like, a *unit-count* system is used. It is similar to character counting except that instead of counting every letter as one character, the letters are assigned units according to their width. Some degree of accuracy is sacrificed to keep the system from being too cumbersome. Letters are assumed to fall in one of four categories: *thin, normal, wide,* or *extrawide.* Normal letters are assigned one unit, thin letters one-half unit, wide letters one-and-one-half units, and extrawide letters two units. Therefore, for display type containing capitals *and* lower-case letters, the following allotments are usually made:

All lower-case letters and numbers 1 unit

except

m and *w*	1½ units
f, 1, i, t, and *1*	½ unit
All capital letters	1½ units

except

M and W	2 units
I	½ unit
Spaces	1 unit
Punctuation	½ unit

Depending upon the design of the type, occasionally *j* and *r* are assigned only a half unit. Other variations can be made, but the assignments above meet most situations.

The specific value given to basic letters could be any amount, provided that the same values are used when line maximums are figured. For example, two units could be given for each basic lower-case letter and with proportionate value to the thin and wide letters; the only difference would be that the maximum number of units that would fit in any line measure would be twice the maximum with one assigned unit.

It follows that the unit count for headlines of *all capitals* is different than that of both capitals and lower case. For simplicity in counting, the basic capital letters are assigned one unit in all-cap heads. The unit allotments in all-capital display lines are:

All letters	1 unit
except	
M and W	1½ unit
I	½ unit
Spaces	½ unit
Punctuation	½ unit

Note how the two headlines in Figure 11-6 are counted.

FIGURE 11-6. Unit count for headlines. Note that unit values assigned to letters and spaces differ between all-cap and cap-and lower-case headlines. The fact that the first line totaled seven units in both cases is only coincidence.

Virtually all the work connected to display types involves writing lines to fit a given space. It is therefore a matter of ascertaining the maximum number of units for the line, and then writing within that limitation. In newspaper offices these maximums are shown on a headline schedule. Originally they are derived by setting lines composed of a normal assortment of letters and spaces and counting the units in these lines. Character counts shown for display type in printers' type specimen books may also be used as line maximums.

Whatever the source, the maximum count per line has to be observed. The temptation to squeeze an extra half unit may be strong if the wording of the title or headline seems especially good—and occasionally such fudging on the count pays. But when it fails, the waste of time for the writer to rewrite and for the compositor to reset the line is inexcusable. The gamble is not worth the effort and expenditure.

12 Photographs and other illustrations are copy to the photoengraver or lithographer, just as text and titles are copy to the letterpress printer. As copy, they require careful editing and preparation for the craftsman to produce the desired quality.

Processing illustrations is the same for letterpress and lithography to a certain point, then the differences between the processes call for individual procedures. Identical techniques will be discussed first followed by the special aspects of copy preparation for photo-offset lithography.

CROPPING PHOTOGRAPHS

Photographs, like news stories or magazine articles, are sometimes verbose, poorly constructed, too large, or too small. They must be edited to tell only what they are supposed to tell, reconstructed to give emphasis where emphasis is needed, reduced or enlarged to fit space.

The basic part of picture editing is called *cropping*. It is the figurative cutting of the original photograph to eliminate the above-mentioned faults when it is in plate form on a printing press.

Cropping is "figurative" cutting because portions of a photo will rarely be cut away with scissors or blade; marks made with a grease pencil are used to indicate the finished dimensions. These are usually placed in the white border around the photograph, or on the mounting board used for backing.

CROPPING FOR CONTENT. As photographic prints come from a photographer, they often contain shortcomings that should be corrected. Unnecessary or disturbing detail should be removed, attention may need to be shifted to the important feature, composition may need improvement.

In most cases judicious cropping can eliminate these weak points. To decide what should be cropped, it is helpful to use two L-shaped pieces of cardboard that can be moved over the face of the photograph until they frame the most desirable portion. Crop marks at these areas later direct the platemaker to use only that portion.

CROPPING TO FIT SPACE. Photographs are usually in two standard sizes: 8 by 10 inches or 5 by 7 inches, but editors often

COPY for the PHOTOENGRAVER and LITHOGRAPHER

have to work with snapshots in a multitude of sizes. Regardless, it is rare when a photo can be reproduced in its original size by a publication.

Platemakers can make enlargements and reductions with their cameras. But, because enlargements and reductions are done photographically, platemakers have no magical way of changing the *shape* of a photograph. If the original forms a wide horizontal rectangle, the plate will be in the same shape. In other words, the plate is a *scaled* version of the original.

Therefore, the depth of a vertical photo that must fit into a horizontal and rectangular spot on a page, must be cropped sufficiently so the original obtains a horizontal shape.

There are two basis systems of finding how much must be cropped in such instances, one involving arithmetic, the other the measuring of lines. Working these is called *scaling*, or *proportioning*.

SCALING ILLUSTRATIONS

The scaling of illustrations is the equivalent of copy fitting. Common problems include finding: (1) the depth of a plate when the width is known; (2) the width when the depth is known; (3) the amount to cut (crop) when the depth and the width of the finished product are known. These problems are most apt to be involved in reducing photos to smaller plate sizes, because platemakers get better quality with reduction than they can with enlargements. Scaling provides the information for either enlargements or reductions.

ARITHMETICAL SYSTEM. A rectangle is shaped by the relationship of its adjoining sides. For example, a photograph 4-inches-wide and 2-inches-deep is the same shape as a rectangle 2-inches-wide and 1-inch-deep. In both cases the width is twice the depth.

This relationship in a photo can be expressed as a fraction: photo width/photo depth. The same can be done with an engraving: engraving width/engraving depth. By setting up these fractions as an equation, any missing dimension can be found with simple arithmetic. The following are typical examples.

Example 1. Finding the engraving depth when width is known. Assuming a photo to be 8-inches-wide and 10-inches-deep and the cut to be 2-inches-wide, the equation is

$$\frac{8}{10} = \frac{2}{x} .$$

To solve, cross multiply 8 by x to get $8x$, and 10 by 2 to get 20. If $8x = 20$, then x (engraving depth) = 2.5.

Example 2. Finding the engraving width when depth is known. Assuming a photo to be 7-inches-wide and 5-inches-deep and the cut is to be 3-inches-deep, the equation is

$$\frac{7}{5} = \frac{x}{3}$$

By cross multiplying, $5x = 21$. The engraving width is then 4-1/5.

Example 3. Finding how much to crop from a photo to give it dimensions that will reduce to fit a specific layout area. Some students seem to have difficulty with this type of problem for they fail to visualize which of the four dimensions in the equation is the unknown. A vertical photo that is to fit a horizontal space has an unknown depth; a horizontal photo that is to fit a vertical space has an unknown width.

If a photo is 8-inches-wide and 10-inches-deep and is to be made into a plate 5-inches-wide and 4-inches-deep, the depth of the photo must be cropped for it is the unknown. Therefore,

$$\frac{8}{x} = \frac{5}{4}; \ 5x = 32; \text{ and } x = 6 \ 2/5.$$

The photo's depth must be cropped *to* 6-2/5 inches from 10 inches wide. The 3-3/5 inches to be cropped can be taken from the top, bottom, or partially from each, depending on the content. If the content will not permit this much cropping, the layout or the photo must be changed.

There are some disadvantages to the system described here. Working with strange fractions can be too time consuming. There is a possibility that errors will occur and result in unusable, costly engravings.

USE OF SPECIAL SLIDE RULES OR CIRCULAR SCALES. Most of the danger of human error can be eliminated by scaling with slide rules and circular scalers that supply ready-made mathematical answers. These handy gadgets are often furnished free by printers and engravers, or can be purchased quite reasonably. Both work on the same principle; two of the dimensions are lined up across from each other on the scale; the missing dimension is then located directly across from the third known dimension (Figure 12-1).

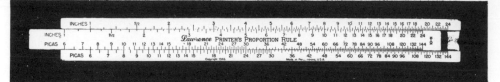

FIGURE 12-1. A proportion rule for scaling photographs. The center portion slides to any position. If two dimensions are placed opposite each other, the fourth dimension will be found directly across from the third known dimension. Note solution of Example 1 on preceding page.

USE OF A DIAGONAL LINE FOR SCALING. Another method, somewhat inaccurate but usable in most instances, employs a diagonal line to find any unknown dimension in picture scaling. No mathematics are involved; the work is done entirely by drawing and measuring lines on an overlay sheet, not on the photograph. Care must be taken so that the pencil does not press a line into the emulsion of the photo, for such lines show in the finished engraving.

The diagonal method, illustrated in Figure 12-2, starts with the bisection of a rectangle by a line drawn diagonally from one corner to another. Any smaller rectangle formed by right-angle lines drawn from adjacent sides of the large rectangle to the diagonal line is proportionate to the large rectangle.

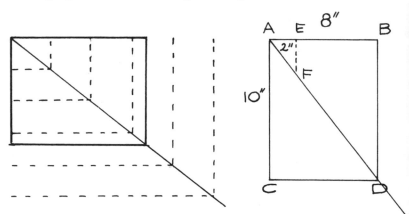

FIGURE 12-2. Diagonal system of photograph scaling.

FIGURE 12-3. Finding depth when width is known.

In Figure 12-3, the diagonal is used to work the first problem solved earlier by the arithmetical system. The larger rectangle represents the 8- by-10-inch photograph. The known engraving width of 2 inches is measured across the top. The perpendicular line dropped to the diagonal at that point (line *E-F*) is the depth the plate will be. If the illustration were drawn to unreduced dimensions, the line would be approximately 2.5 inches. "Approximately" because this method is only as accurate as the drawing of the lines. If the perpendicular is not at exactly 90 degrees, the measurement will be slightly off. All inaccuracies in drawing lines affect the answer.

Figure 12-4 shows the use of the diagonal to find the width when depth is known. Procedure is identical to that used in Figure 12-3, except that the perpendicular is drawn from the side (because the depth is known) to the diagonal.

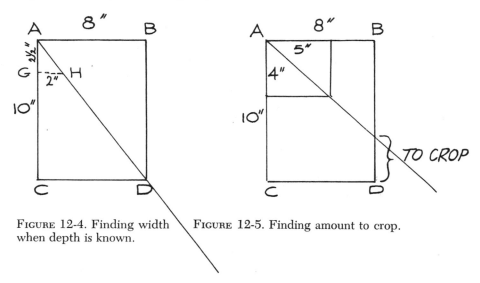

FIGURE 12-4. Finding width when depth is known.

FIGURE 12-5. Finding amount to crop.

The third example used earlier in explaining the arithmetical system (finding amount to crop) is worked out by the diagonal method in Figure 12-5. In this example both dimensions of the engraving are known (it thus becomes the starting rectangle) and the diagonal constructs the rectangle representing the *cropped* picture. The amount to be cropped is found by measuring the distance between the intersection of the diagonal with the line *B-D* and the corner *D*.

FINDING THE PERCENTAGE OF REDUCTIONS OR ENLARGEMENTS

Platemakers usually translate the relationship of original photo to finished plate size in terms of percentages because camera settings are determined by the percentage to which copy is enlarged or reduced.

It is often beneficial to do the same thing when editing photographs. One of the costs of platemaking is the camera work, and if several original photos can be shot (photographed) at the same time a same-focus reduction in price is given. Because plate dimensions can often vary without harming a layout, it may be wise to change them slightly so several photos can be reduced to the same percentage of the original size.

For example, if five photographs are to be reduced respectively to 48, 49, 50, 50.5, and 51 percent, they might all be made at the 50 percent reduction in order to claim the same-focus price benefit.

The percentage of reduction or enlargement is determined simply by dividing one dimension of the photo into the same dimension of the plate. In Example 1, above, a photo 8-inches-wide was to be reduced to a plate 2-inches-wide. By dividing 8 into 2, the reduction is found to be 0.25, or reduced to 25 percent.

OTHER METHODS OF ALTERING PHOTO CONTENT

Cropping is not the only method by which the content of a photo can be changed. An artist can *air brush* photographs to remove disturbing background or to emphasize certain portions of the subject. The platemaker can also do this and can manipulate his camera settings to *highlight* (make white) some sections of the picture subject that might otherwise be gray and dull.

Through the use of special plate finishes as described in Chapter 6 (silhouette, partial silhouette, vignette, geometrical shapes), the appearance and shape of photographs can be changed when they appear in print.

Although air brushing and retouching require special skills, the journalist can get special plate finishes without an artist's assistance. Through the use of overlay sheets he can adequately communicate his desires to the platemaker who creates the special effect as he makes the plates.

To order silhouettes, for example, an overlay sheet is fastened snugly to the photo and then the subject to be silhouetted is lightly outlined with soft pencil. To avoid misunderstanding, "outline" or "silhouette" should be written in the area surrounding the line.

Vignettes can be indicated in similar fashion. The beginning and ending of the fade-out area can be drawn on an overlay.

Mortises, notches, and geometric shapes (circles, ovals, irregulars) can also be shown on an overlay. The change in size brought on by enlargement or reduction in platemaking *must always be considered* when working with overlays.

High-light (also called "drop-out") halftones are so named because they permit reproduction of pure whites in photographs and other continuous-tone illustrations. The dots present in all areas of a halftone are dropped out of the light areas of the copy by special camera exposures, or are painted out of the negative. Whichever procedure is followed, high-light halftones are expensive (about three times the cost of regular halftones). They are imperative for some types of art work, and are often used to give true-to-life reproduction of the products of advertisers.

A cheaper method of highlighting is achieved with line engraving of a screened photographic print made on special *Velox* paper. These halftones are called Veloxes and are used mainly for newspaper reproduction. After the original copy has been photographed through a screen, the photo print (the halftone print) is retouched to get the high-light effect. Grayed blacks can be painted to pure blacks, and type or other line copy can be superimposed on the print before it is processed by the engraver as a Benday line cut. The cost of the Velox print plus the line engraving is considerably less than a high-light halftone, especially if the plate contains both line and halftone copy.

An overlay sheet is again used to show desired high-light areas for these special plates, whether they are done completely by an engraver or with Velox prints. Location of line work on combination plates, both reverse and surprint, is indicated in the same manner.

Combination plates are expensive, but on many occasions are especially effective. If type matter or line illustrations must appear over a halftone (in white or in the color of the halftone) a combination plate is required. Along with the halftone copy, reproduction proofs of type matter or sharp black-on-white line drawings must be provided to the engraver so that he can make good combination plates.

These techniques are also used in offset lithography, but they do not, of course, involve special *plates*. The special treatment needed in each case centers around the *negative* preparation in lithography printing.

For any method of printing, a size allowance must be made if illustrations are to run off the edge of the page. These *bleeds*, as they are called, must be given an extra eighth-inch for each edge that goes off an outside edge of the paper. This allowance is necessary so that the illustration will still bleed after the printed piece is trimmed; otherwise, folding, trimming, and binding operations cannot insure that a thin white streak will not appear on what were meant to be bleed edges.

Photomontages (composite pictures made by combining several photos into one) are usually made by pasting the photos together on mounting board. They can also be made by the photographer, in which case the negatives are used to print several subjects on one sheet of photo paper.

The edges of the component photos can be sharp or blended into each other by an air brush or retouching. They require no special instructions to the engraver unless he is to tool a fine white line around each photo in the composite. There is a slight extra charge for this.

SPECIFYING SCREEN AND METAL FOR HALFTONES

The fineness of screen, which determines the quality of reproduction, must be specified for halftones that are to be duplicated by either the letterpress or offset processes.

Generally speaking, the finer the screen the better the reproduction. In letterpress printing, however, this statement is true only in so far as the fineness of screen and quality of paper are properly matched. Fine screens require smooth papers in letterpress; in offset lithography good reproduction of fine screens can be obtained on rough papers. The earlier chapters on photoengraving and paper should be helpful in guiding proper matching of screen and paper. The screen desired may be indicated on the back of copy or with grease pencil on an unused portion of the surface in this fashion: 55-line, 65-line, 133-line, and so on.

For letterpress engravings, the platemaker must also be told the metal that is desired. The more expensive copper plates are usually requested if fine screens and/or long runs are desired; otherwise zinc is adequate.

OTHER TYPES OF ILLUSTRATIVE COPY

Discussion to this point has been mainly limited to black and white photographic copy. Communication by graphic arts today requires the knowledge and effective use of color and special art techniques. This does not infer that the journalist must be an artist or a color photographer; it simply means he must know the special effects at his disposal and be acquainted with the mechanical methods involved in putting them to use.

PEN AND INK DRAWINGS. These are relatively inexpensive to produce as line drawings. In offset lithography, these and other line illustrations scaled with type matter can be positioned on the paste-up and photographed along with the type matter, in which case there is no extra charge for their processing. If the drawings have to be reduced or enlarged to a percentage other than that of the type, they must be photographed separately at a moderate cost.

FIGURE 12-6. A pen and ink drawing, reproducible as a line plate. (Courtesy Kimberly-Clark Corporation)

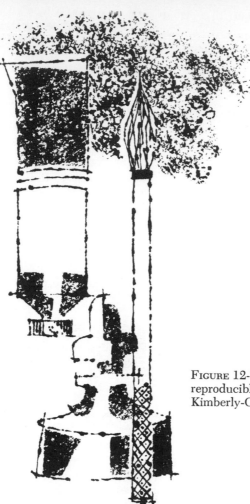

FIGURE 12-7. A brush and ink drawing, reproducible as a line plate. (Courtesy Kimberly-Clark Corporation)

Pen and ink drawings are usually done on bristol board, and will reproduce well if the lines are sharp and definitely black. Shading can be introduced (Figure 12-6) with hatch marks or by the Benday process. When the art work is not on a 1 to 1 scale with the plate, allowance in size and spacing of hatch marks must be made for enlargement or reduction.

BRUSH AND INK DRAWINGS. Also made as line engravings, these illustrations have a somewhat different flavor from those made with pen and ink. The artist, using a brush carrying ample quantities of ink, gets only blacks and whites, and lines are not as distinct as with pen and ink. The result might be called a painting without shades of grays. Rough illustration board and water-color paper are often used for the original art work.

The *dry-brush* technique differs from brush and ink only in that the artist uses a brush that is virtually dry. To get ink coverage, he rubs the ink on the paper instead of flowing it on. By using rough illustration board for his surface, he introduces grays into the drawing because the ink does not seep between the high spots of the paper (Figure 12-7).

Dry-brush drawings are produced as line engravings, not halftones, although they may seem to contain variations in tone.

SCRATCHBOARD DRAWINGS. Using a bristol board coated with chalk, an artist can produce a drawing by covering an area with ink and then scratching the ink and chalk from the surface of the board. The ink that remains forms the black areas of the drawing; the scratched area is white. These are reproduced as inexpensive line engravings.

DRAWINGS MADE ON TEXTURED BOARD. Surfaces with various textures are available in drawing board and can produce attractive results. *Coquille* board, for example, has a surface composed of scores of small raised dots. By drawing on it with crayon or ink, the artist creates a halftonelike illustration. Tones are created by the dots. When only the peaks of these dots are coated, the line engraving made from the drawing has a dot structure like one obtained by a halftone screen.

The use of pencil on a special velvety paper and charcoal on a rough paper specially made for that purpose also create interesting effects, as shown in Figure 12-8.

Pencil, crayon, and charcoal drawings on smooth paper usually require halftone plates. Without a screen in his camera, the engraver cannot capture the grays that characterize these drawings. If made as line engravings, they lose their distinguishing softness of tone.

WASH DRAWINGS. Tones are "washed" onto water-color paper or illustration board by the artist with brush and ink or water color. Their effect might be described as a water-color painting done in a single color.

Wash (Figure 12-9) is frequently employed in combination with other methods described above; it is often in a color, while the line drawing is in black. These drawings are made as halftones, either regular or high-light.

FIGURE 12-8. A pencil and charcoal drawing sometimes must be reproduced as a halftone or highlight halftone. (Courtesy Kimberly-Clark Corporation)

COPY FOR FULL-COLOR REPRODUCTION. As pointed out in the chapter on photoengraving, an engraver can produce process plates from several kinds of copy. Full-color paintings (oil or water color), color transparencies, color prints, and hand-painted black-and-white photos can serve as copy. In the latter case, the original black-and-white print is made to be "high-key" (printed light).

Engravers also convert black and white photos to full-color plates with a *fake-process* technique adequate only in some instances. It should ordinarily not be attempted if exact color values are needed.

Individual engravers have definite preferences for the type of color copy they prefer; it is wise to learn first from one's engraver which type of copy he needs for the best results.

READING ENGRAVER'S PROOFS

Although the errors in photoengraving differ from the misspellings, wrong fonts, transposed lines, and the like, that creep into type matter, they nevertheless demand careful attention. Photoengravers provide proofs of their work, just as printers do, and these should be checked in time for necessary corrections to be made before deadlines.

Discerning some photoengraving errors is difficult; some are easy to spot. With a little care and practice, anyone can detect the common failings that include:

(1) Wrong-size plate. This error often can be traced to the person who marked the original copy, but occasionally an engraver's production chief will err in figuring the percentage of reduction, or a cameraman will shoot the copy incorrectly. Regardless of the cause of error, the plate must usually be remade to fit the space planned for it.

FIGURE 12-9. A wash drawing, reproducible as halftone or high-light halftone. (Courtesy Kimberly-Clark Corporation)

(2) Imperfections on the edges. Plates with jagged edges need not be tolerated. If edges are not straight and true, the engraver will correct the fault or make a new plate.

(3) Content not as desired because plate dimensions do not follow crop marks. Again, this may be the fault of the person who marked the photograph, and it usually requires the making of a new plate.

(4) Scratches. Engravers try to handle plates with care, but unsightly scratches do appear on plates. Circle them on the proof so the engraver can spot them quickly.

(5) Spots. These should also be circled on the proof. Although spots may be only the result of a bad proof, it is possible that they are actually on the plate. If they are on the proof, the engraver can prove the fact with a good proof; otherwise he must correct the error.

(6) Proof too gray or too contrasty. A good halftone plate requires accuracy in the determination and making of several camera exposures. Bad camera work or etching can cause the plate to be a poor reproduction of the original. Mark the proof "too gray" or "too contrasty," and the engraver will deliver a better plate if the evaluation was reasonable.

Some imperfections in plates can be seen only with a magnifying glass; others may show up only when the plate is subjected to press pressures. But most shortcomings that can cause serious difficulties can be detected by careful inspection of proofs. Time so spent is certainly worth-while.

It is also worth-while to use care in editing photographs so that flaws in the finished plate cannot be traced back to improper handling by the editor. Photos should not be rolled, as rolling may put cracks in the emulsion that will be visible in the plate. Paper clips can also mar a photograph. So can the indentations made when a pencil is pressed too heavily as instructions are written on the back. Any mark that can be photographed by a camera will show up in the engraving.

ILLUSTRATIONS FOR OFFSET LITHOGRAPHY

From the discussion of the printing processes in Chapter 2, it will be remembered that separate plates for illustrations are not needed in photo-offset lithography. Instead, all material—type, line illustrations, photographs—are made into photographic negatives and combined in position in a sheet of goldenrod paper. This flat is then printed photographically on a single light-sensitive sheet of metal.

PASTE-UPS FOR LITHOGRAPHY. It is possible to provide a lithographer with a dummy, the written copy, and all illustrations as is done in letterpress printing. The lithographer can then assemble all the elements in page form himself. This procedure, however, does not provide the full cost advantage of this process.

It is customary for users of lithography to prepare page paste-ups, thereby doing for themselves what is equivalent to the composing-room page make-up of letterpress printing. All line material, including text and display type and any illustrations that would be reproduced as line engravings in letterpress, are pasted in position on a suitable white cardboard. Photographs or other continuous-tone illustrations must be treated separately. Although the paste-up must be done accurately, anyone using a T-square, triangle, and drawing board with care can do the job so none of the elements are out of line. Type proofs must be handled so the ink does not smear, because any smears and blemishes will appear in the final copy. These page paste-ups are then photographed by the lithographer and the resultant negatives are stripped into the sheet of goldenrod.

All photographs and continuous-tone illustrations must be scaled and cropped for lithography just as they are for letterpress printing. They are photographed separately through a screen in order to reproduce their tonal variations. Each is then separately stripped into the sheet of goldenrod.

One of the most exacting details in doing a paste-up is the indication of the space for illustrations that are to be stripped separately. For square-finish halftones, the space is usually indicated by accurately ruled lines or by a rectangle of black or red paper pasted in place. Lithographers will usually indicate their preference for either of these methods.

When line and halftone matter are to be combined (as in letterpress combination plates) an acetate overlay containing the line work is usually registered over the halftone as if for color application (see Chapter 13).

Other special halftone finishes, such as silhouettes and vignettes, can be specified through the use of tissue overlays as indicated earlier for letterpress. To make sure they will be positioned properly on the plate, two paste-up techniques are commonly used. In one of these, a *cameral lucida* is employed. This device projects art work at desired scale to a drawing surface on which the subject can be outlined. This outline can then be accurately positioned on the paste-up. Otherwise a photostat to size is used on the paste-up to show location of the illustration.

The procedure for adding color to illustrations is described in the next chapter.

13 Esthetics is as much a consideration when selecting and arranging colors as it is when positioning printing elements. Failure to observe principles can be disturbing to the reader, while proper handling of elements can bring about a pleasant reaction. For this reason a fundamental knowledge of color is essential to the typographer.

The scientific aspects of color have been largely developed by physicists through their study of light. Their findings are of little *direct* help to most people involved in graphic communications, but inasmuch as they foster an understanding of the psychological effects of color, they are important and will be summarized here.

THE NATURE OF COLOR

The source of all color is light. When we look at a red rose, we see it only because light reflects from it into our eyes, making the rose and its color discernible. But why are the rose and its surroundings, seen through the same source of artificial or natural light, not all the same color?

Light is visible radiant energy made up of various wavelengths. It is one of several electromagnetic waves listed in order of their frequency and length: long electric, radio, television, radar, infrared, visible light, x-rays, cosmic rays, and gamma rays. The longest waves are invisible. As waves shorten and their frequencies climb, they are felt as heat—infrared, for example; then reach visibility in a varying range we know as color. Magenta red is first as the longest; as the waves shorten they move from oranges, yellows, into greens, blues, indigo to violet. Beyond violet, at shortest lengths and highest frequencies are invisible ultraviolet rays.

As the several wavelengths of light are separated—by raindrops as in the rainbow or by a glass prism—the colors appear. The white light of the sun contains all of them. When it falls on a surface that reflects all the white light, the surface appears white to our eyes. When it falls on a surface that absorbs all the white light, we see the object as black. When some of the rays are reflected and some absorbed, color is evident. The red rose reflects only red rays; in like manner, the color of everything depends upon which color rays are absorbed and which reflected.

Color, then, is a property of the light waves reaching our eyes, not of the object seen. The latter has the property to absorb some wavelengths while allowing others to reflect.

THE PRIMARY COLORS. There are three colors in light and three in pigment called primary colors. The familiar pigment primaries are red (actually magenta), yellow, and blue (actually a blue-green referred to as "cyan"). The light primaries are green, red-orange, and blue-violet. All pigment colors are derived from mixtures of the pigment primaries; all light colors from mixtures of the light primaries. But the primaries themselves can be derived only one from the other. A pigment primary is caused by the reflection of two light primaries; a light primary by the reflection of two pigment primaries. This means a pigment primary is a secondary color of light, and *vice versa*, since secondary colors are the result of a mixture of two primaries.

Complementary colors are colors that neutralize each other when combined. That is, two light color complementaries in combination make white light; two pigment complementaries make gray. Colors made from any two primary colors are complementary to the third primary. For example, when blue-violet is absorbed, the light primaries of green and red-orange are left, and these combine in the eye to make yellow.

Two pigment primaries mixed result in a secondary color that is a light primary because the two pigment primaries absorb the other two light primaries. For example, when pigment red and yellow are mixed, yellow subtracts its complementary blue-violet, and red subtracts its complementary green. The outcome: orange.

The mixture of three primary pigments deletes all visible energy to produce black. Three light primaries mixed create white.

Chemists have found it impossible to develop three primary substances that can be mixed to produce all other colors. A number of chemicals can be used for producing the various primary pigments but none is exact enough to correspond precisely to the secondary colors of light.

COLOR DIMENSIONS

In order to apply color effectively, typographer, artist, engraver, and printer need a basic understanding of the various dimensions of color—hue, value, and chroma.

HUE. Hue is a synonym for color. We distinguish one color from another because of the quality of hue. For purposes of identification, hues are classified by arrangement in a circular scale

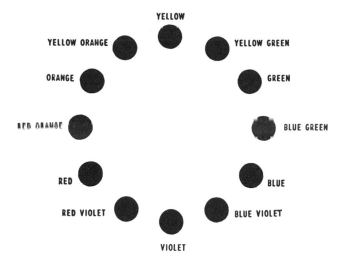

FIGURE 13-1. The color wheel.

(Figure 13-1). The hues of red, yellow, and blue are considered the primary colors.

The three secondary colors, orange, green, and violet, can be obtained by mixing the primaries to either side; for example, green is made with blue and yellow.

The intermediate colors result from mixing a primary with a secondary. For example, yellow and green make yellow-green. Intermediate colors can also be made by mixing adjoining colors; for example, yellow and yellow-green.

VALUE. Value refers to the lightness or darkness of a hue. A color can be lightened by being mixed with a lighter hue of the same color or by the addition of white. Lightening a color produces a *tint*. The printer can lighten a color by mixing the color ink with white ink or by screening the printing plate with a tint block.

A darker value is called a *shade*, achieved by adding either a darker hue of the same color or black. The printer can reduce the value by mixing a color ink with black or by overprinting the color ink with a screened black.

CHROMA. Chroma refers to the purity or strength of a color. *Intensity* and *brightness* are similar terms. To alter chroma is to change the *tone* or to weaken, dull, or neutralize a color. This can be accomplished by adding the complementary color or gray. Gray is actually a color without hue and can be developed by an equal mixture of black and white.

psychological aspects of color

As stated in Chapter 1, the three objectives in preparing graphic communication are: (1) to attract attention; (2) to be legible and comprehensible; and (3) to make an impression. The use of color is justified only to the extent it contributes to the realization of these objectives.

Form and color are basic elements of visual stimulation. They have a vital share in man's emotional life. An object familiar in the daylight can seem to have a different form at night and becomes capable of arousing negative feelings.

In Chapter 10 some design principles that affect psychological reactions were discussed. Colors, too, can affect viewers in similar ways. The typographer must understand this aspect in order to use color to its greatest advantage.

The psychological impact of color has been researched primarily through several means of testing: (1) observation; (2) instrument; (3) memory; (4) sales and inquiry; and (5) unconscious-level. These have been useful also in developing many workable principles of layout.

Observation tests study the reactions to color by subjects who are unaware that their behavior is being viewed and evaluated. The testers are often hidden behind one-way glass.

Instrument tests employ eye cameras, the tachistoscope, and lie-detector equipment. The psychogalvanometer is best known of the latter. It measures reactions to color as revealed by somatic variations, such as pulse, blood pressure, and sweat-gland activity.

Memory tests involve questioning persons to determine how much and what they recall of items in print. These tests might show, for example, that advertisements using color rate higher than ads in black and white.

Sales and inquiry tests measure the effect of color on merchandise sales or on offers to the readers of advertisements. A common technique is to advertise items for sale through the mail, running some ads in black and white, some in color. Not only can color *versus* no color be tested in this way, but so can one color *versus* another, one color *versus* two, and so on. Inquiry tests seek the same information on offers of booklets, samples, and the like. The numbers of inquiries are considered indicative of the effectiveness of the different applications of color.

Unconscious-level, or indirect, testing uncovers attitudes that subjects cannot or will not reveal. People are not generally conscious of the effects of color. This is why the value of opinion testing—asking people directly how they react to colors—is questioned by most experts. Indirect testing, on the other hand, attempts to reveal unconscious reactions by depth interviews and projective techniques, such as word association.

Often the decision to use color is based on the assumption that it is better than black and white. The decision is never that simple. Many factors should be given careful consideration before the right color or colors can be selected. Once determined and properly applied, color can contribute substantially to effective communication.

The artist's knowledge and skill in use of color are valuable aids in planning color printing. But it should be remembered that the end result of the planning should be the scientific application of color to the communications task and not a form of abstract expression in color.

FUNCTIONS OF COLOR

Color can be utilized in printing to accomplish the following functions:

(1) To attract attention.
(2) To produce psychological effects.
(3) To develop associations.
(4) To build retention.
(5) To create an esthetically pleasing atmosphere.

Let us consider each function in turn, bearing in mind that they are interrelated and that they contribute to the three goals of graphic communication.

To ATTRACT ATTENTION. This is the major use of color. Contrast is the basis of attention. Thus the addition of a bright color to a piece printed in black increases the attention-getting value of the piece.[1] Tests have shown conclusively that the amount of people noting a printed communication is increased by use of color.

Color should be applied to elements of greatest significance. Since emphasis results from contrast, color should be placed with

---

[1] In printing terminology, anything printed in black plus a color is called a two-color job. Black is considered a color in the printing field.

discretion. One color plus black offers the greatest contrast, for a color is always its most intense with black.

To effect contrast without black, several color schemes are possible. They are, in order of descending contrast: complementary, split-complementary, analogous, and monochromatic.

The *complementary scheme* uses colors opposite each other on the color wheel. Colors can be divided into two groups in terms of psychological suggestion—warm and cool. One complementary is warm, the other cool. Cool colors are blue, or predominantly blue. They are relaxing and recede on the page. Warm colors are red, or red and yellow. They are stimulating and advance to the foreground. Green and red-purple lie between the warms and cools and are thus relatively neutral.

Selecting colors takes care. Full-value complementaries can be disturbingly vibrant. A rampant hue can be controlled by changing its value or chroma, or by selective use in a limited area.

The *split-complementary scheme* contrasts three colors. A color is used in contrast with the colors adjoining its complementary on either side. For example, the split complements of red are yellow-green and blue-green.

The *analogous scheme* uses colors that neighbor on the wheel—green, blue-green, and blue; or red-orange, orange, and yellow-orange. Related colors are either warm or cool. Analogous colors are less exciting than complementaries since contrast is missing.

The *monochromatic scheme* calls for the use of different values and strengths of a single hue. Generally in this arrangement weak, dull areas are the largest; small, bright areas provide the contrast.

Four helpful hints for planning color contrasts are:

    (1) The tint of a hue is stronger on a middle gray than on a full strength of the hue.

    (2) Warm colors are higher in visibility than cool.

    (3) Contrast in values—light *versus* dark—is greater than contrast in hues—blue *versus* yellow.

    (4) The darker the background, the lighter a color appears against it.

To PRODUCE PSYCHOLOGICAL EFFECTS. The colors that predominate in an ad or other printed piece should fit the over-all mood of the message. The color suggestions of coolness and warmth in turn suggest formality and informality. Red implies life and many moods and ideas associated with life, such as action, passion, gaiety. Blue connotes distinction, reserve, serenity. Green is nature; purple, splendor and pomp; white, purity.

To Develop Associations. It is natural for people to associate certain colors with different products. Red is readily associated with cherries; while the thought of green with fresh meats is not pleasant. But many associations are not so obvious, and research may be called for before a color selection is made. Personal judgment cannot always be trusted: although one might suspect that pink is preferable to blue for a face-powder message, an error could be made without a more tangible basis for the choice.

To Build Retention. In describing something we are likely to refer to its color. This is because color has high memory value, a feature that the communicator can capitalize upon. A color should predominate because it helps the reader remember what he saw. Advertisers are, of course, particularly interested in reader recall of message and repeat certain colors in their campaigns in order to establish product identification.

To Create a Pleasing Atmosphere. Misuse of color in a message is worse, from the viewpoint of the communicator, than the use of no color at all. Color may get the initial attention, but unless this is sustained and developed into interest, the reader will not spend time to absorb the message. Poor choice and application of colors can repel the reader immediately after his attention has been aroused.

Colors, including black, gray, and white, in the printed piece should be arranged in accordance with the same basic principles of layout: balance, contrast, proportion, rhythm, unity, and harmony.

Balance comes from the judicious placement of elements in terms of weights. Color adds further weight to elements. Bright colors appear lighter; dark colors, heavier. When used with black for a two-color job, the color should be given a relatively light weight so it will not draw undue attention from the black. Normally it should be run in large areas at a 30, 40, or 50 percent level; that is, screened to that amount. Solids of the color should be reserved for emphasis.

Contrast is necessary for legibility. Contrast in values is more significant than contrast in colors. For this reason, where color serves as a background, care should be given to its treatment so it will not detract from other elements. If the latter are dark, the background should be light, and *vice versa*.

Proportion refers to relationships between colors. Proportional arrangement calls for a pleasing balance of (1) dark colors and light colors; and (2) dull or weak colors and bright colors.

Rhythmic use of color is achieved through repetition at various points in the printed piece. Spots of a second color can be used effectively in this manner to guide the reader's eye through the message.

Color, as well as form, can contribute to the unity of a printed piece. Misplaced, it can disintegrate the total effect, even cause the message to seem divided.

Harmony in its broadest sense results from abiding by the other principles of color use—balance, contrast, proportion, and so on. More specifically, harmony applies to the so-called color schemes. Thus one speaks of monochromatic, complementary, split-complementary, or analogous color harmony. Complementary colors are not automatically harmonious together, however, unless some consideration is given to their use.

Psychological tests have uncovered personal color preferences. Blue is highly popular, being *the* color preferred by men and second only to red by women. Tests also show that women are more color conscious than men and tend more to prefer tints and softer colors. Color preferences vary according to age, education, and geographic location of readers. Bright colors appeal to young people, soft colors to older persons—and to those with high levels of education.

Preference tests are of some value to the designer if he knows the specific group to which his message will be directed. But the value of general tests is questionable in view of the fact that researchers have also found that "favorite" colors can be unattractive in certain uses.

 types of color printing

Color printing can be divided into two types: spot color and process color. Process, meaning the various ways to reproduce color copy—photographs, drawings, or paintings—was discussed in the chapter on photoengraving.

Copy is usually full-color, is reproduced with four inks by the *four-color process*. Occasionally *three-color process* is used for full-color copy by eliminating the black plate. This effects a substantial savings, but not all copy lends itself to the treatment. Subjects in a light key, such as outdoor scenes, are adaptable, but portraits, people, and indoor scenes are better reproduced by four-color process, since the black plate gives definition and detail needed for a more realistic effect.

Paintings or other copy done in two colors are subjected to camera separation and *two-color process printing*.

Spot color refers to multicolor printing (two or more colors), by methods other than process. The simplest form is *flat-color printing*. A message with text in black and headlines in red is an example. In this form, colors do not overlap to form new colors—red is red, blue is blue, black is black, and so on.

Flat tones can be used with solids. In addition to headlines in red, red tints can be placed behind certain portions of the type or perhaps behind halftones of photos printed in black.[2] If the flat-color spots do not touch, the entire ad can be prepared by the printer as if it were all one color.

In letterpress printing, at the time of lockup, the printer can "break for color." This means that the elements to print black remain in the black printing form. The color elements are removed to the color form and are replaced with spacing material.

If the printing is to be done with stereotype plates, two casts are made. The color elements are routed from the black plate; that is, removed with a rotating cutting blade. The black elements are routed from the color plate.

The lithographer can break for color by making two plates from a single flat or mask, allowing the proper elements to be exposed at the time each plate is burned.

To indicate this type of color work to the printer, the layout can be done in the desired colors, indicating headlines and tints in red, for example, the remainder in black. Or the entire layout can be done in black. A thin transparent paper (an overlay) can be laid over the layout with the color indicated on it.

Much spot-color work calls for laying one color over another to form additional color. Tints and solids can be used in this way. The Sunday color comics are an excellent example.

Often *color register* is significant. The term "register" refers to the positioning of the impression on the sheet. For example, when a book page is viewed against a light, both sides should be aligned.

---

[2]To say that the color tint is "printed behind" the type does not mean that the color is necessarily printed first. Often the black is laid on the sheet, and the color is then printed. The one requirement is that the colored ink be transparent.

If so, they are registered, or properly *lined up*. Color register refers to the alignment of one color with another.

If the colors do not touch and are not closely interrelated, the printer can break for color. This is called *loose register*.

When colors touch or overprint, the register is described as *tight, hairline,* or *close*. Modern printing equipment is capable of maintaining the position of impression at a tolerance of 1/1000 of an inch. An almost imperceptible lap can be given where spot colors come together.

There are several ways to indicate the necessity for color register to a printer. One technique of copy preparation requires the use of a clear acetate overlay. This is fastened over the *key plate*, which is a drawing of the copy to which other colors will be registered. This drawing is the copy for the black plate.

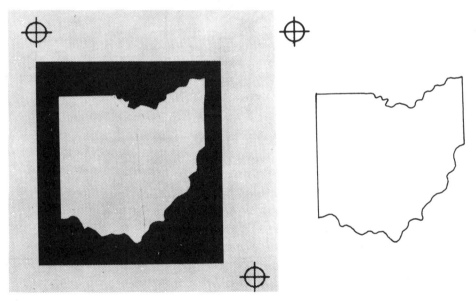

Figure 13-2. Color copy prepared with an overlay (left). Register marks are shown on the key drawing and on the overlay.

Art for the additional color is drawn on or pasted to the overlay, separate overlay being used for each color. Register marks are added to key and overlay art and must coincide exactly when the overlay is positioned over the key. These marks bring about the proper positioning of copy on the printing plates. Figure 13-2 shows key art, an overlay for second color with register marks.

Another common method of copy preparation is the *key line*

technique. Black and color art are drawn on a single board or paper. Separation between colors is indicated by a key line. The areas to appear in color and in black are painted with black ink to within one-quarter to one-eighth of an inch of the key line.

When plates are made, the space up to the line is filled in for each color including black. The key line thus becomes the invisible. Figure 13-3 shows a key-line drawing for a circle, one side of which will be blue solid, the other side 60 percent black.

FIGURE 13-3. Keyline drawing for color register.

the cost factor in color printing

The added cost factor is usually an important consideration in the decision of whether to use multicolor printing. Expense piles up because the paper has to go through the press as many times as there are colors. Between impressions, time must be taken for press wash-ups, changes of ink, additional make-ready. Extra designing, camera, and plate charges are often involved. Multicolor jobs can be run through two-, four-, and six-color presses. This can mean some savings, but such equipment is used only for long runs. The manner in which color is used adds little to the cost. A small spot or a more expansive spread of a second color applied to a sheet affects the total expense very little.

Designers and buyers of printing frequently hesitate to spend the extra money required for two-color or full-color printing. Yet there is abundant evidence everywhere of the significance of color in modern life. The market place is alive with it acting to sell products. The practical business world is under the influence of color now, as bright, warm reception rooms replace the austere, walnut-paneled ones of the past.

Color acts as a warning: do not park; stop; go. It promotes efficiency and safety through scientific application to work areas. It is used in modern architecture to an extent undreamed of a generation ago.

These are signs the communicator cannot well ignore. There are evidently plus values to be gained from the use of color—but he needs to know as precisely as possible what he gains from the extra cost.

Memory tests have shown that on the average readers increase with the addition of color. There is no conclusive evidence, however, that the ratio of increase is greater than the increase in cost, so this may not justify the added cost. Other functions must account for the difference, but the dollar value of pleasing atmosphere, psychological effect, esthetics, and other intangibles cannot be appraised.

The communicator can solve the added cost problem only by resolving to apply the color allowable under his budget in the way that most efficiently accomplishes its particular functions.

FIDELITY IN PROCESS COLOR

There are certain basic weaknesses in process color printing that mean the purchaser cannot expect exact reproduction or fidelity. These weaknesses occur because of: (1) differences between colors in light and in inks; (2) ink deficiencies; (3) the nature of halftone dots; and (4) the quality of paper.

PHYSICAL COLORS AND PIGMENT COLORS. The colors that enter the engraver's camera at the time of color separation behave according to the physical properties of light. The printer, on the other hand, must use pigmental or surface colors in his reproduction. To understand the difficulties this leads to, let us review the separation process. As explained in Chapter 6, a violet filter is used in preparing the yellow plate. As shown in Figure 13-4, this filter allows the red and the blue light to pass and record on the negative. Areas on the negative where these rays strike are dense. Yellow, the complement of the color in the filter, is held back. Thus the yellow areas become the most transparent on the negative. When the plate is made, a reversal of values occurs—yellows are the darkest, reds and blues are lighter.

The orange filter passes reds and yellows, holds back blue; the green filter passes yellows and blues and holds back red. These fil-

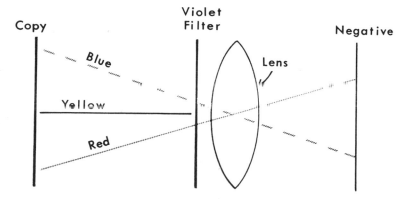

FIGURE 13-4. Use of violet filter for making a yellow negative.

ters are used respectively for the blue and red plates.

The filters are analagous to the primaries of light in absorption and transmission, and they are complementary to the printing colors.

If art work could be submitted in standardized colors, the engraver's chores would be much simpler. There is, however, no standardization, and there are countless colors available from many different sources. For example, the violet filter is used for all yellows, of which there is an infinite variety.

The printer's surface colors represent white light minus a color primary, since the three color primaries together represent white. Thus yellow is white minus blue, reflecting red and green. Cyan is minus red, and magenta is minus green. If a color in the art work, say a certain yellow, does not absorb all the blue light, the result on the plate is a distortion, a weakening, of the true value of that color. Similar distortions of other colors result in the separation process.

INK CHARACTERISTICS. The process inks used by the printer give rise to similar difficulties. Cyan is furthest from perfection, reflecting some red, which it should absorb completely, and absorbing much of the blues and greens, which it should reflect completely. For this reason colors requiring blues, notably purples and greens, suffer in reproduction. Magenta absorbs some of the blues and reds and reflects a high percentage of green. Yellow is the most effective of the process inks, since it absorbs nearly all blue and reflects green and red very effectively. True red, which should be effected by using magenta and yellow, also suffers in reproduction.

HALFTONE DOTS. The nature of the halftone process is a further obstacle to full fidelity of reproduction. Color photographs are reproduced with three layers of superimposed, continuous-tone primary colors. In an area of a halftone print where orange is being reproduced, for example, some of the magenta and yellow dots fall side by side, others overlap. The result is a variation in hue from the original.

EFFECT OF PAPER. Paper for process reproduction should absorb all colors equally—at least as nearly as possible. A pure white, which reflects all colors with a minimum of absorption, is preferred. Reflecting more light from its surface through the inks, it adds a brilliance to the reproduction.

Research, however, has led to the development of coordinated inks and papers to make process printing possible on pastel-colored stock with noteworthy results.

COLOR CORRECTION. Despite the above, it should not be assumed that process printing is ineffective. If straightforward separations were made, reproductions *would* fall far short of the original. However, the engraver's color-correction methods minimize the deficiencies by special treatments of negatives and plates.

 practical pointers in the use of color

A number of practical pointers help the designer plan printed pieces with color. By no means an exhaustive list, the following cover many frequently overlooked considerations, applicable to monochromatic *and* multicolor printing:

(1) When using more than one color, reserve the darkest for the basic message, using the additional color or colors for emphasis or for setting a mood.

(2) Color used behind type should be light to insure easy legibility. In general the smaller the type, the lighter the color should be. This is accomplished, of course, by having the color screened.

(3) Running type in color demands care. Some colors are too light ever to be so used on white stock—yellow, for example. If the type size is large, color has a better chance of supporting legibility. It is safest, however, to use color on type to emphasize a few words in a headline.

(4) If both front and back covers of a large folder—8½ by 11 inches, for example—are to run in a solid color with a white rectangle of fair size—say 5 by 3 inches—centered on the front, a dark streak may follow the rectangle entirely across the back page. This is due to the fact that the plate takes no ink from the form rollers in the area of the rectangle. This excess, then, builds up behind the open area. A similar situation can occur when a wide band of color completely surrounds an open area on a single page. The areas parallel to the rollers may appear darker than those at right angles. Such designs need not necessarily be avoided. But it is wise to discuss the problem ahead of time with the printer.

(5) If a number of large dark halftones or solids appear in a booklet, it is wise to secure an imposition sheet before planning their location. If they fall at the head of the sheet (that which prints first), they may so rob the form rollers of ink that areas falling behind them may be starved and receive underinking.

(6) If four-color process and black-and-white halftones appear in the same form, the printer should be consulted before planning the layout or ordering engravings. If the black-and-white halftones are large and dark, they may require such heavy inking for satisfactory printing that, as a result, the black process plates will have to carry excess also, thereby muddying the color reproductions. Consultation with the printer and engraver in the planning stage can often solve this problem.

(7) Care is required when running type in color (other than black) on a sheet on which process printing appears. Let us assume a red or an orange is desired. This necessitates printing type from two plates—magenta and yellow—in exact register. A satisfactory result is possible if the type is large. If it is small or light in weight, even the slightest imperfection in register will be obvious.

(8) Likewise, when printing in reverse is to appear on a color formed by overprinting two or more plates—for example, on a dark green formed by printing a screened black on a light green, the reverse printing must be on both plates. Unless they are printed in very close register, the type will not appear as a clean white. Naturally, the smaller the type, the more critical the problem.

(9) Type printed in reverse should be within a fairly dark area to preserve legibility. As a general rule it is best to avoid reverses in a tone below 40 percent. If type is to appear in one color against a background of another—red on a black panel—the color on the type should be bright.

(10) A band of color running and bleeding across the top or bottom of a page can leave a sort of smudge of color on the page

opposite when a book or booklet has been folded and is being trimmed. This is often erroneously thought of as "offset of ink." It is more likely to have been pressed onto the white page by the clamps in the trimmer. This can be avoided either by running a similar band of color on the opposite page or by avoiding the bleed and not taking the color any closer to the edge of the page than one-half inch, the distance required by the clamp that holds the booklet in position while it is being trimmed.

(11) Often the artist prepares art for reproduction by over-printing one screened color on another and applies the screens to the art work, using screen tones on self-adhering acetate sheets. Improper angling of the screens must be avoided for it results in an undesirable moiré pattern.

(12) Several halftones printed on a page with a second color occupying the remainder of the space except for an even, narrow white border around each photo will mean that even the slightest variation in register will be discernible, since the white borders become uneven.

(13) It is sometimes possible to get full-color effect from two-color process plates made from full-color photos. This technique is not a substitute for full-color process, but startling results can be obtained under controlled conditions. The color photos should be composed of hues that are predominantly the same as those of the inks to be used in printing. For example, a color photo of a pair of dark brown shoes worn by a model dressed in a brown suit, posed against a red background might be effectively reproduced with process red and black.

(14) Restraint must reign in the use of additional color. Because of cost, there is often a feeling that color ought to be applied lavishly to get one's money's worth. But overuse can defeat the reason for the extra expense. Often a single spot of color is sufficient; or two spots can be utilized, one to contrast with the other, and the two together to contrast with the basic color. Too much color, however, can create a weak communication.

14

A newspaper's main commodity is the news. How reliably and thoroughly it presents the news should be *the* factor by which to appraise its performance. But a newspaper's appearance is of considerable importance, too. Its typography and make-up decide whether or not it can attract and hold readers.

Newspapers are like people in that each has its own personality, expressed by its physical appearance. Like people, whose habits of dress reveal age, background, and associates, the make-up of a newspaper also reveals these very same factors.

Some papers are more than a century old, and their typographical dress shows their age. They are likely to be more concerned with showing their conservatism and reliability than they are with projecting any other personality traits.

Other newspapers came into existence to fight for a particular cause or to appeal to a special class of people, and the circumstances of their founding may still be apparent in their typography and make-up. And there are others who are newcomers just forming their personalities, or who have been around for some time but are flexible enough to adopt modern styles.

INFLUENCE OF HERITAGE AND NEWS POLICY ON MAKE-UP

The typographic dress of *The New York Times* bespeaks the character that its news policy substantiates. Its headline patterns are holdovers from a bygone era; they tell readers that the *Times* is an institution of long standing. There is nothing in its make-up to lure the great mass of readers who are more interested in film stars than foreign policy. Instead, the balanced, dignified, and dull arrangement of material on its pages seems to say here is all the news *if* you have the intellect, the sophistication, and the time to dig it out.

A comment that the make-up of the *Times* is on the dull side is actually not a significant criticism, of course. The *Times* is the *Times*, a valuable newspaper property with one of the most precious reputations in the world. And, although it may seem to be paradoxical, the *Times* can be cited as an example of the good application of a sound typographical principle despite its quiet mien that breaks many "rules" devised by experts in graphic communications. If there are cardinal precepts in newspaper typog-

NEWSPAPER TYPOGRAPHY AND MAKE-UP

raphy, this is one: *a newspaper's appearance should appeal to its selected public and should truthfully reflect its own character.* The loyalty and support of its followers are proof of the *Times'* success in this regard.

Other newspapers, such as the members of the Scripps-Howard group, appeal to a different audience and are quite different in character from the *Times*. Their typographic dress reflects this difference, as it should. As crusading and fighting newspapers appealing mainly to the masses, most Scripps-Howard publications use a bold and vigorous make-up featuring strong headlines.

Still other newspapers—members of the Hearst group are notable examples—use massive display that shouts their wares loudly enough to attract even the most unattentive reader. They give the impression of having so much shocking news that it is difficult to get all of it on their pages. Day in and day out they seem to be in the position of the circus master who must keep three rings going in order to squeeze all his good acts into one show.

In many cases, the direction a newspaper is taking today was determined years ago. The *Times*, for example, was founded during the era of the penny press. At that time, penny papers such as James Gordon Bennett's *Herald* were offering New Yorkers a steady story diet of murder, sex, and violence. These papers had come into existence to provide the new audience of factory workers, created by the industrial revolution, with daily newspapers at a price they could afford. Henry J. Raymond and his cofounders of the *Times* recognized another need of these new newspaper readers for a daily publication higher in tone but at the same low cost. Thus the *Times* was founded with the definite intent to draw discriminating readers away from other penny papers. Later in its history, when it was on the verge of bankruptcy, the *Times* was given the motto "All the news that's fit to print" by Adolph S. Ochs and was rededicated to its philosophy of appealing to a select group of readers.

E. W. Scripps set off on his own in 1878 to start his first newspaper of typical penny-press character but with special emphasis on bold crusades to improve the status of the mass factory laborers. In the first issue of that paper, *The Penny Press* (now the *Cleveland Press and News*), he set the tone that has been characteristic of most subsequent Scripps-Howard papers.

The Hearst newspapers still show the effects of their roots in the yellow journalism days of newspaper history. In the 1890s, William Randolph Hearst led his *New York Journal* and other papers into a raucous journalism that flourished on sensational news announced by sensational typographical display.

✓ types of headlines and their importance

Headlines are perhaps the greatest outward manifestation of a newspaper's personality. They are its most striking facial characteristic and have several jobs to do in addition to contributing to a newspaper's personality. They help sell newspapers, index the news, grade stories according to importance, summarize the news for hasty readers, and help to make the paper more attractive.

The first newspapers in the United States used no headlines because there was no need for them. Colonists lucky enough to get a newspaper could be expected to read all of it without the salesmanship urging of display type. Newspapers were extremely small, and readers had a built-in interest in everything that could be put on their pages.

As newspapers attained size, it became apparent that readers needed some help in selecting which portions to read and in getting the gist of stories quickly. Headlines then became fixtures. Like Topsy, many of their patterns just grew. These, for want of a better term, are called "traditional patterns" in this text. Others, more recent in origin, are labeled "modern patterns."

TRADITIONAL HEADLINE PATTERNS

There are four basic traditional headline patterns: (1) *bar line*; (2) *inverted pyramid*; (3) *hanging indention*; and (4) *step lines* (sometimes called *drop lines*).

The first typographical pattern for headlines was the bar line (Figure 14-1), a single line of type centered over the story. To tell more of the story in a headline, several bar lines separated by dashes were used.

RULING IS 6 TO 1   Figure 14-1. A bar line.

As the editor-printers of pre-Civil War days set bar lines, they often found that what they wanted to say would not fit into a single line. In these instances, they usually carried over the extra word or two to a second line and centered that line under the first, thus creating an inverted pyramid (Figure 14-2).

FIGURE 14-2. Inverted pyramid.

The Proceedings In Washington

The Civil War gave editors news of unusual importance, and the subsequent need for greater headline display. Using the two headline patterns known to them, they gave more display to big stories by adding more decks to the headlines. Bar lines and inverted pyramids were usually alternated as the headlines were constructed.

The hanging indention joined the other headline forms during the latter part of the Civil War and took its place in the multideck headlines prevalent at the time. It is composed of a top line flush to both sides, and usually two additional lines uniformly indented from the left (Figure 14-3). Like the inverted pyramid, it is seldom used today except as a subordinate deck.

FIGURE 14-3. Hanging indention.

Producers Schedule 570,000 Assemblies; June Activity Up 1% Despite Ford Strike

For years the bar line merited undisputed claim to the top spot in headlines. Perhaps a few more bar lines were mixed with inverted pyramids and hanging indentions as the headline progressed down the column, but the top deck was always a single bar line. In this position, it was given the greatest display—the largest type size. Consequently, it was impossible to get more than one or two words in the top deck, making it a mere label that told little about its story.

The desire to tell more in the top deck resulted in the introduction of the step line in the late 1800s. By adding a second line set flush to the right and moving the top line flush to the left, editors created a new pattern that quickly became popular (Figure 14-4).

FIGURE 14-4. Step line (drop line).

Wall St. Hails Action by U.S.

It gave editors a neat, orderly arrangement and enabled them to get more information into the top deck. The step line is still used by both newspapers that have redesigned their make-up in recent years and by papers retaining their traditional appearance.

In order to show some grading of the news on their pages, editors in the early years of headlines had no choice but to add more decks to stories of importance. These were the days of the Hoe type revolving machine, a rotary press that depended on wedge-shaped column rules to hold the pieces of type in place on a rotating cylinder. It was impossible to break across columns without having type fly everywhere as the cylinder rotated.

This problem was solved with the introduction of curved stereotype plates by Charles Craske at the New York *Herald* in 1854, but multicolumn headlines did not become common until the heyday of yellow journalism.

MODERN HEADLINE PATTERNS

When William Randolph Hearst and Joseph Pulitzer engaged in their monumental struggle for circulation during the Spanish-American War, typographical display took on new significance for newspapers. Street sales, on a cash-per-copy basis, had grown in importance since the method's introduction by the penny papers several years earlier, and it did not take long for publishers to realize that headlines sold newspapers.

As direct salesmen, headlines received more attention in newspaper offices and greater size in each day's issue. *Banner* lines (headlines spreading across every column of a page) became common. Many banners during the Spanish-American War were two-line step lines.

Although newspaper make-up became more conservative and restrained again after the war, the use of headlines spreading over more than one column had become an accepted practice. Some papers preferred the vertical impression created by single-column heads of several decks, but even these put spread headlines over particularly important stories.

During World War I, editors again made extensive use of banner lines because of the extraordinary importance of the news resulting from the conflict. They became so much a fixture for many papers that after the war some papers continued to use a banner on page one regardless of the news value of the day's top story.

The banner line is, of course, simply a bar line that extends over all the columns on the page. In that sense it is a traditional pattern

FIGURE 14-5. Flush left.

Charter Suit
Asks State
Redistricting

FIGURE 14-6. Modified flush left.

**Representation
Called Unfair
And Unequal**

adapted to modern needs. There are some typographical patterns of relatively recent vintage, devised for two reasons: (1) to make headline writing easier; and (2) to put more white space around headlines so that each will have better contrast and readability.

The basic form for modern headlines is *flush left*. All lines are started at the extreme left side of a column, and substantial variation in line length is tolerated (see Figure 14-5). Flush-left headlines are easier to write because of the greater variation permitted in line length, and because each line has the potential of going to the full column measure. Drop lines, in order to allow room for the step, must always be shorter than full measure.

A common variation of the flush-left headline is the *square indention,* often called *modified flush left* (Figure 14-6). Instead of starting at the extreme left side, all lines are indented uniformly.

To get more white space around headlines, many newspapers use a short line above the main deck of flush-left or square-indention headlines. The line is usually in smaller type, may be flush to the left or centered (Figure 14-7), and is usually underlined with a thin rule. This headline form goes by many names, including "astonisher" and "kicker."

Estes Investigation Continues
New Witnesses Found

FIGURE 14-7. Kicker headline.

Reds Defeat Entire Battalion
S. Viet-Nam Forces Lose

SOME SPECIAL HEADLINE USES

When portions of stories are carried over (*jumped*) to other pages, headlines must be placed over the continued portion of the story. These are called *jump heads*. They may take any typographic form as long as they are in harmony with headlines throughout the rest of the paper. Jump heads were originally scaled-down versions of the headline at the top of the story, but most newspapers have simplified them as much as possible. Figure 14-8 shows some representative jump heads.

U. S. Seeking Information On Steel Men

Continued from First Page

Department is not at liberty to disclose them."

JET CRASH

Continued from Second Page

the eve of an air show to celebrate the introduction of a

MINISTERS' TALKS ON BERLIN HINTED

Continued From Page 1, Col. 1

standing of United States attitudes on iseaes conncected with the European economic and political union that is expected to

Feud

(Continued from page one)

approximately existing levels. But this provided no money for planned new undertakings — the labor retraining program,

FIGURE 14-8. Some representative jump heads.

A *folo head* is used over a story related to a main story above it. A national weather round up, for example, may be followed by one or two items giving details about regional weather. Some newspapers use rules to set off their folo heads.

Boxed heads take several forms (Figure 14-9) and are used to give special display for small stories. They provide effective contrast when they are placed between two headlines of larger type size.

Who's News
• • •
• • •

Management—Personnel Notes

dent engineering. of Formica Corp., a sub-

Jet Helicopters Slice Travel Time Between New York, Airports
• • •

They Cut Local-Service Line's Cost; New York-Philadelphia 35-Minute Service Planned

Dividend News

G.C. Murphy Proposes 100% Stock Dividend; Plans Rise in Payments

FIGURE 14-9. Typical boxed headlines.

Editors like special headlines to signal a feature or humorous story. Italic type formerly did well at this but has been used so generally for all types of news that it no longer serves. Headline arrangements employing double kickers, stars, asterisks, and other decorative devices, now perform as *feature heads.*

Standing heads appear in issue after issue over columns, departments, or other regularly repeated features of a newspaper. Many newspapers use both a standing head and a working head for this purpose. The standing head identifies the feature, while the work-

FIGURE 14-10. Standing heads can be used as kickers for working heads.

These Days

What Is The Compulsion?

GEORGE SOKOLSKY

ACROSS THE BORDER   By J. A. Stevenson

Pearson Flays Diefenbaker's Timetable on Next Parliament

COURT NEWS

4 Jailed For Lagging In Support

Men Appear Without Funds For Payments

ing head is supposed to attract readers to that day's output. It is common for the standing head to be of the kicker variety (Figure 14-10).

HEADLINE SCHEDULES

Headline schedules (*hed skeds*) are a collection of all the headlines to be used by a particular newspaper. They are relatively inflexible, although on some papers editors are permitted to concoct an occasional special headline.

A headline schedule gives a newspaper continuity of character; readers can recognize their paper day to day by the uniformity of headline display issue to issue. The hed sked also saves time on the copy desk and in the composing room.

A well-planned schedule provides headlines for every purpose. Banner lines, *top* heads (headlines for the top of columns), secondary, spread, folo, feature, and departmental (sports, society, and so on) headlines are specified.

From the schedule, headline writers can find for each headline the number of decks, the unit count for each line, the number of lines, the style and size of type, and any special typographic treatment. Rather than spell out each characteristic, the writer can simply mark his copy with a number, letter, or other symbol to identify it for the composing room. A "#1" label, for example, may tell the composing room that the headline is flush left, capitals and lower case, with a top deck of three lines, 36-point Erbar, and a second deck of two lines, 24-point Erbar indented one em.

HEADLINE CAPITALIZATION AND PUNCTUATION

Uniform capitalization and punctuation are as essential for headlines as they are for the text material of a newspaper. Either the headline schedule, the style sheet, or both should set the rules to follow.

Of course, all-caps headlines give the writer no problem with capitalization. But when they are capitals and lower case, considerable variation occurs. Most newspapers use capital letters to begin all words in a headline; some make an exception for certain prepositions.

One of the most interesting recent developments in this regard has been the growing acceptance of standard sentence capitalization for headlines. Edmund C. Arnold, editor of *Linotype News* and author of *Functional Newspaper Design*, has been a vigorous leader in the movement. In his book and in clinics he conducts throughout the country, Mr. Arnold has advocated "down-style" headlines because: "They are easier to read by eyes accustomed to down-style in all our text material. They are easier to write because of the extra units saved by fewer caps."[1]

His opponents argue that capitals are needed for emphasis, that their long strokes enhance readability by setting the words apart, especially when the spacing between words is tight.

Council selects Taylor as temporary chairman

UPI news
Forces to return to Port Matadi

Stolen tombstone brings probation to two students

FIGURE 14-11. Some typical down-style headlines.

Figure 14-11 shows some down-style heads. How much acceptance they will receive is unknown. But their practicality may some day bring them into the same general use that the standard capital-and-lower-case headline now enjoys. The old and extensive debate of "all caps" versus "c. & l.c." has virtually been resolved in favor of the latter.

Punctuation of headlines differs from text punctuation in these ways: (1) periods are not used at the end of headlines; (2) semicolons are used instead of periods to indicate the end of a skeletonized sentence within the headline; (3) a comma is often substituted for "and"; (4) single, instead of double, quotation marks are usually used.

MODERN TRENDS IN HEADLINES

Although some newspapers have retained old headline patterns and practices, many have revamped their headline schedules to keep pace with modern developments. In these revampings,

---

[1]Edmund C. Arnold, *Functional Newspaper Design* (New York: Harper & Row, 1956), p. 64.

several changes have been so universally applied that they have emerged as basic principles of modern newspaper typography. They include the following:

(1) The number of decks in a headline should be kept to a minimum. The tendency has been to eliminate secondary decks except for occasional use with banners and other large heads. Even then, one secondary deck is usually considered sufficient for a gradual scaling down in type size to make an easy transition from large display type to body type.

(2) To compensate for the reduction in number of decks, headlines are spread across columns for additional display, thus creating a horizontal rather than vertical impression.

(3) Jim dashes (short, plain, centered dashes) should not be used between decks; they are superfluous and disturbing. Use of rules of all types is kept to a minimum because white space performs the usual functions of rules more efficiently.

(4) Capital-and-lower-case heads are better than all caps. They permit the headline writer greater unit count and are easier to read.

(5) Decks should not exceed three lines; they become confusing as more lines are added.

(6) Flush-left headlines are preferable to other patterns because of their flexibility of unit count. They also save time in the composing room because spacing is no problem; it is not necessary to center the middle lines as in three-line step lines.

 ## other make-up components

In addition to headlines, there are a number of other components of newspaper make-up. Some, such as body type, name plate, ears, column width, column separators are more or less constant. Other decorative devices are called upon for special occasions.

NEWSPAPER BODY TYPE

No decision on the typography or make-up of a newspaper is more important than the selection of body type, for most of what a newspaper has to say is said in the small 7- or 8-point type used for body copy.

Selection should be based entirely on practical considerations. It is doubtful that any newspaper reader has ever given any real thought to the esthetic properties of a body type, but all are concerned with its legibility.

Some aspects of the mechanical production of newspapers have a direct bearing on type selection. The coarseness of newsprint, the need for stereotyping by the large dailies, and the highly fluid nature of newspaper inks create special problems.

Before 1900, the most commonly used type for this purpose was a face called "Roman No. 2." It retained its popularity after the turn of the century and was joined in 1904 by Century Expanded as a widely used news body face. These served adequately until dry-mat stereotyping and faster presses became common. The increased pressure to which type was subjected by the new stereotyping method caused the fine lines of Roman No. 2 and Century Expanded to break down. With the rough newsprint traveling through presses at greater speed, ink had a tendency to fill up some areas of letters.

After extensive research and experimentation, the Mergenthaler Linotype Corporation produced a face designed espcially to surmount the problems of newspaper printing. The new face, called "Ionic No. 5," became immediately popular when it was introduced in 1926. It was followed by other specially-designed news-body faces: Excelsior in 1931, Opticon in 1935, and Corona in 1940. In each case, maximum attention was given to the special mechanical requirements of newspapers and the desire to get maximum viewing area with greatest space economy. These faces are shown in Figure 14-12.

The Intertype Corporation has also produced efficient and popular news faces, including Ideal News, Regal, and Rex. No matter what his composing machines, the newspaper publisher has the choice of several excellent faces for body type.

SIZES OF BODY TYPE. The early newspapers in America were set in agate or 6-point type. Although some newspapers or portions of them (the classified section, for example) are still set in such small sizes, the trend has been toward the larger.

Wartime scarcity of paper and the current high price of newsprint has slowed the development somewhat, but several factors maintain the pressure for the increased legibility of somewhat larger sizes. Competition from other media, increasing numbers of elderly readers, and a greater realization of the physical effects of eyestrain have caused many newspapers to go to 8- and 9-point sizes. Other sizes still in use include 6½-, 6¾-, 7-, and 7½-point.

There is an appealing touch of human nature in the story of this stolid English merchant, who in his fiftieth year turned aside from his prosperous undertakings to devote himself to learning and practising the new-born art of printing. Caxton was living at Bruges, so well thought of by his compatriots that he had been elected "Governor of the English Nation in the Low Countries," when, to please his pa-

There is an appealing touch of human nature in the story of this stolid English merchant, who in his fiftieth year turned aside from his prosperous undertakings to devote himself to learning and practising the new-born art of printing. Caxton was living at Bruges, so well thought of by his compatriots that he had been elected "Governor of the English Nation in the Low Countries," when, to please his pa-

There is an appealing touch of human nature in the story of this stolid English merchant, who in his fiftieth year turned aside from his prosperous undertakings to devote himself to learning and practising the new-born art of printing. Caxton was living at Bruges, so well thought of by his compatriots that he had been elected "Governor of the English Nation in the Low Countries," when, to please his pa-

There is an appealing touch of human nature in the story of this stolid English merchant, who in his fiftieth year turned aside from his prosperous undertakings to devote himself to learning and practising the new-born art of printing. Caxton was living at Bruges, so well thought of by his compatriots that he had been elected "Governor of the English Nation in the Low Countries," when, to please his pa-

FIGURE 14-12. Linotype's group of newspaper legibility faces. (Courtesy Mergenthaler Linotype Company.)

There is an appealing touch of human nature in the story of this stolid English merchant, who in his fiftieth year turned aside from his prosperous undertakings to devote himself to learning and practising the new-born art of printing. Caxton was living at Bruges, so well thought of by his compatriots that he had been elected "Governor of the English Nation in the Low Countries," when, to please his patroness the

An increasing use of extra white space (leading) between lines has accompanied the movement toward larger type sizes.

COLUMN WIDTH

The average newspaper page is set off in eight columns 22-inches-long. For years, the standard column width was 12 pica ems, but now column widths vary. In order to cut newsprint costs, many publishers started using narrower columns and, in 1953, the American Newspaper Publishers Association and the American Association of Advertising Agencies agreed on 11½ ems as the standard.

Therefore, newspapers that kept the larger dimension have actually been giving away some space to advertisers because the same rate per column inch is paid for the narrower columns. Ads are provided in sizes based on the 11½ em column; the space left over is just wasted newsprint.

Although problems exist with narrow columns, some newspapers have adopted 11 or 11.3 em columns. It is quite likely that columns will tend to be narrower, rather than wider, in the future.

Newspapers using teletypesetting have another problem with column width. As described earlier, teletypesetting is machine composition by a perforated tape. If a newspaper is to receive tape perforated telegraphically from another point by Associated Press or United Press International, its column widths ought to coincide with the standard adopted by the press association. As the tape operates a composing machine, it signals the start of new lines according to a predetermined measure.

Originally the standard measure for TTS was 12 ems but it now has been changed to 11¾. Newspapers with 12-em columns have never had any problem with teletypesetting. But those with narrower columns had to find a type face that would set the same number of characters in its columns as TTS was transmitting for each 12-em line.

This problem was solved by composing-machine manufacturers who redesigned news-body types to give them a narrower *set*. Set of type refers to width only, not height. It is measured according to the width of the matrix for a capital *M*. Thus an 8-set type has a capital *M* that is 8-points-wide; a lower-case alphabet for 8-set uses 118.1 points of space. Because most newspapers used 8-set faces, the AP transmitted tape for 8-set faces in 12-em columns. Mergenthaler Linotype redesigned its basic news body faces to a 7.66 set so that newspapers with 11½ pica columns could accommodate the lines as transmitted by TTS.

TTS users have a selection of several sizes of type; the only critical characteristic is the set. In other words, 7-, 7½-, and 8-point type can have the same 7.66 set for 11½-pica-em columns or 8 set for 12-em columns.

VARYING COLUMN MEASURE FOR SPECIAL EFFECT. Although eight columns are the standard, it is possible to change column measure for special effects. Even with TTS, this make-up device can be manipulated to good advantage for locally punched tape.

Often type is set to a one-and-one-half or two-column measure on editorial or other special pages. Type size usually increases in wider columns, and the result is a pleasing and readable page.

Also common are the so-called *2-10 leads,* an effective make-up device. "Spread leads" is a more technical name, but the term "2-10s" is used because they are generally set two-columns-wide in 10-point type. They can be carried across more than two columns and can be in a different point size. They serve well to separate headlines (see Figure 14-13) so that each gets good display.

TEN-DAY EXTENSION

Judge Extends Air Strike Ban

NEW YORK—(AP)—A federal judge has ordered a 10-day extension of his temporary ban against a strike by Pan American World Airways' 500 flight engineers.

Daniel Kornblum, counsel to the engineers' union, said he would seek an immediate review of U.S. Dist. Judge George Rosling's action by the U.S. Court of Appeals.

Juvenile Correction Assailed

CLEVELAND—(AP)—Ohio is failing to rehabilitate its youthful offenders despite its

Rosling ordered the extension Tuesday 20 minutes before the expiration of his order which last Saturday ended a strike against Pan Am four hours after it started.

Rosling called counsel for Pan Am and the union back before him again today for continued argument on the airline's application for a full-fledged injunction.

Eastern Air Lines — shut

FIGURE 14-13. A two column lead is used to separate and give contrast to headlines.

Extending the column measure for body type also creates a horizontal flow of layout masses, a characteristic sought by many newspapers of modern design.

COLUMN SEPARATORS. The traditional method for separating columns is with a hairline rule on a body sufficiently thick to provide adequate white space on each side of the line. A 6-point body is most common. Debate persists on whether the black line created by the hairline rule is needed between columns. Many designers prefer white space to do the job. One of the interesting aspects of the debate is that the opposition calls column rules old-fashioned. However, the first newspaper in the United States used only white space. Ben Harris separated the columns of his *Publick Occurrences* with white space, and James and Ben Franklin did the same with their *New England Courant* of the early 1700s. Other early newspapers including the second newspaper in the colonies, the *Boston News-Letter,* used rules. Ample precedent for either course of action exists. As far as appearance is concerned, the question is moot; but there are some mechanical factors worth considering.

Column rules present somewhat of a problem because they must be carefully cut and mitred so that they form neat joints with other rules. The smaller papers that must reuse column rules also have a problem with nicked, bent, or blunted rules, for they can make a sloppy appearance. Many weekly papers have abandoned column rules because they found reglets easier to work with.

Regardless of the means, column breaks must be adequate to give the reader a place to start and end his reading. Generally, one pica of space is considered the minimum without rules; with hairline rules at least a 6-point body is needed. To conserve newsprint during World War II many newspapers used less, but not with good results.

Most newspapers without column rules have found it necessary to return to rules for separating some advertisements. Borderless ads run together in confusing fashion without some means of specific demarkation. Confusion also exists for the reader unless rules and dashes cut across columns properly. There is a tendency to eliminate these devices when there are no column rules, but some layout problems can not be solved without them. Most common are the *cut-off rules,* "*30*" *dashes,* and *jim dashes.*

As the name implies, the cut-off separates layout units in any instance where the reader might not otherwise know where to stop. A picture and cutline must be cut off from the unrelated story below it. Headlines of more than one column need cut-off rules to direct the reader into the column where the story begins.

Cut-off rules ordinarily extend to full-column measure and form a plain, light, single line. Wavy rules, oxford rules, parallel rules, and decorative devices, such as star dashes, are also used depending upon the newspaper's "layout personality." The type of rule and the extent of its use should harmonize with other make-up practices.

The "30" dash is appropriate in traditional make-up to signify the end of a story. It is usually plain, centered in the column, and long enough to be more than half but less than two thirds the column width.

The jim dash is shorter than the "30" dash and is used to separate the decks of headlines or items within stories. Both tho jim and "30" dashes are being replaced by white space in newspapers of modern design. They are available in decorative forms also, but plain, light lines are most common.

THE NEWSPAPER NAME PLATE, OR FLAG

Every newspaper needs a quick means to identify itself. The *name plate,* or *flag,* performs this function. Its basic component is the name of the newspaper; its traditional position is at the top of page 1. It should not be confused with the *masthead,* the statement of ownership and other pertinent information that usually appears on the editorial page.

Because it is in a prominent position in every issue and has a specific job to do, the name plate is an important part of a newspaper's make-up. Originally they were hand-set in a large size of the body-type style because that was all the printer had. Today they can be highly decorative since they are electrotypes made from type proofs or artist's drawings. Unless a paper goes through a wholesale redesigning, name plates do not change in order to maintain their primary function of immediate identification for the newspaper.

When a new name plate is being designed, these factors must be considered:

(1) It should have enough display or boldness to get instant recognition.

(2) It should be appropriate for the newspaper and the community it serves.

Most newspapers use Text (Black Letter) for name plates. Its boldness and its impression of reliability stemming from its traditional association with religious printing are desirable characteristics.

Figure 14-14 shows some typical name plates. Note that some have *ears* (display elements at the side of the name plate). Ears can draw readers' attention to inside features, give weather news at a glance, state price for newsstand sales, and so on, but many newspapers have dropped them.

WEATHER
Occasional rain. High
tomorrow, 36.
(Details on Page 2)

The Detroit News 4

STAR
★★★★
HOME
EDITION

THE WEATHER
U. S. Weather Bureau Forecast
Philadelphia and vicinity
Cloudy and warmer today with
occasional showers. High
temperature 48. Southwesterly
winds, 25 to 35 miles an hour.
COMPLETE WEATHER DATA
ON PAGE 16

The Philadelphia Inquirer

An Independent Newspaper for All the People

**LATE CITY
EDITION**

Something's A-Mess
WEATHER BUREAU FORECAST
Cloudy tonight with snow later or
freezing rain turn to 27-32. Saturday, snow
or sleet changing to rain, high 35-40.
BINGHAMTON TEMPERATURES

BINGHAMTON PRESS

Friday Evening, Feb. 24, 1956   *THE TRIPLE CITIES' NEWSPAPER*   Vol. 77—269   26 Pages   5 Cents

★ ★ ★
Living Nightmare
Britain is now living a nightmare of
controls. Restrictions are the tightest
since the darkest days of World War 2.
Page 6.

ON TODAY'S EDITORIAL PAGE
Uranium for Peace. *Editorial.*
Yesterday's Red God: *Cartoon.*
Confusion in the Missile Program:
Mirror of Public Opinion and Editorial.

ST. LOUIS POST-DISPATCH

FINAL
★ ★ ★
(Closing New York Stock Prices)

Weather Forecast
Snow or sleet late tonight,
changing to rain tomorrow. Low
tonight 26, high tomorrow 43.
Chances of precipitation 5 out
of 10 tonight.
Travelers Weather Service Report

The Hartford Times.

Wall Street
Net Paid Circulation
Jan. 26, 1956   **118,026**

THE WEATHER
Fair. Slowly rising temperature through tomorrow. High today, 73 to 78; low tonight, 63
to 67. Moderate east to south-
east winds.
Extremes Past 24 Hours: 72-61.
Weather Report and Map on 3D

MIAMI DAILY NEWS

Today's News Today

**FINAL
EDITION**

**OKLAHOMA'S
GREATEST
NEWSPAPER**

TULSA DAILY WORLD

**RELIABILITY
CHARACTER
ENTERPRISE**

THE MILWAUKEE JOURNAL

Los Angeles Examiner

FIGURE 14-14. Some typical name plates with and without ears.

Name plates formerly extended fully across the top of the page, but that practice is no longer followed by many newspapers. Smaller name plates, some only two-columns-wide, are now common. Their chief advantage is that they can be moved to different positions to permit greater variety of top-of-the-page display. Many newspapers have name plates in several widths for maximum flexibility. Whether a paper retains its name plate in traditional width and position depends upon its willingness to adopt this and other modern changes designed to make design more functional.

Small newspapers are apt to use an electrotype until it is so worn that the name plate is no longer sharp and crisp. Duplicate electros should be kept on hand so replacements can be made before wear is noticeable. Another fault is the undue separation of the elements of the name plate (name, ears, slogans, date lines) so that each stands apart instead of in one unit. The result is a distracting busyness.

ILLUSTRATION AND DECORATION

Photographs and illustrations are more important to newspapers today than ever before; in all likelihood this emphasis will continue. Types of illustrations and plots have been discussed in earlier chapters. There are a few other typographic devices available to make-up editors that need attention. Some are merely decorative, others have more specific functions. In general, they complement photographs and headlines in adding tone variations to a newspaper page.

Subheads, special *paragraph beginnings,* occasional *boldface paragraphs, boxes* and *simulated boxes, thumbnail* cuts, large *initial* letters, and numerous types of *dingbats* (stars, asterisks, and the like) can add spice to dull layout areas. Some of these are shown in operation in Figures 14-15 and 14-16.

Subheads often relieve overly large gray areas. They are short lines of contrasting type inserted between groups of paragraphs in a story. Subheads supply contrast by being set in the boldface of the body type, either capitals and lower case or all capitals. They may be set flush left, centered, or flush right, although the latter is rare. Equally rare is the *cut-in* subhead composed of several lines of type cut into the column rather than inserted between paragraphs.

Special paragraph beginnings achieve the same purpose as subheads. The first two or three words of the paragraph can be set in boldface capitals, with the rest of the line in either bold or medium face. A star or asterisk dash is often used ahead of the paragraphs begun in this way. Samples of both subheads and paragraph beginnings can be seen in the design of this textbook.

Behind the Flood Wall

Harold Martin, machinist in The Times composing room and oldest printer in terms of service, was

mission. He charged he had been turned down on racial grounds.

MANY DELAYS

After many delays, the case was tried on its merits last Jan-

what the employees believe."

Missouri 'Climate' Changed

John R. Thompson, executive vice-president of the Missouri State Chamber of Commerce,

IT'S surprising to see Williams inconclusive and hesitant where always he has been certain and direct, no matter

FIGURE 14-15. Cut-in, flush left, centered subheads and boldface paragraph beginnings are used to brighten gray areas.

Vet's Book On 'Patients' Entertains

PARK AVENUE VET, by Louis J. Camuti and Lloyd Alexander; Holt, Rinehart and Winston, 184 pp., $4.
WHOLLY CATS, by Faith McNulty and Elisabeth Keiffer; Bobbs-Merrill, 208 pp., $3.50.

By WALTER B. GREENWOOD

CENSUS FIGURES on the matter are unreliable, but there is general agreement that in the last decade the cat has become the most popular of household pets. Remarkably independent and adaptable, they adjust better to the teeming uncertainties of urban life.

Novel Loss Was Gain
From Famous Fables, by E. E. Edgar

SHORTLY after he took up writing as a career, Sir Arthur Conan Doyle dashed off a novel and mailed it to a publisher. The amateurish effort was lost en route and never was recovered.

Years later, when he was an established author, Doyle was asked how he felt about the loss.

"Are you still worried by the thought that it will never be found?"

"No," replied Doyle, "I am worried that it might be."

Humor Lost When Novel Is Too Long

LEARNER'S PERMIT, by Laurence Lafore; Doubleday, 308 pp., $4.50.

LAURENCE LAFORE, a professor of history at Swarthmore College, has a good joke going in "Learner's Permit" but he suffers from interminabilia, a disease invented for the express purpose of classifying people who don't know when to stop.

The scene is Parthenon College in Acropolis, N. Y. This college doesn't

ning of a new series of atmospheric tests.

The new flurry of activity at this desert proving ground coincided with the recent

A mighty underground blast—most powerful set off in the United States and the first announced use here of an H-bomb type device—shattered the desert calm today.

resumption of testing in the Pacific and with announcement of plans to lob a dum-

counties, cities, and city school districts thereof." Another statute designates the Personnel Board of Review as the agency to enforce civil service.

So it is hard to see how the board has any choice but to investigate the union's charges and, if it finds them true, to order the cities to comply with the law.

Some politicians of the old school still prefer the patronage setup that was common in Ohio before 1912, but

FIGURE 14-16. Boxes, large initial letters, half-column cuts, and bold-face paragraphs are also used as page brighteners.

Occasional boldface paragraphs add a touch of life to long gray columns of type. These paragraphs are often also indented to make them stand out still more.

Boxes can break the gray tone while displaying small interesting items that might otherwise be lost among stories of greater length. A true box is ruled on all sides, but seen more today are boxes simulated by rules at top and bottom only. The text is usually indented for boxes; if side rules are used, the indention is necessary to allow space.

Photographs and line drawings of half-column-width occasionally provide a spot of boldness in columns. These *thumbnails*, as they are called, present a problem because type must be specially set to run around them. Their most frequent appearance is to present a likeness of the author of a column.

Available dingbats are so numerous they cannot all be described here. There are stars, asterisks, bullets (like large periods), squares, diamonds, and many specialty designs. Dingbats in the form of dashes act as paragraph separators; singly they often serve as spots to draw attention to items in tabulated matter.

Large initial letters begin a major segment of copy in many books and magazines, but are also found on some editorial or other special newspaper pages. They may be either *set in* so that the top of the initial lines up with the top of the body matter or they may be permitted to rise above the text. The latter method is used more in newspapers, because it poses no lining up problems.

✓ make-up: putting the parts together in an attractive package

The student, armed with a knowledge of the components of make-up, is ready to put the parts together in attractive, functional page units. As was said at the beginning of this chapter, physical appearance is extremely important to a newspaper. Make-up is the art of creating the desired appearance for a newspaper; it conveys a certain personality that in turn directly affects the make-up practices a paper will follow. All editors, therefore, work within certain limitations as they design each day's pages. By so doing they give continuity to their newspaper's appearance.

Make-up has other functions. First and foremost, it should help the reader get the maximum amount of information in the shortest possible time. It should grade the news—let the reader know which stories are most important and least important, which are serious and which are light in nature. It should help him move easily from one item to another and provide quick and handy summaries of the news at a glance.

In theory it seems necessary to put various front-page layouts into specific categories; whether this is done in practice is questionable, to say the least. Although a few make-up men may have definite patterns in mind as they decide a front-page format, most of them approach their task with only two objectives: *function* and *attractive design*. Seldom do their pages meet the specifications of any prescribed category.

Each front page is, and should be, somewhat different from that of any other day because its news is somewhat different. When the make-up editor is doing his job well, his page design naturally evolves through the sound application of basic design principles and without regard for stereotyped patterns. How he does this is explained in the following paragraphs. Specific categorizing is purposely kept incidental, rather than primary, to the discussion.

PREPARATION OF A DUMMY

Like a pattern for the dressmaker, a *dummy* is the first step for the make-up man. In its preparation, he assigns a page position to each story and illustration. A copy schedule supplies all the information he needs. It is an inventory of the day's news, and identifies each story, describes each headline, gives the length of each item, and lists each piece of art (photograph or illustration). To a degree, the news has already been evaluated by copy-readers who weighed the importance of items and assigned headlines accordingly. A few of the stories competing for top ranking are sometimes without headlines and page position awaiting last-minute developments to determine placement.

MAIN FOCAL POINT ON FRONT PAGE. The make-up man's first job is to decide which story is to get "top play." He then dummies in his main story in the front-page focal point—the upper-right corner. The importance of this position is traditional, based upon the usage of banner headlines. It is logical for the reader to trace a banner from column one to column eight, and follow the story down column eight. The key position for inside pages is the same as that for all other printed designs—the upper left. It is covered in detail later in the text.

On the front page, the upper left is usually considered the place for the number-two (second-in-importance) story. From that point on, stories are placed according to their worth as indicated by the headlines assigned to them.

A rule of long standing is that large heads go high on the page. In other words, the largest single-column headline is used higher on the page than other single-column heads; the largest two-column headline is higher than all other two-column heads, and so on. Boxes, because they are treated as illustrations, are used contrary to this rule as are some feature heads that stand out because of special typographic dress.

TO JUMP OR NOT TO JUMP. As main stories are put into position, the make-up man must decide how much of each story is to run on page 1 and how much, if any, is to be jumped to another page.

FIGURE 14-17. A no-jump front page. Small dailies can close all inside pages early if no stories are carried over from the front page.

Most newspapers have a basic policy regarding jump stories. Some insist that all front-page stories be complete (see Figure 14-17), some merely try to keep jumps to a minimum, and others insist that most major stories carry over to provide complete coverage. It is agreed that the "no-jump" front page is an ideal worth seeking because readership loss comes with any carry over.

CREATING AN ATTRACTIVE DESIGN

On some newspapers, the make-up man dummies in only a few of the day's main stories. The remaining spots are filled while he directs the forming of the page on the stone. Generally speaking, make-up is improved with thorough dummying.

After the main stories are in position, the other items are arranged on the page according to the dictates of good design. These are basically the same for a newspaper page as they are for any other printed matter: *contrast, balance, harmony, unity,* and *motion.*

HOW TO ACHIEVE DESIRABLE CONTRAST

Contrast comes from opposites: light and dark, large and small, tall and short, fat and thin, straight and crooked. It is the element that makes graphic communication possible: contrast between lightness and darkness makes type and illustrations visible.

Because we start with a field of white, it is easy to fall into the trap of thinking that contrast automatically comes from dropping large dark areas onto this field. It is true that the first of these will give maximum contrast, but what happens with consecutive additions? Contrast is steadily reduced, of course.

CONTRAST AMONG HEADLINES. With this in mind, two rules of contrast apply to headlines.

(1) *Headlines should be separated by white space, gray matter, or illustrations.* Some newspaper make-up men put teeth into this rule by insisting that two headlines never be placed together on a page. There are a number of ways to separate them. Spread leads provide gray matter between spread headlines and the headlines of stories below, as shown in Figure 14-13. Photographs, illustrations, and boxes serve likewise. Most make-up men, by the way, treat boxes as if they were illustrations because they perform the same functions in layout.

Separation of headlines on a horizontal plane is especially important. If two headlines of like size and style are next to each other horizontally, they form a so-called *tombstone.* As can be seen in Figure 14-18, tombstones reduce the contrast for each

GUIDO EXPECTED TO VOID PERONIST ELECTION GAINS IN ARGENTINA

Navy Decides to Back Army in Pressuring President — Military Leaders at Midnight Conferences.

U.S. SPACECRAFT FIRED AT MOON; 229,541 MILES, 60 HOURS AWAY

10-Story Rocket Takes 750-Pound Ranger IV Aloft, With Television and Scientific Apparatus.

FIGURE 14-18.
A tombstone.

headline so much that the reader can be tricked into reading the two headlines as one. Obviously these should be avoided.

(2) *If headlines must be together, they must be individually distinctive so as to retain some contrast.* Their difference can be in type size, type style, or the typographical pattern of the headline.

Two spread heads in large type can be separated by a single-column head in smaller type. An italic head may be placed next to a roman, or a lightface next to a boldface. Boxed heads or feature heads can stand out from adjacent heads by white space and size-difference. Spread heads with a broad horizontal sweep are distinct from single-column heads in a vertical shape, but again difference in type size or style helps (Figure 14-19).

Chamber Declares Economic Growth Hinges on Tax Cut

By the Associated Press
WASHINGTON, July 7—The
U. S. Chamber of Commerce

Probe Spreads to Boston In $100,000 Swindle Case

Brooklyn Realtor Tells of Introducing Parties in Mexico Gold Refining Deal

By the Associated Press
NEW YORK, July 7 — New name was rented in Mr. Schermond's

U. S. ASKS SOVIET JOIN IN LOWERING BARS TO TOURISTS

WASHINGTON, July 7 (UPI) —The United States advised Russia Friday it is lifting its travel ban for Soviet tourists and exchange visitors, and invited the

SOVIET VETO KILLS U.N. KASHMIR PLAN

Dissent, 100th in Council, Stirs a Wrangle Between Stevenson and Russian

Salan Calls for End Of Algerian Terror But Attacks Resume

By ROBERT C. DOTY
Special to The New York Times.
PARIS, June 22—Raoul Salan, serving a life sentence for leading the Secret Army Organ-

A FARM STOPGAP IS SENT TO HOUSE

Would Extend Emergency Plan—Freeman, Beaten, Looks to Next Year

FIGURE 14-19.
Tombstones can be avoided if adjacent headlines are varied in form, face, or size.

CONTRAST IN BODY AREAS. The practice of changing the line measure for editorials is a good example of contrast in body areas. With lines in single-column measure on the rest of the page, editorials two-columns-wide get special visual attention.

Change of measure for contrast is not restricted to the editorial page, of course. Front-page feature stories and major interpretive efforts displayed under a *skyline* (a banner on a story above the name plate) or a spread head at the bottom of the page are frequently given the additional eye appeal of wider columns.

Indention of lines, quite often accompanied by dropping the column rule in favor of white space between columns, is often put to similar purposes. The boldface paragraphs, special paragraph beginnings, and other typographical decorative devices shown in Figures 14-15 and 14-16 represent other methods for acquiring contrast in body areas.

A WORD OF WARNING. Contrast is essential to good design, but it can have undesirable aspects. Imagine a page with every headline a different face, and body copy varying widely among stories. There would be plenty of contrast, but the over-all result would be distasteful. Effective contrast makes each component stand out on its own without destroying the equilibrium, harmony, and unity necessary for an attractive design.

Newspaper make-up that concentrates so much on contrast it neglects other parts of good design is called "circus make-up." It is characterized by spread headlines, often in excessively large type, all over a page with little or no thought to the total picture. As can be seen in Figure 14-20, there is no doubt that circus make-up creates an impression of action and noise—but so much from so many directions that the reader can barely see or hear any of it.

BALANCE IN NEWSPAPER MAKE-UP

Balance is primary in the make-up of some newspapers and purely secondary for others.

Newspapers trying to project a conservative, steady, and reliable personality are inclined to make balance dominant in their page design. "Shouters" may deliberately try to subordinate balance lest their readers think the day's news a trifle dull. Most newspapers try for a middle ground.

Balance on a newspaper page is acquired by placing relatively equal weights on both sides of an imaginary line splitting the page

FIGURE 14-20. Make-up that is full of contrast but ignores harmony, unity, and balance is often called circus make-up.

into vertical halves. Balancing opposite corners is also considered. When these weights are virtually identical, the make-up is in *formal balance,* or *symmetrical.* When they are only relatively alike, the balance is *informal.*

Headlines and illustrations have the most inherent contrast, which means they exercise the strongest influence on equilibrium; therefore, their placement is especially important. A formally balanced newspaper page has every headline and illustration on one side of the page perfectly matched in weight and position by others on the opposite side.

But because make-up acts to grade the news for readers, formal balance necessitates news stories to develop in import by pairs. Naturally this is rare, and as a result much use of formal balance is negated.

Functionally, in newspaper make-up, headlines are balanced by pictures, headlines of one pattern by those of another, lighter elements by heavier elements placed closer to the center, like the heavier child sitting closer to the center of a teeter-totter.

Newspaper front pages with varying degrees of balance are presented in Figures 14-21, 14-22, and 14-23.

FIGURE 14-21. This page is balanced, but the balance is not obvious.

FIGURE 14-22. (At right.) Balance on this page is not symmetrical.

FIGURE 14-23. (At right.) Formal, or symmetrical balance is immediately apparent. (Courtesy *The New York Times.*)

HARMONY IN NEWSPAPER MAKE-UP

The make-up man is concerned with three kinds of harmony as he lays out newspaper pages: (1) the general appearance of the pages with the character or personality of the newspaper; (2) typographic; and (3) special pages with their subjects and readers.

HARMONY OF APPEARANCE AND CHARACTER. Because harmony in a paper's personality concerns the basic character, it is usually controlled by specific management policies. Only minor decisions on detail are made in this respect from day to day.

The range of headlines, the emphasis on illustration, and preferred make-up patterns are a matter of policy. The make-up man must simply translate his news judgments into assigning headlines, display for photographs, and page arrangements that do not depart from the predetermined paths.

TYPOGRAPHIC HARMONY. Newspapers have more difficulty achieving typographic harmony than the other printed media do.

FIGURE 14-24. Sports page typography should be bold and masculine.

FIGURE 14-25. Women's page typography should be graceful.

The large size of the pages and the great number of individual units of type display almost require that the selection of display be *monotypographic* within any *section* of a newspaper. Some newspapers still have headlines in two or, at the most, three type families, but their ranks steadily decrease. Restricting the use of display type to one family assures harmony, and the large number of variations within any type family offer many ways to avoid monotony.

Type families can and should change from department to department. One family may be used for basic news pages, another for the sports pages, another for women's pages, and perhaps another for the editorial page.

HARMONY WITH SUBJECT AND READER. Type families can be changed in different sections because their subjects and readers differ. The heavy sans-serifs of a sports page are inappropriate for a women's section; the thin lightface sans-serifs in the women's section are equally inappropriate for pages read mainly by men.

Compare the typography of the sports and women's pages of Figures 14-24 and 14-25; these pages have display faces that are completely different, but each is harmonious with subject and reader.

UNITY RESULTS FROM HARMONY

A page with harmony most likely has unity. If all its components are compatible and in keeping with the paper's character, the make-up of a page will be harmonious unless the factors below creep in:

(1) The design breaks pages into sharply defined sections.

(2) Individual components have so much contrast that they stand separately and not together.

(3) The design creates a feeling of movement that directs the reader off the page.

THE ELEMENT OF MOTION

It is difficult to know just how much the arrangement of display elements on a page contribute to the reader's eye-movement pattern. Some precaution is taken to put headlines and other display elements in lines intended to give the reader a directional boost. This effort is most apparent in a type of make-up called "focus" or "brace." When one story dominates a day's news, it is given heavy display top right. To focus attention to that story, headlines are staggered from the lower-left corner to the upper-right. The resulting line leads to the main story and forms a brace for the heavy weight that has been given to it, in much the same way that a triangular brace gives support to shelves (Figure 14-26).

MAKE-UP OF INSIDE PAGES

The same principles of functional, attractive design for the make-up of front pages apply to the inside pages of newspapers with one complicating factor, the placement of advertising.

Although the editorial staff may not like it, advertising governs the size of any issue and to a great extent controls the appearance of most inside pages. If the biggest news day in several months happens to be Saturday, the editorial staff may have less space than it could fill because the advertising is heavy for that day. Sports and other department editors would like to have their number of pages determined by the amount of news, but the amount of advertising space sold decides their allotments.

When the editorial department begins dummying inside pages, the advertising department has already made their placements.

FIGURE 14-26. Brace makeup gives emphasis to heavy display in the top right corner and braces the weight in that corner.

Make-up men can only do their best to make the page look as attractive as possible with sound planning of the space that remains.

Advertising is usually arranged in one of three basic patterns: *pyramid to the right* (which is most preferred), *double pyramid,* or *well.* Shown in Figures 14-27, 14-28, and 14-29, they act to get as many ads next to news matter as possible. Advertisers do not want their messages buried beneath other ads.

FIGURE 14-27. Ads arranged in a pyramid to the right.

As mentioned earlier, the key focal point on inside pages is the upper left, and, with ads pyramided to the right, this portion of the page is left for news display. Adherence to the following makes inside pages more functional and attractive:

(1) Balance, contrast, harmony, unity, and motion matter as much to these pages as they do to the front page.

(2) Plan a sufficient number of spread headlines, illustrations, boxes, and other major elements to give each page adequate eye stoppers.

(3) Avoid wraps (carry overs to adjacent columns) that might confuse readers. Enough spread headlines reduce this problem.

(4) Keep in mind the display effect of advertising at the bottom of the page as you plan the display of news at the top.

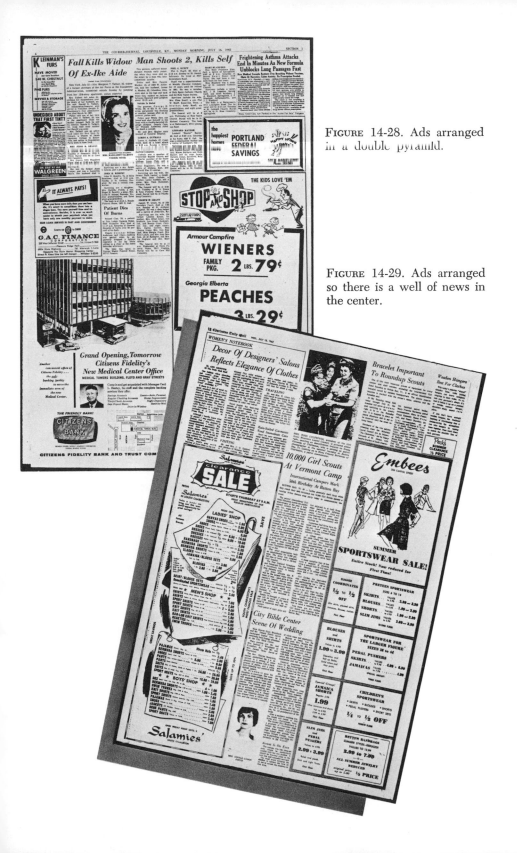

FIGURE 14-28. Ads arranged in a double pyramid.

FIGURE 14-29. Ads arranged so there is a well of news in the center.

(5) Avoid naked columns (which start at the top of the page without a headline). Spread heads and pictures eliminate this problem also.

TABLOID MAKE-UP

For many people the term "tabloid" means a particular kind of journalism. In reality it describes a page size usually 5-columns-wide and 15-inches-deep. The secondary meaning has come about because the better-known newspapers in tabloid format have been in the bigger cities and have been a rambunctious breed. The newspaper with the largest circulation in the United States is the *New York Daily News*, a tabloid.

The tabloid format has one strong advantage: it is easier to handle because of its smaller size. It can also be produced on ordinary newspaper equipment because it is just half the size of the standard format. In many respects it is a hybrid—part newspaper and part magazine. Some tabloids, such as the *Daily News*

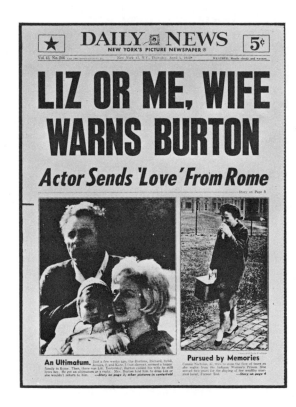

FIGURE 14-30. Some tabloids use the front page to emphasize only one, or perhaps two, major stories. (Courtesy New York *Daily News*.)

FIGURE 14-31. Tabloids, especially those in suburbs, also can use traditional treatment for their front pages.

(Figure 14-30), have front pages that resemble magazines more than they do newspapers. Others are patterned after standard-sized newspapers (Figure 14-31).

There has been a marked tendency for new newspapers to adopt the tabloid format. This has been especially true in the burgeoning suburban press, an area of journalism that is expected to grow in importance in future years. Along with the functional tabloid format, these newspapers are emerging as leading practitioners of the most modern and functional journalistic principles. As suburban journalism grows, we can expect greater respectability for the tabloid format, and greater attention paid to it.

15 As far as layout and design are concerned, newspapers and magazines are alike in some ways but strikingly different in others. Certainly the basic visual elements are the same: white space, illustrations, display type, text type, and some typographical decorations. It could even be said that the basic form itself are the same for both media; certainly layout men for newspapers *and* magazines try to entice and hold readers.

But this latter statement is an oversimplification. Newspapers deal in facts, and the natural thirst for news on the part of their readers gives them a head start. Most magazines deal in entertainment, abstractions, and concepts. Whereas newspapers may display thirty or more items on a page, magazines often devote several pages to one article. Magazines also appeal to a somewhat more discriminating audience, at least as far as appearance is concerned. Rough paper, poor illustrations, hastily-put-together pages are generally not acceptable. Maximum use of graphic techniques in building reader appeal is not merely desirable for magazines, it is essential. Hence, although the typography and design principles may be identical, their application must be different.

Magazine layout principles are more closely related to those of advertising than of newspapers. In both cases considerable effort has been advanced to get the utmost selling power through the use of the best visual techniques. Magazines must constantly sell and resell themselves.

The importance placed on physical appearance is readily apparent as one glances through the scores of magazines on any drugstore magazine rack. Full-color photographs, quality paper, and elaborate illustrations are the rule. This emphasis becomes even more striking when a magazine, for one reason or another, gets into a precarious situation. Those hit especially hard by the competition of television in the fifties and sixties indulged in an orgy of typography and design experimentation. How effective such changes in appearance can be in keeping a magazine alive is undecided, but there is no doubt that a forceful use of graphic techniques is vital if a magazine is to reach a maximum level of success.

Because magazines do indulge in a great deal of experimentation with graphics, it is difficult to reduce a discussion of periodical layout and design to the level of basic principles. Establishing a relationship of physical form to function, however, can provide us with a starting point for suggestions on magazine design that can pass the test of time.

MAGAZINE LAYOUT AND DESIGN

THE FIRST "F" OF MAGAZINE LAYOUT: FUNCTIONS

The functions of magazine layout are not difficult to find, nor are they in any way unique. Briefly stated, they are (1) to get the immediate attention of the reader to the magazine or any part thereof; and (2) to hold that attention so the reader can and will read the material presented.

Any layout obviously must succeed at both. If attention is not attracted, all is lost; if attention is not held or the reader is somehow prevented from reading, achievement of the first function is valueless.

ATTRACTING ATTENTION. Perhaps the most useful elements for attracting attention are *color, photographs* or *illustrations,* and *titles.* Whatever the device, the eye stopper must do its job quickly. A potential reader who is leafing through a magazine will spend no more than an estimated ten seconds with a display element. Unless his attention is attracted within that time, he moves on.

Color is especially effective because it brings forth an instant reaction. The various uses of color discussed in Chapter 13 can be applied to magazines.

The picture magazines, such as *Life* and *Look,* brought photographs to the fore as attention getters. Their influence on magazine layout has been so pronounced that magazines by the scores depend primarily on photographs to stop a reader. Many employ a standard layout (a large photo with cutline followed by title and text) for most of their articles, issue after issue (see Figure 15-1). Stereotyped as it may be, this arrangement is sufficiently functional and simple to remain repeatedly effective.

The photo-cutline-title-text formula has worn well with magazines of all types because it is tailored to the two basic functions of magazine make-up. It depends on a large appealing photo to catch the eye, then the reading matter in logical sequence to hold the interest of the reader. From the photograph, the reader can be expected to move to the cutline for explanation. His interest is renewed by the title, which also leads him to the body of the article.

Headlines or titles, especially when combined with ample white space, can also halt the scanner long enough to get him interested. They work well in conjunction with photographs or illustrations, and also do the job on their own.

Flirt with a Fluttery Fan

FIGURE 15-1. A strong picture attracts attention when followed by cutline, title, and text. (Courtesy *Life* Magazine © 1962 Time, Inc.)

The important principles to remember about titles on magazine pages are: (1) they must be sized large enough to dominate; (2) there must be ample white space surrounding them to make them stand out in contrast; (3) as attention getters, they can be treated like illustrations and can be used anywhere on a page or spread.

Most magazine titles are short and must be in large type to be effective. Contrast the display power of the titles used in Figure 15-2 and Figure 15-3. The title in Figure 15-3 is definitely undersized. Also note the need for more white space with the title in Figure 15-3. A title often calls for one-third, one-half, or even a full page of white space surrounding to create good contrast.

The journalism student reared on newspaper make-up must resist the tendency to squeeze titles into a minimum space as he has been accustomed with newspaper headlines. He must also be prepared to change his thinking about the location of titles, as he does his first work with magazine layout. Magazine titles can be located anywhere on the page if they have sufficient display power through size and white space. Note the varied placements of titles in the illustrations in this chapter.

Type selection for magazines requires a different approach also. Monotypographic harmony is excellent for newspapers, but it tends to be monotonous for magazines. Again, titles for magazines should be treated as illustrations—each one suitable for the article it describes and, in most cases, each one different from the others. If two articles are not alike, their titles should not be alike. It is also common to use more than one type face in a single-line title on a magazine spread; this is virtually unheard of for newspapers. Figures 15-2 and 15-4 show how different styles and sizes of type can be combined in titles that attract attention and act to illustrate their articles.

KEEPING THE READER. The second function, to hold the reader and aid him in reading, is accomplished by applying the principles of good typography and layout described in earlier chapters. Some of these merit additional mention here.

(1) Use a serif type with roman posture in capitals and lower case for large text areas. It is difficult or impossible to find a maga-

FIGURE 15-2. A large title sur-rounded by ample white space. (Courtesy *Systems* Magazine.)

zine whose contents have been set in all-caps, italics, or a sans-serif type. These are not used because they make it more difficult for the reader to stay with the written matter.

(2) Avoid running type vertically. This is fine in China, but Americans are accustomed to reading from left to right, and type contrary to this cannot help the reader. Although layout men have not intentionally run type from right to left, there are many who have a penchant for using type reading from top to bottom.

(3) Place the key element of the layout in the upper left. Whether the area is a single page or a spread, custom again indicates that the reading start in the upper left. From first-grade primers through all the books needed to acquire an education, the reader has started in that section of a display area. This custom can be broken with the help of special display. When the main title, photograph, or color spot is in another area of the layout field, reader eye movement must be made to follow the path we want.

(4) Place captions close to their illustrations. Descriptive matter for illustrations must be virtually a part of the illustrations. They may be placed at either side or at the bottom, but separated from their illustration with too much white space, they are lost. Captions run above an illustration only as an emergency measure because the placement is contrary to normal eye movement.

(5) Select column widths so line length is suitable for the type size being used, keeping in mind the principles discussed in Chapter 9. Columns that are too narrow or too wide can hinder the reader.

THE SECOND "F" OF MAGAZINE LAYOUT: FORMAT

The *format* (shape and size) of a magazine is a basic factor in its layout and is not subject to artistic whims. Magazines vary considerably in shape and size, ranging from small enough to tuck into a pocket to dimensions that equal the tabloid newspaper. Its format is the result of one or more of three practical considerations: (1) ease of handling; (2) adaptability of content to format; and (3) mechanical limitations of printing-press sizes.

Ease of handling is the chief advantage of the pocket size of the *Reader's Digest* and many others. Easy to hold and to store, it is particularly suited to contents consisting mainly of text with the illustrations secondary.

The large sizes are best for emphasis on pictures, for the larger the photographs, the greater their impact.

Most magazines present text and illustrations on a relatively equal basis, and use a format adequate for both—8½ by 11 inches —or in that vicinity. Since this is the same size as standard typing paper, filing of these pages is made possible, and the dimensions are comfortable for the reader.

Most magazines are vertical rectangles, a traditional shape substantiated by the difficulty of handling horizontal formats.

A THIRD "F": FRAMES

Frames (margins) are an important part of magazine layout for two reasons. First, they are the ending and/or beginning marker for copy. Try cutting the margin from both sides of copy in a magazine and note the reading difficulty incurred without the frame of white that demonstrates line endings.

Second, they help make pages and spreads attractive and unified by wrapping the elements on a page into one package with the border of white margins. In this respect they act like the frame around a work of art.

Margins are mandatory for type matter. The need for a beginning and ending for lines requires type to stay within the margins of the page or spread.

Use of Bleeds. Pictures may break the margins of course. The use of bleed photographs helps in the following ways:

(1) To provide a change of pace.
(2) To give more room on a page by adding the marginal space to the content area.
(3) Perhaps most important, to offer extra magnitude for photographs; without frames photos seem to go on and on.

The exact size of margins and the extent to which bleeds are used are matters of magazine art-department decisions. However, a generally accepted work rule keeps the four margins of a page in a relationship keyed to the optical center of the layout area.

Optical Center Helps Set Margins. The optical center of a layout area is slightly higher than the geometric center. Intersecting lines drawn to opposite corners of a rectangle mark the geometric center, but the spot in the page that actually seems central to the eye is one twentieth higher than the page depth.

Type pages are centered according to the optical center; in other words, they ride slightly high on the page. Therefore margins are allotted by first making the bottom margin the largest on the page. The outside margin is smaller than the bottom, and either larger or the same size as the top. The inside, or gutter, margin is always the smallest, because it is doubled by its opposite on the facing page. This strip would hurt the unity of a spread if it were too wide. Width can be desirable when the material on the two pages is unrelated, but magazines are usually laid out in spreads, rather than in single pages. As a rule, the gutter margin should never be more than half the bottom margin for maximum cohesion.

REMEMBER: READERS ALWAYS SEE TWO PAGES

With the exception of the outside cover, the magazine is viewed two facing pages at a time. For the reader's sake, it is wise to design facing pages as a single unit, and no page should be designed without a consideration of the one it faces. The two may not be a unit, but they cannot help influencing each other's design.

FIGURE 15-5. Spreads can be tied together by titles which cross the gutter at word breaks. (Courtesy *The Michigan Bell*, Michigan Bell Telephone Co.)

OVERCOMING THE GUTTER. To build effective spread layouts takes a mastery over the natural obstacle of the gutter margins. Facing pages can be tied together by the following: type, illustrations, color, white space, and/or typographical devices.

Extending a title across the gutter forms a workable bridge, but demands attention so that the spacing between letters is not disrupted. If a title is large enough and is positioned with the gutter falling between words (Figure 15-5), the tie-in is accomplished without interfering with readability.

Except for a center spread in a saddle-stitched magazine, the printer has an eternal problem of putting the linking elements of a spread in proper alignment across the gutter. Some deviation must be allowed for when planning tie-ins.

A single horizontal photograph crossing the gutter is a good link, but the margin must be broken on both pages so the segments of the photo seem to abut each other. The content of the photo or illustration determines whether any misalignment might be too disturbing to risk. Good linkage is also possible with a series of illustrations that cross the gutter, leave the margins intact (Figure

FIGURE 15-6. A tie-in achieved by having a series of photographs carry over to another page leaving space for the gutter intact. (Courtesy *The Beacon*, The Ohio Oil Company.)

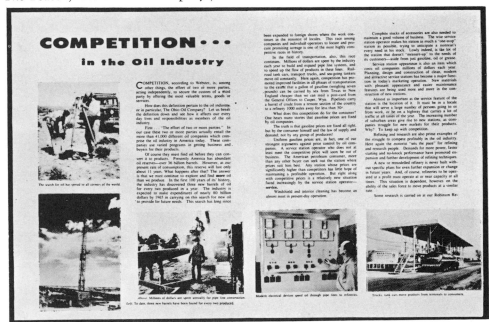

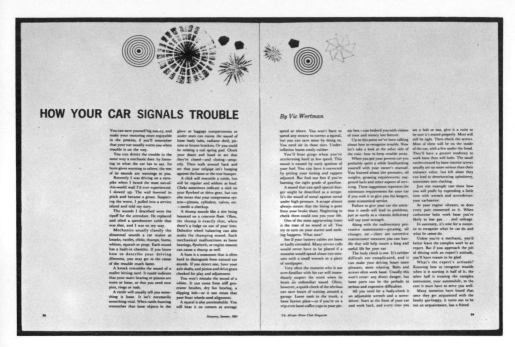

The illustration within shows the article:

HOW YOUR CAR SIGNALS TROUBLE

By Vic Wortman

FIGURE 15-7. Illustration and white space work together to bridge the gutter and unite two pages. (Courtesy *Discovery,* Allstate Motor Club.)

15-6), and make the misalignment far less grave.

Strips of white space, alone or aided by illustrations, can unite two pages (Figure 15-7), as can rules, borders, dotted lines, and the like, which give horizontal direction across the pages (Figure 15-8).

Combining spread pages need not be so obvious as in these examples, of course. In fact, more subtle methods should be sought. There is no limit to the techniques a fertile imagination can produce.

EMPHASIZING THE GUTTER. When facing pages contain two different subjects, the reader must not be confused by a visual connection between the subjects. The layout must accent each page by exploiting the gutter divider or by other means. Techniques for bridging the gutter should be scrupulously avoided. Instead, white space may be needed in the gutter area. Certainly each of the pages must be given contrast in order to stand out as separate units.

APPLY BASIC DESIGN PRINCIPLES

Magazine spreads and pages should be attractive as well as functional. They can be made pleasing to the eye by applying the good design principles discussed in Chapter 10. A review of this material by the student is feasible at this point, for the requirements of balance, contrast, harmony, appropriateness, and motion are as important to magazine layout as they are to advertising, newspapers, or any other form of graphic communication.

To the requisites of good design is added the necessity for simplicity of page layout. In spite of the design gymnastics practiced by a few magazines in the fifties and sixties, most magazines are still committed to a quiet approach. Pages that shout "here is a design" may be a joy to their creator, but to the reader may only represent a collection of blocks to the enjoyment and enlightenment they hope to get from the content.

Generally speaking, the fewer the display elements on a page or spread the greater the chance of success in attracting and holding

FIGURE 15-8. A Ben Day rule is the chief unifying factor for this spread. All kinds of rules can be used for bridging the gutter. (Courtesy *The Trading Post*, Timken Roller Bearing Company.)

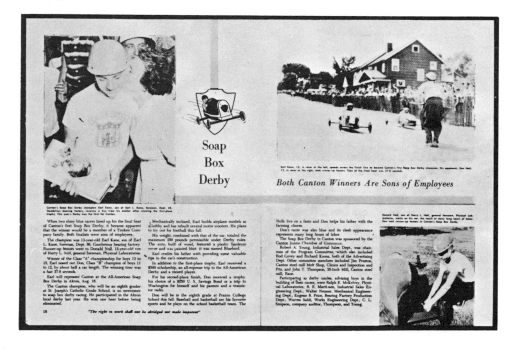

the reader to the material. Avoiding a cluttered, busy, disorganized effect becomes more difficult as the number of elements increases. Furthermore, simplicity provides the reader with a definite starting point; one element should overshadow all others at the point where the reader should begin.

Emphasizing the need for simplicity does not in any way imply that pages should be formal, dull, or monotonous. Indeed, when pages are laid out with the need for appropriateness in mind, variety is a natural outcome. Pages should reflect the character and flavor of the material presented upon them; they should be alike only if their subject matter is alike. A benefit perhaps to be derived from the recent extreme design experiments among magazines may be a happy compromise between the wild and the commonplace. The need for appropriateness should rule out the commonplace; the need for simplicity should rule out the bizarre.

A WORD ABOUT SPECIAL PAGES
AND PROBLEM PAGES

Front covers and table of contents pages require special layout attention. Covers because they are so important; contents pages because they tend to be dull and uninspiring.

THE FRONT COVER. A magazine's front cover is like a store's front display window, a building's entrance, an automobile's exterior styling. It should encourage attention and create the desire to go inside.

The functions suggested by these comparisons are vital, and there is the additional need for the instant identification of the magazine from its competitors and of its issue, as distinct from its previous issues.

Covers consist of type display alone or of type and illustration combined. The latter is employed most today. The principal identifying characteristic is usually a distinctive name plate, but design and/or color may be used for the same purpose. A name plate must be unique and of enough size to merit quick recognition. Design, as an aid to recognition, should be flexible so that necessary variations in the shapes of illustrations can be accommodated from issue to issue. Cover illustrations selected from the interior content can entice a reader into the magazine, but type is needed as well to direct the reader to specific articles inside. Reference to page numbers is an added lure.

Issues may be set apart from each other by changes in color,

FIGURE 15-9. A long horizontal sweep can be attained if facing pages are split and each is carried across the gutter. (Courtesy *Forward*, Dayton Power & Light Company.)

design, and the use of volume and issue numbers. No cover is complete without the latter, of course, but such information is usually so subordinate that instant issue identification must be aided in other ways.

Because some magazines sell their front covers to advertisers at a premium price, the editorial department is compelled to create covers so valuable in maintaining readership that the business office will not appropriate this vital part of a magazine to add to income. This pressure, plus the cover's important functions, makes cover designing especially important.

TABLE-OF-CONTENTS PAGES. Any magazine large enough for the reader to have logical difficulty in locating material should have a table of contents. Its information may consume only a portion of a page, but must have sufficient display to be found instantly, which usually necessitates placement well forward in the magazine.

Paid-circulation magazines using second-class mail distribution are required to put certain basic information regarding entry as second-class matter, office of publication, and so on, somewhere within the first five pages. Since such masthead data is commonly on the table-of-contents page, the position of the latter is more or less predetermined.

The combination of masthead information and a long list of titles can mean a dull page. Therefore, many magazines now (1) make an effort to use illustrations on the page; (2) give special typographical display to some listings in the contents; and (3) bury the mailing and masthead information where it can be found when necessary but where it does not represent a major element on the page.

Small photographs, taken from important articles in the issue and used adjacent to the listing in the contents table, can help spruce up the layout and point out the significant features.

Checks, bullets, and other typographical dingbats can be used (perhaps in color) to give variety to the listing of titles and tempt the eye. Whatever the device, monotony caused by a long list of items equal in display, should be avoided.

Special display should be reserved for what is new in each issue; material that appears regularly, such as mailing information and titles of content departments, should not be emphasized.

PROBLEM PAGES. Advertising on split or fractional pages creates layout difficulty for magazines as well as for newspapers. These pages are not a serious problem if their editorial portions are treated as separate design areas. They can be made attractive and functional by realizing that their shapes may be quite different from the ordinary page shape.

The extreme vertical often left after ads have been placed cannot be laid out like a two-page spread, but its dimensions can be exploited. Titles, illustrations, or other layout elements must simply be made to conform to the area. Two facing verticals can be brought together in the center of a spread by ads located on the outsides. Or, with ads spread across the bottom, the upper portions of two pages can be linked for a horizontal layout field. In such cases, the techniques used for spreads are applicable.

Many fractional pages are used for carry-over material, but continuations are being avoided more and more. Most magazine articles can be confined to full pages up front, by adjusting the space for display (titles, and so on) to make the text fit. Fractional pages can then be used attractively for short items with adequate reader interest.

ALLOCATING SPACE: "BREAK OF THE BOOK"

The allocation of space to various articles and ads—usually called the "break of the book"—has an important effect on readership and appearance.

Because advertising determines the existence of a magazine, it is usually placed first, with consideration allowed for editorial-department needs. Although advertisers may request, pay for, and get special position, they are vitally concerned with the success of the editorial portions. As a matter of fact, their requests are often in connection with placement at or near certain portions of a magazine. Cooperation between business and editorial offices negates difficulties arising from advertising placement. It is common practice for ads to be located front and back with the center reserved for the main editorial section.

One of the minor layout problems associated with this practice is to alert the reader to the beginning of the content. The reproduction of the name plate is often used on the first editorial page to signal the reader.

Several studies have shown that a large percentage peruse a magazine backwards. (This can be checked in a classroom survey.) Some magazines have, therefore, found it expedient to place some strong features as complete single-page units at the end of the editorial section. These serve as a starting point for the "backward" readers.

As the main editorial section develops, the pace should change frequently. Long articles should not be lumped together but should be relieved by single or fractional page articles.

EFFECTS OF PRODUCTION REQUIREMENTS ON LAYOUT

The mechanics of production must be an everpresent thought during make-up. Both appearance and cost are affected by the method that produces the magazine.

The importance of signatures and imposition (Chapter 8) should be reemphasized here. Charges for color can be kept down by placing color in signatures and imposition for minimal additional press runs. Through careful planning, an editor can use color on editorial pages in the same form with advertising color pages for virtually no extra cost.

Binding is important, too. Problems of alignment for the spread that crosses the two center pages of the magazine are eliminated in saddle-stitch magazines. For side-stitch-bound magazines, allowance must be made for the loss of some of the gutter margin during the binding.

Printers usually assess a special charge for breaking the margins, which must be considered as layouts are prepared. This does not mean bleeds should be forsworn. It may mean only that with the charge incurred for one spread, the margin can be broken completely for that particular spread. It is important to know how to make the most of extra costs.

This same realization should apply to the extra cost of special photoengraving plates. Combinations, silhouettes, and so on should be used where their value to the layout merits the extra cost; they should not be used just to suit a whim.

Special fold-out pages and other like contrivances should be reserved for special occasions that rate unusual production costs.

The emphasis on simplicity of design arises from artistic considerations, and is strengthened by the production problems that accompany attempts to be different.

 summary

Magazines demand meticulous layout and design by their nature. When sold on newsstands, their appearance is all-important in seizing readership.

The principles of layout and design, described in Chapter 10, should be applied as magazine pages are constructed. These and the knowledge of magazine make-up result in attractive, legible pages.

For the beginner, the best source of layout ideas is the work of others. A study of magazines on store racks and those of a specialized nature found at home or in libraries provides many good examples of the principles presented in this chapter—and a few violations to recognize.

16

Some factors of producing effective graphic communications are beyond the control of the designer who is preparing materials to appear in the established media. He has to fit his layout to prescribed size limitations; he must use the printing process by which the medium is produced; the paper is predetermined, and this in turn affects his use of continuous-tone art work.

It is in the printing field outside the media that the communicator finds fewer restrictions and can exercise the fullest creative use of the principles of graphic communications. Here he controls the selection of:

(1) Printing process.
(2) Color.
(3) Paper.
(4) Fold.
(5) Size and shape.

Because this product goes directly to readers, it is referred to as "direct literature." It may be mailed, distributed by individuals, or placed at convenient locations where readers can help themselves. The most common means is by mail, and when so handled, it is referred to as "direct-mail literature."

 types of printed pieces

Printed pieces take many forms. The scope of this text cannot include them all. In broadest terms they divide into two groups: (1) flat and folded sheets; and (2) booklets.

LETTERS AND FOLDERS

The printed form letter is the most typical of the first group. It is usually folded prior to delivery, and when opened, presents its message on a single flat sheet. It is frequently typed, reproduced by offset, and closely resembles a typewritten letter. Letters may also be printed by letterpress from line cuts of typed copy or from line-cast body set in a typewriter face.

Production is also possible on the Multigraph. Metal type resembling typewriter faces is composed, a piece at a time, by sliding each piece into slots on a drum. An inked ribbon is wrapped around the drum over the type. As the drum revolves, the type is printed through the ribbon onto the paper. The result is so much like an individually typed letter that a *fill-in* (name, address, and salutation) is scarcely discernible from the body of the letter.

Other common types of flat pieces are the *card,* the *blotter,* and the *dodger.* The latter is an unfolded sheet, also called a *flier* or *enclosure.*

The simplest kind of folder is the *leaflet,* a small sheet printed on one or both sides and usually folded once. It can be treated in its design as having four separate pages (the two inside often used as a spread) or as being two pages, one on each side of the sheet.

The so-called *folder* is a larger sheet folded more than once— generally three or four times. A *broadside* is a kingsize folder, usually 19 by 25 inches or up to 25 by 38 inches, which unfolds to a smashing center-spread concentrated on a single idea. It is typical that as folders unfold, each newly revealed part becomes a layout or design unit. Some common types of folds used for leaflets, folders, and broadsides are shown in Chapter 8.

BOOKLETS

Booklets are sometimes called "pamphlets" or "brochures." Essentially they are "small books," and are made up of eight or more pages bound together, usually either saddle- or side-stitched or mechanically bound. Booklets differ from books primarily in format and style of design.

Book format is traditionally standardized. It has roughly three main divisions: (1) the preliminaries, or front matter; (2) the text; and (3) the reference.

The preliminaries include the *half title,* the book's first printed page on which appears only the book's title; the *title page,* which includes the title and the names of the author, publisher, and place of publication; the *copyright page;* the *preface;* the *acknowledgments;* the *contents;* the *introduction* when it is not a part of the text proper; and often, a second half title. Tradition governs the order of these pages and whether they fall on a left- or a right-hand page. *Folios,* or page numbers, are Roman numerals, appearing first on the opening preface page, although the actual numbering starts from the half title.

The text section contains the chapters; the reference section consists of appendices, bibliography, glossary, and index. In text and reference sections folios are Arabic. They may be either at the top or at the bottom of the page. *Running heads* usually appear at the top of each page, and the content is apt to be different on the right- and left-hand pages.

Throughout, the progressive margins in use remain consistent although text on facing pages may run a line or two long or short depending upon make-up.

Booklets, on the other hand, are much less rigid in layout. Tradition plays no part. Because a story unfolds through succeeding pages, as in a book, a continuity of style must be maintained by the designer, who works with units of individual or facing pages.

The arrangement of elements in a booklet can differ from page to page. Cuts can bleed, copy block widths and margins be varied, display and color used with a lavish hand.

The front page of a booklet, generally referred to as the *front cover*, should be particularly attractive to invite readership within.

what type of printed piece?

An important creative decision is the type of printed piece to be produced. The following factors favor the use of a booklet:

(1) Lengthy copy requiring continuity of presentation.

(2) Need for a number of illustrative examples.

(3) Highly technical material.

(4) Catalogue material.

The folder, on the other hand, lends itself when these conditions exist:

(1) A series of illustrations is to be presented, as the number of different models of a product.

(2) Short but crisp text is offered.

(3) The unfolding naturally builds a climactic impression.

(4) Production speed and economy are required. Booklet production means time-consuming, extra folding-and-binding operations, while folders can be *self-mailers*. With the latter, one section is left open for addressing and for the printing of postal *indicia*, an indication that the sender has a permit to pay postage at time of mailing in lieu of affixing stamps. Booklets are usually mailed in envelopes, thereby entailing the dual expense of envelopes and insertion.

(5) *Imprinting* of, for example, various dealer names is called for. Such work can be done economically on the flat sheets prior to folding.

standard unit sizes

An early step in planning the printed piece is the preparation of the dummy. At this point the designer must remember that the size of the piece has a significant effect on final production cost because manufacturers, in the interest of economy, produce certain standard sizes of paper, available through printers. Thus only certain sized pamphlets and other forms of direct literature can be cut advantageously from these stock sheets. Following are these standard sizes:

Bond: 17 by 22 (substance), 17 by 28, 19 by 24, 22 by 34, 28 by 34, 34 by 44 inches.
Book: 25 by 38 (basis), 28 by 42, 28 by 44, 32 by 45, 35 by 45, 38 by 50, 17½ by 22½, 19 by 25, 23 by 29, 23 by 35, 36 by 48 inches.
Cover: 20 by 26 (basis), 23 by 35, 26 by 40, 35 by 46 inches.[1]

Suppose an eight-page booklet, 4½ by 6 inches, is being planned. What size stock can be used? Remember these points before solving this problem:

    (1) One-half inch should be subtracted from the short dimension of the stock to allow for press grippers, which hold the paper on the impression cylinder. This is three-eighths of an inch on some presses. Printing can extend to but not beyond the grippers.

    (2) One-eighth inch should be allowed for bleed trim on every edge of the piece.

Thus we can determine that sixty-four pages can be printed on a 25-by-38-inch sheet, thirty-two on each side, as shown in Figure 16-1. This means a total of eight eight-page booklets per sheet of paper.

The finished booklet should be 4⅝ by 6¼ inches to allow trim of one-eighth inch on top, bottom, and outside to open the pages. The fractions along the right side of the sheet in Figure 16-1 indicate trim allowances. As long as the print area falls at least one-

---

[1]The basis size of cover stock (20 by 26 inches) is slightly larger than 19 by 25 inches, one half of the basis size of book paper (25 by 38 inches) to allow for *overhang covers;* that is, covers with dimensions larger than the inside of the booklet.

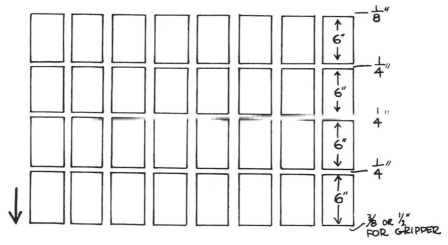

FIGURE 16-1. Thirty-two 4½ by 6-inch pages imposed on one side of a sheet.

half inch below the top of the sheet, 25 by 38 inches is adequate.

But when bleed pages are in the design, the printed booklet should be 4¾ by 6½ inches. When trimming is done, the cut to make the finished 4½ by 6 inches is then deep enough to insure inclusion of the bleed art. The piece should be printed on a 28-by-42-inch sheet for bleeds.

COMMON SHEET SIZES

Size of piece in Inches	Cuts with Trim from (in Inches)	Cuts with Bleed from (in Inches)	Number of Pages
3⅜ by 6¼	28 by 42	28 by 44	96
3¾ by 5⅛	32 by 44	35 by 45	128
4¼ by 5⅜	35 by 45	38 by 50	128
4½ by 6	25 by 38	28 by 42	64
4 by 9⅛	25 by 38	28 by 42	48
5¼ by 7⅝	32 by 44	35 by 45	64
5½ by 8½	35 by 45	38 by 50	64
8½ by 5½ (oblong)	23 by 35	25 by 38	32
6 by 9⅛	25 by 38	28 by 42	32
7¾ by 10⅝	32 by 44	35 by 45	32
8½ by 11	35 by 45	38 by 50	32
9¼ by 12⅛	25 by 38	28 by 42	16

A piece can be printed from other than standard-sized paper. Manufacturers make paper in special sizes, and quantities in excess of 5000 pounds can be purchased economically. For smaller amounts, extra costs usually dictate fitting the design to a standard size.

Presses and envelopes are keyed to accommodate all of the standard-sized pieces. Special envelopes can be made to order. Certain standard printed pieces fit with a letter in the widely used No. 6¾ envelope (3⅝ by 6½ inches) and the No. 10 envelope (4⅛ by 9½ inches). Others can be mailed in *booklet envelopes* available in various sizes.

special paper considerations

In addition to size, certain other aspects of paper need the attention of the designer. These are: (1) kind; (2) color; and (3) weight.

KIND OF PAPER

Bond lends itself well to folders because of its good folding quality. It is strong and durable. Offset prints well on its hard surface; but it should be avoided for most letterpress work. Common weights in use are 20- and 24-pound, equivalent to the book paper weights of 50- and 60-pound respectively.

Coated book stocks are high-priced and tend to crack in folding. Letterpress reproduction is best, but coated stocks are available for offset.

COMPARATIVE WEIGHTS OF STOCK

Book Paper in Pound Weight	Cover Paper in Pound Weight	Bond in Pound Weight
30	——	——
35	——	13
40	——	16
45	25	——
50	——	20
60	35	24
70	40	28
80	43	32
90	50	36
100	35	——
120	65	——
150	80	——

Uncoated book stocks are less distinctive than coated—and less expensive, enough so that in a long run the cost savings is substantial.

Offset stocks, which are also book paper, fold excellently and are thus particularly adaptable to folders. The weights of 60-, 70-, and 80-pound are most used.

Cover stock is particularly useful for the addition of separate covers to booklets, and is also used for folders and pamphlets. Weights above 80-pound usually require scoring before folding.

Cover is also available in 90-, 100-, and 130-pound weights. Paper is not made in weights above 150.

COLOR

White has been the traditional color for paper since the earliest days of printing, and black ink on white paper will probably continue most popular in the future. But for some time interest in color stocks has grown. There are several reasons for this:

(1) The contrast of color stock to white. With the bulk of printing done on white paper, messages on color stock get attention.

(2) Increased understanding of the psychological effects of color. As discussed, color stimulates positively and negatively. Skillfully used, color stock creates atmosphere and builds retention. Because black and white are in a sense the absence of color, they lack the psychological impact of printing color ink on color stock.

(3) Research in developing compatible inks and papers. Paper and ink manufacturers, with the assistance of psychologists, ophthalmologists, and lighting engineers, have uncovered pleasing combinations of color ink on color paper. Four-color process printed on a color stock has proved startlingly effective when the key color black is substituted by a dark color ink compatible to the paper.

The reading task is simplified when the message is printed color-on-color. There is less reflection than black-on-white. Many experts contend this reduction in contrast is a welcome relief for the reader. Because the cost of color-on-color is not much greater, the continued improvements in paper and ink manufacture will no doubt mean expanded use.

WEIGHT

The weight of stock must be considered primarily because of its effect on mailing costs.

which printing process?

Letterpress, offset, gravure, photogelatin, and silk screen are all used in the production of direct literature. The latter two are limited to short runs. The chief advantage to silk screen is the startling effect of bright ink. Its flat color work is good, and with a small folder of a relatively short run—perhaps 2000 to 3000—the expense is worthwhile.

Photogelatin is practical for runs up to 5000. Special stock is required. Plate size is large—40 by 60 inches—and if a single mailer is to be printed, the high cost can be justified by gang running.

Gravure offers rich color and soft tone, with sheet-fed preferable to rotogravure. The latter is best for extremely long runs into the several hundred thousands.

Because type is screened in rotogravure, this process is not usually selected for jobs of mainly text. On the other hand, its excellent near-screenless reproduction of art and photos makes it adaptable for long-run pictorial work, even on relatively inexpensive papers. Production costs are comparatively high but are absorbed by long runs.

Letterpress makes sense for the quality reproduction of type-dominant jobs. In many cases printing is done directly from the composed type. The presses for this work are slower, and, when volume and speed are significant, the additional costs of electros for rotary equipment is a factor.

Letterpress cannot print fine screen halftones on rough stock.

When pictures, tints, and other elements that require engravings for letterpress are a major portion of the finished piece, offset is favored. Moreover, these elements can then be printed on any quality of paper, and offset is faster, and adaptable to gang running several pieces at a time. But, probably the most beautifully reproduced halftones are done letterpress on a superior coated stock.

checking press sheets

Once a message is released to a medium, opportunity for controlling the printed result fades. In the case of direct literature, however, there is an opportunity to check the printed piece as it comes from the press. At this point it is possible to find and correct *fill-in,* or *plugging,* of halftones and fine lines; streaks, slurs, and other blemishes; improper make-ready and inking.

Press sheets, or *press proofs,* are marked by an arrow that indicates change of position. It is drawn to point out where type or art is to be moved. A circle is drawn around areas where make-ready is faulty or where some other imperfection is spotted, and the proof reader's delete symbol draws attention to the circle.

conclusion

The communicator faces his greatest challenge with direct literature. Not only must he bring into play all the principles of typography and design, but he must also make important production decisions that he is spared when dealing with media.

a final word

In the four centuries following the invention of movable type, master craftsmen established standards of excellence for letter forms and for books that still endure. Many of the earliest type faces remain popular today, and beautiful books printed centuries ago are still regarded as models of typographic excellence.

The coming of the Industrial Revolution brought new demands on the printer. Printing that was to "sell"—whether ideas or products—could no longer follow the standards for books, which were designed to inform and be read in leisurely comfort. To persuade, printing had to be made to call attention to the message it would impart. Thus, a century or so ago printers turned to decorative or ornate type faces and typographical ornaments and to bizarre and overwhelming presentation in an attempt to meet the demands made of them.

Once again, design has returned to printing; not design for design's sake but rather design to meet the physiological and psychological needs of the readers. Increased effectiveness in graphic communication will be brought about in the future when we better understand what these needs are.

But it will always remain true that to be able to fashion graphic communication to meet current requirements, one must have a basic and comprehensive knowledge of the mechanics of printing as well as a fundamental knowledge of sound design. Only then can today's communication needs be met. This book has this purpose as its aim.

Allen, John E., *Newspaper Designing* (New York: Harper & Row, Publishers, 1947).

American Photoengravers Association, *Line, Halftone & Color—An Introduction to Modern Photoengraving* (1959).

Arnold, Edmund C., *Functional Newspaper Design* (New York: Harper & Row, Publishers, 1956).

Burt, Sir Cyril, *A Psychological Study of Typography* (London: Cambridge University Press, 1959).

Butler, Kenneth, *Practical Handbook on Effective Illustration in Publication Layout* (Mendota, Ill.: Butler Typo-Design Research Center, 1952).

———, *Practical Handbook on Headline Design in Publication Layout* (Mendota, Ill.: Butler Typo-Design Research Center, 1954).

———, George C. Likeness, and Stanley A. Kordek, *Ken Butler's Layout Scrapbook, 101 More Usable Publication Layouts* (Mendota, Ill.: Butler Typo-Design Research Center, 1958).

———, ———, and ———, *101 Usable Publication Layouts* (Mendota, Ill.: Butler Typo-Design Research Center, 1954).

———, ———, and ———, *Practical Handbook on Double-Spreads in Publication Layout* (Mendota, Ill.: Butler Typo-Design Research Center, 1956).

Carter, Thomas Francis, *The Invention of Printing in China* (New York: Columbia University Press, 1925).

Cheskin, Louis, *Color for Profit* (New York: Liveright Publishing Corporation, 1951).

Clodd, Edward, *The Story of the Alphabet* (New York: Appleton-Century-Crofts, Inc., 1918).

Dain, Carl, *Design with Type* (New York: Farrar, Straus & Co., Inc., 1952).

de Lopatecki, Eugene, *Advertising Layout and Typography* (New York: The Ronald Press Company, 1952).

Devoe, Merrill, *Effective Advertising Copy* (New York: The Macmillan Company, 1956).

Eighth Graphic Arts Production Yearbook (New York: Colton Press, Inc., 1948).

George, Ross F., *Speedball Textbook for Pen & Brush Lettering*, 18th edition (Camden, N.J.: Hunt Pen Company, 1960).

Golden, Cipe Pineles, Kurt Weihs, and Robert Strunsky, *The Visual Craft of William Golden* (New York: George Braziller, Inc., 1962).

Hoe, Robert, *A Short History of the Printing Press* (New York: The Gillis Press, 1902).

How to Prepare Artwork for Letterpress, for Lithography (Neenah, Wis.: Kimberly-Clark Corporation).

Hunter, David, *Papermaking* (New York: Alfred A. Knopf, Inc., 1947).

Hymes, David, *Production in Advertising and the Graphic Arts* (New York: Holt, Rinehart and Winston, Inc., 1958).

Jackson, Hartley E., *Newspaper Typography* (Stanford, Cal.: Stanford University Press, 1947).

———, *Printing: A Practical Introduction to the Graphic Arts* (New York: McGraw-Hill Book Company, Inc., 1957).

Jahn, Hugo, *Hand Composition* (New York: John Wiley & Sons, Inc., 1931).

Karch, R. Randolph, *How To Plan and Buy Printing* (Englewood Cliffs, N.J.: Prentice-Hall, Inc., 1950).

Kubler, George A., *A New History of Stereotyping* (New York: J. J. Little & Ives Company, 1941).

Lithographers National Association, *The Story of Lithography* (New York).

Longyear, William, and Richard S. Chenault, *Advertising Layout* (New York: The Ronald Press Company, 1954).

McMurtrie, Douglas C., *The Book* (New York: Oxford University Press, 1943).

Melcher, Daniel, and Nancy Larrick, *Printing and Promotion Handbook* (New York: McGraw-Hill Book Company, Inc., 1956).

Mott, Frank Luther, *American Journalism* (New York: The Macmillan Company, 1962).

Ninth Graphic Arts Production Yearbook (New York: Colton Press, Inc., 1950).

Olson, Kenneth E., *Typography and Mechanics of the Newspaper* (New York: Appleton-Century-Crofts, Inc., 1930).

Partridge, C. S., *Stereotyping, The Papier Mâché Process* (Chicago: Mize & Stearns Press, 1892).

Paterson, D. G., and M. A. Tinker, *How To Make Type Readable* (New York: Harper & Row, Publishers, 1940).

Pocket Pal, 6th edition (New York: International Paper Company, 1960).

Pollack, Philip, *Printing: Careers and Opportunities for You* (Philadelphia: Chilton Company-Book Division, 1959).

Printer 1 & C (Washington: U.S. Government Printing Office, 1954).

Printing, Its Forms and Designations (Boston: S. D. Warren Company, 1961).

Printing Layout and Design (Albany, N.Y.: Delmar Publishers, Inc., 1955).

Printing, Papers and Their Uses (Boston: S. D. Warren Company).

Printing, The Processes of Reproduction (Boston: S. D. Warren Company).

Printing, Types and Typography (Boston: S. D. Warren Company).

Stanley, Thomas Blaine, *The Technique of Advertising Production* (Englewood Cliffs, N.J.: Prentice-Hall, Inc., 1954).

Stevens, William J., and John A. McKinven, *How To Prepare Art and Copy for Offset Lithography* (Maywood, N.J.: Dorval Publishing Company, 1948).

Sutton, Albert A., *Design and Makeup of the Newspaper* (Englewood Cliffs, N.J.: Prentice-Hall, Inc., 1948).

Tarr, John C., *Printing To-Day* (London: Oxford University Press, 1949).

Type Faces and Production Techniques (Milwaukee, Wis.: *The Milwaukee Journal,* 1957).

Westley, Bruce, *News Editing* (Boston: Houghton Mifflin Company, 1953).

CHARACTERS PER PICA OF SELECTED TYPE FACES

Copy fitting can be accurate only when the peculiarities of the individual type design are taken into account. Types of the same size but of different faces use more or less space according to the design of the face. A further complication, the space required also varies according to the manufacturer. Hence, not only will Baskerville differ from Bodoni, the Baskerville of one manufacturer will not take up the same space as the Baskerville of another maker.

The character-per-pica counts for a number of selected type faces are presented below. No attempt has been made to make this list complete; instead only a few of the more common body and display faces are included. The manufacturer of each face is given, but it should be understood that faces by the same name may be offered by several other firms. The information is presented here as a tool for practice in copy fitting; information about other type faces can be obtained from printers and type manufacturers when needed.

Key to abbreviations of manufacturers: L=Linotype; I=Intertype; A=American Type Founders; B=Bauer.

Face	Man-ufac-turer	Point Sizes							
		8	9	10	11	12	14	18	24
Baskerville	L	3.22	2.96	2.64	2.46	2.3	2.01		
Bernhard Gothic Medium	A	3.75		2.96		2.64	2.29	1.75	1.33
Bernhard Gothic Medium Italic	A	3.61		2.94		2.61	2.17	1.74	1.31
Bernhard Modern Roman	A	3.59		2.99		2.54	2.15	1.74	1.31
Bodoni with Italic	I	3.13		2.6		2.36	2.11	1.64	1.28
Bookman	L	3.11	2.88	2.6	2.37	2.21	1.84		
Caledonia	L	3.12	2.87	2.63	2.44	2.26	2.00		
Caslon 540	A	3.39		2.91	2.56	2.21	1.86	1.49	1.06
Caslon 540 Italic	A	3.39		3.16	2.76	2.38	1.99	1.59	1.16
Century Schoolbook	A	2.97		2.43		2.12	1.75	1.4	1.1
Century Schoolbook Italic	A	2.99		2.46		2.17	1.81	1.44	1.13
Cheltenham	L	3.56	3.2	2.99	2.72	2.53	2.15		1.42
Cloister	L	3.56		3.11	2.97	2.75	2.45	1.93	1.46
Cooper Black	A	2.6		2.03		1.75	1.42	1.09	.83
Franklin Gothic	A	2.66		2.1		1.89	1.63	1.26	.98

Face	Man-ufac-turer	Point Sizes							
		8	9	10	11	12	14	18	24
Futura Medium	I	3.6		2.87		2.42	2.11	1.61	
Futura Medium Oblique	I	3.6		2.87		2.43	2.11	1.61	
Garamond with Italic	I.	3.37	3.18	2.95	2.7	2.59	2.3	1.77	1.38
Goudy Old Style with Italic	I	3.36		2.74		2.42	2.01		
Kaufman Script	A			3.12		2.84	2.54	1.94	1.5
Lydian	A			2.72		2.28	2.00	1.6	1.2
Lydian Cursive	A							1.91	1.47
Lydian Italic	A			2.97		2.51	2.22	1.77	1.35
Park Avenue	A					2.83	2.54	2.07	1.64
Scotch Roman	A	3.18		2.85	2.7	2.26	1.87	1.45	1.12
Stymie Bold	A	2.92		2.29		2.02	1.67	1.31	1.03
Stymie Bold Italic	A	2.86		2.22		1.98	1.63	1.29	1.01
Times Roman Bold	L	3.14	2.90	2.73	2.53	2.31	2.07		
Times Roman Italic	L	3.14	2.90	2.73	2.53	2.31	2.07		
Ultra Bodoni	A	2.18		1.97		1.56	1.46	1.12	.82
Ultra Bodoni Italic	A	2.18		1.98		1.57	1.43	1.13	.84
Vogue	I	3.51		2.93		2.44	2.12	1.67	1.28
Wedding Text	A	3.71		3.01		2.7	2.47		
Weiss Roman	B	3.76		3.16	2.93	2.58	2.27	1.7	1.37
Weiss Italic	B	4.54		3.51	3.38	2.92	2.66	2.09	1.69

SOME COMMONLY USED TYPE FACES

The type faces shown on the following pages represent the designs commonly used for body and/or display in all forms of printed matter. They are set in a moderate size to reveal their suitability for these purposes. By analyzing the distinctive characteristics of various letters, the student can soon learn to recognize many of these common designs.

Most of these specimens have been reproduced from *Design With Type,* copyright © 1955 by American Type Founders, Inc. The exceptions are: Baskerville, Bookman, Caledonia, Cheltenham, Cloister, Craw, Futura, Kennerly, Lightline, Scotch, Times Roman, Venus, Vogue, and Weiss.

BALLOON EXTRABOLD

A B C D E F G H I J K L M N

O P Q R S T U V W X Y Z

$ 1 2 3 4 5 6 7 8 9 0

P. T. Barnum

A B C D E F G H I J K L M N
O P Q R S T U V W X Y Z &
$ 1 2 3 4 5 6 7 8 9 0
a b c d e f g h i j k l m n o p q
r s t u v w x y z

Baskerville

ABCDEFGHIJKLMNOPQR
STUVWXYZ&
abcdefghijklmnopqrstuvwxyz
$1234567890

Baskerville Italic

ABCDEFGHIJKLMNOPQR
STUVWXYZ&
abcdefghijklmnopqrstuvwxyz
$1234567890

Bernhard Modern Roman Italic

ABCDEFGHIJKLMN
OPQRSTUVWXYZ&
$ 1 2 3 4 5 6 7 8 9 0
a b c d e f g h i j k l m n o p q
r s t u v w x y z

Bernhard Gothic Medium

ABCDEFGHIJKLMN
OPQRSTUVWXYZ&
$1234567890
a b c d e f g h i j k l m n o p q
r s t u v w x y z

Bodoni

ABCDEFGHIJKLMN
OPQRSTUVWXYZ&
$ 1 2 3 4 5 6 7 8 9 0
a b c d e f g h i j k l m n o p q
r s t u v w x y z

Bernhard Gothic Medium Italic

ABCDEFGHIJKLMN
OPQRSTUVWXYZ&
$1234567890
a b c d e f g h i j k l m n o p q
r s t u v w x y z

Bodoni Italic

ABCDEFGHIJKLMN
OPQRSTUVWXYZ&
$ 1 2 3 4 5 6 7 8 9 0
a b c d e f g h i j k l m n o p q
r s t u v w x y z

Bernhard Modern Bold

ABCDEFGHIJKLMN
OPQRSTUVWXYZ&
$ 1 2 3 4 5 6 7 8 9 0 ¢
a b c d e f g h i j k l m n o p q
r s t u v w x y z

Bookman

ABCDEFGHIJKLMNOPQ
RSTUVWXYZ&
abcdefghijklmnopqrstuv
wxyz
$1234567890

Bookman Italic

ABCDEFGHIJKLMNOPQ
RSTUVWXYZ&

abcdefghijklmnopqrstuv
wxyz

$1234567890

Caslon Italic

ABCDEFGHIJKLMN
OPQRSTUVWXYZ&
$1234567890
abcdefghijklmnopq
rstuvwxyz

Caledonia

ABCDEFGHIJKLMNOPQRS
TUVWXYZ&
abcdefghijklmnopqrstuvwxyz
$1234567890

Century Schoolbook

ABCDEFGHIJKLMN
OPQRSTUVWXYZ&
$1234567890
abcdefghijklmnopq
rstuvwxyz

Caledonia Italic

ABCDEFGHIJKLMNOPQRS
TUVWXYZ&
abcdefghijklmnopqrstuvwxyz
$1234567890

Century Schoolbook Italic

ABCDEFGHIJKLMN
OPQRSTUVWXYZ&
$1234567890
abcdefghijklmnopq
rstuvwxyz

Caslon

ABCDEFGHIJKLMN
OPQRSTUVWXYZ&
$1234567890
abcdefghijklmnopq
rstuvwxyz

Cheltenham Medium

ABCDEFGHIJKLMNOPQRS
TUVWXYZ&
abcdefghijklmnopqrstuvwxyz
$1234567890

Cheltenham Medium Italic

ABCDEFGHIJKLMNOPQRS
TUVWXYZ&
abcdefghijklmnopqrstuvwxyz
$1234567890

Craw Modern

ABCDEFGHIJKL
MNOPQRSTUV
WXYZ&
abcdefghijklmn
opqrstuvwxyz

Cloister

ABCDEFGHIJKLMNOPQRS
TUVWXYZ&
abcdefghijklmnopqrstuvwxyz
$1234567890

Dom Casual

ABCDEFGHIJKLMN
OPQRSTUVWXYZ&
1234567890
abcdefghijklmnopq
rstuvwxyz

Cloister Italic

ABCDEFGHIJKLMNOPQRS
TUVWXYZ&
abcdefghijklmnopqrstuvwxyz
$1234567890

Franklin Gothic

ABCDEFGHIJKLMN
OPQRSTUVWXYZ&
$1234567890
abcdefghijklmnopq
rstuvwxyz

Cooper Black

ABCDEFGHIJKLMN
OPQRSTUVWXYZ&
$1234567890
abcdefghijklmnopq
rstuvwxyz

Franklin Gothic Italic

ABCDEFGHIJKLMN
OPQRSTUVWXYZ&
$1234567890.,-:;!?'
abcdefghijklmnopq
rstuvwxyz

Futura Medium

ABCDEFGHIJKLMNOPQRSTU
VWXYZ&
abcdefghijklmnopqrstuvwxyz
$1234567890

Goudy

ABCDEFGHIJKLMN
OPQRSTUVWXYZ&
$1234567890
abcdefghijklmnopq
rstuvwxyz

Futura Medium Italic

ABCDEFGHIJKLMNOPQRSTU
VWXYZ&
abcdefghijklmnopqrstuvwxyz
$1234567890

Goudy Italic

ABCDEFGHIJKLMN
OPQRSTUVWXYZ&
$1234567890
abcdefghijklmnopq
rstuvwxyz

Garamond

ABCDEFGHIJKLMN
OPQRSTUVWXYZ&
$1234567890
abcdefghijklmnopq
rstuvwxyz

HUXLEY VERTICAL

ABCDEFGHIJK
LMNOPQRSTU
VWXYZ
$1234567890

Garamond Italic

ABCDEFGHIJKLMN
OPQRSTUVWXYZ&
$1234567890
abcdefghijklmnopq
rstuvwxyz

Kaufmann Script

ABCDEFGHIJKLMN
OPQRSTUVWXYZ&
$1234567890¢
abcdefghijklmnopqrss
tuvwxyz

Kennerly

ABCDEFGHIJKLMNOPQRS
TUVWXYZ&
abcdefghijklmnopqrstuvwxyz
$1234567890

Lydian Cursive

ABCDEFGHIJ
KLMNOPQRS
TUVWXYZ&
abcdeefghijkl
mnopqrstuvw
xyz
$1234567890

Lightline Gothic

ABCDEFGHIJKLMNOPQRS
TUVWXYZ&
abcdefghijklmnopqrstuvwxyz
$1234567890

News Gothic

ABCDEFGHIJKLMN
OPQRSTUVWXYZ&
$1234567890
abcdefghijklmnopq
rstuvwxyz

Lydian

AĀBCDEFGHIJKLM
NOPQRSTUVWXYZ&
$1234567890¢
abcdefghijklmnopq
rstuvwxyz

Lydian Italic

ABCDEFGHIJKLMN
OPQRSTUVWXYZ&
$1234567890¢
abcdefghijklmnopq
rstuvwxyz

News Gothic Condensed

ABCDEFGHIJKLMN
OPQRSTUVWXYZ&
$1234567890
abcdefghijklmnopq
rstuvwxyz

Park Avenue

A B C D E F G
H I J K L M N O
P Q R S T U V W
X Y Z &
a b c d e f g h i j k l m n o
p q r s t u v w x y z
$ 1 2 3 4 5 6 7 8 9 0

Scotch Roman

ABCDEFGHIJKLMNOP
QRSTUVWXYZ&
abcdefghijklmnopqrstuvw
xyz
$1234567890

Scotch Roman *Italic*

ABCDEFGHIJKLMNOP
QRSTUVWXYZ&
abcdefghijklmnopqrstuvwxyz
$1234567890

Stymie Bold

ABCDEFGHIJKLMN
OPQRSTUVWXYZ&
$1234567890
abcdefghijklmnopq
rstuvwxyz

Stymie Bold Italic

ABCDEFGHIJKLMN
OPQRSTUVWXYZ&
$ 1 2 3 4 5 6 7 8 9 0
abcdefghijklmnopq
rstuvwxyz

Times Roman

ABCDEFGHIJKLMNOP
QRSTUVWXYZ&
abcdefghijklmnopqrstuvw
xyz
$1234567890

Times Roman Italic

ABCDEFGHIJKLMNOPQ
RSTUVWXYZ&
abcdefghijklmnopqrstuvwxyz
$1234567890

Ultra Bodoni

ABCDEFGHIJK
LMNOPQRSTUV
WXYZ&
$1234567890
abcdefghijklmnop
qrstuvwxyz

Ultra Bodoni Italic

ABCDEFGHIJK
LMNOPQRSTUV
WXYZ&
$1234567890
abcdefghijklmnop
qrstuvwxyz

Wedding Text

ABCDEFGHIJ
JKLMNOPQR
STUVWXYZ&
$1234567890
abcdefghijklm
nopqrstuvwxyz

Venus Bold Extended

ABCDEFGHIJKLMNOP
QRSTUVWXYZ&
abcdefghijklmnoprstuv
wxyz
$1234567890

Weiss Roman

ABCDEFGHIJKLMNOPQRST
UVWXYZ&
abcdefghijklmnopqrstuvwxyz
$1234567890

Vogue Bold

ABCDEFGHIJKLMNOPQRSTU
VWXYZ
abcdefghijklmnopqrstuvwxyz
1234567890

Weiss Italic

ABCDEFGHIJKLMNOPQRS
TUVWXYZ&
abcdefghijklmnopqrstuvwxyz
$1234567890

Vogue Bold Italic

ABCDEFGHIJKLMNOPQRSTU
VWXYZ
abcdefghijklmnopqrstuvwxyz
1234567890

AGATE Name for 5½ point type; agate line is unit of ad-space measurement, 1/14-inch deep, one column wide.

AMPERSAND The symbol &.

ART Photographs, drawings, and hand-lettering. Also paste-up of materials for camera copy, as in offset and rotogravure.

ASTONISHER Name sometimes used for headlines that include a short line above and/or below the main lines. Also printers' slang for exclamation point.

AUTHOR'S ALTERATIONS Abbreviated "AA's", refers to changes in proofs not due to printer's error. They are extra charges.

BACKBONE Portion of book binding between front and back covers.

BANNER Newspaper headline crossing full width of page. Also called streamer or ribbon.

BASIS WEIGHT The weight of a ream of paper at standard size (book 25 by 38; cover 20 by 26; index 25½ by 30½).

BENDAY PROCESS A method of applying shading and tinting (lines or dots) to line artwork. (Originated by Benjamin Day.)

BINDING In broad sense, any further treatment of stock after printing; includes cutting, folding, trimming, gathering, stitching, gluing, and casing.

BLEED An illustration filling one or more margins and running off the edge of the page.

BLUEPRINT Or blue or blueline, a fast proof on paper from an offset flat or negative; print is blue.

BODY TYPE Type for main message; generally under 12-point size. Also called text type. Opposite of display type.

BOLDFACE (bf) A variation of a type face which is heavier and darker than the fullface or lightface versions.

BOND PAPER A paper stock suitable for business purposes, such as letterheads and forms.

BOOK PAPER A paper stock for periodical printing as well as books and direct literature (promotion, etc.).

BOX Printed matter enclosed in rules.

BREAK-OF-THE-BOOK Allocation of space in a magazine.

BROWNLINE or **VANDYKE** Same as blueprint except print is brown.

BUILD-UP An excess of ink sufficient to cause smudging or filling-in of letters.

BULK Thickness of paper, without reference to its weight.

BULLET Large dot used as an attention-getter.

BUTTED SLUGS Two or more linecaster slugs placed together to form a single line of type. Slugs must be butted when the printed line is to be longer than the machine can set.

GLOSSARY

CALENDERING   A rolling operation during paper making that produces smoothness of surface. Super-calendered paper is rolled between polished steel cylinders to create an especially smooth surface.

CAPS AND SMALL CAPS   Capitals (upper case) and small capitals. Small capitals are the same height as lower-case letters in any type face but have upper case formation.

CAPTION   Text accompanying illustrations. Also used to describe the overlines or "heads" above newspaper illustrations.

CASE   Storage drawer for foundry type. Also the stiff cover of a book and the mold in electrotyping.

CASE-BOUND   A book with hard cover.

CHASE   Metal frame to contain type and plates for printing or for molding duplicates.

COATED PAPER   Paper to which a surface coating has been applied for a smooth finish.

COLD TYPE   Type composed by other than traditional methods (hot type or foundry)—viz., photocomposition, paste-down, or "typewriter methods." Such type is printlike in varying degrees.

COLLOTYPE   *See* photogelatin.

COLOPHON   Symbol or trademark identifying a printer or publisher.

COLOR PRINT   Color photograph viewed by reflected light as compared with a transparency that is viewed by transmitted light.

COLOR SEPARATION   Process of preparing separate primary color prints (plates) which, when printed in register, produce a full-color illustration.

COMBINATION   Line and halftone combined into a single illustration. Also a run of several different jobs at one time on one press.

COMPOSING STICK   A device into which foundry type is assembled and justified into lines.

COMPREHENSIVE   A hand-drawn layout or dummy, carefully prepared and finished to approximate piece in print.

CONTACT PRINT   A print on photo paper from negative or positive in contact, as opposed to enlargement or reduction.

COPY   Text or art to be printed or reproduced.

COPYFITTING   Determining: (1) space required for copy; (2) amount of copy to be written for allotted space; (3) size of type to accommodate an amount of copy in an allotted space.

COPYREADING   Reading copy for errors and marking copy for printer.

COPY SCHEDULE   An inventory sheet kept by copy desk chief of a newspaper; contains sufficient information about each item so a dummy can be made.

COVER STOCK   Special paper suitable for covers of booklets.

CROP To mark artwork or photographs indicating which portions are to be reproduced.

CURSIVE TYPE Any type face resembling handwriting, but with disconnected letters. A form of italic in some recent book faces.

CUT A photoengraving (line or halftone) for letterpress printing.

CUTLINES Text accompanying illustrations. *See also* caption.

CUT-OFF RULE A rule that prints a line used horizontally across columns in newspapers to separate items and guide the reader.

CYLINDER PRESS A press on which paper is held to a cylinder which revolves, rolling the paper across a flat, inked letterpress form to receive impressions.

DEAD MATTER Printing materials (type and illustrations) no longer needed (foul matter).

DIE-CUT A printed piece cut into special shape by dies made by shaping steel blades into the desired form.

DINGBAT Typographic decorative device such as a bullet or star.

DISPLAY TYPE Type larger than body.

DOCTOR BLADE The blade on a gravure press that wipes excess ink from the plate prior to impression.

DOUBLE-BURN In offset, the exposure of light in succession through two separate flats onto the same plate; in many cases one flat contains halftones and the other contains line copy.

DOUBLEPRINT A surprint, i.e., black line appearing on a tone area.

DROPOUT A halftone without dots in unwanted areas; produced by a number of photomechanical means.

DUMMY Proofs of text, illustrations, caption (or measured holes for each element), and display pasted into position on sheets in specific page arrangement for compositor's guidance in making up pages. In newspapers and magazines the elements may be sketched in place.

DUOTONE A two-color reproduction of a halftone from separate plates. When two plates are made from a single black and white photo (one high-key carries color, the other normal carries black) it may be called a duograph.

EAR Small amounts of type and/or illustration on either side of a newspaper name plate. Also refers to the hook on letters r and g.

ELECTROTYPE A metal plate cast from a wax mold of the original type page.

ELROD Machine for making rules, leads, slugs, and borders.

EM The (nonprinting) square of a type body of any size. Also but erroneously used as a synonym for pica.

EMBOSSING Pressing a relief pattern of type and/or art into paper or cover materials.

EN Piece of spacing material half as wide as it is high (half the width of an em).

END PAPERS Paper glued to the inside covers of a book; often left blank but may contain printing.

ENGRAVING A printing plate etched by acid from photographic or other copy; a copper plate into which letters are hand etched in reverse for printing invitations, calling cards, etc. Also a synonym for a cut or photoengraving.

FACE The printing surface or type or plate. Also the name for a specified type.

FAKE PROCESS COLOR Full-color reproduction from a black and white photo, effected by the engraver's manipulation of four separate negatives so they represent the respective primaries and black. (See process color.)

FILLING IN Excess ink builds up to a point where letters, notably those with bowls (g, e, a), plug or close up.

FIRST REVISE A proof of type with corrections made after first proof-reading.

FLAG Name plate of a newspaper.

FLAT A vehicle for holding film positives or negatives in position for exposing onto plates. Offset flats are usually goldenrod paper; photoengraving and gravure flats are usually glass.

FLAT-BED PRESS A direct-from-type (or engraving) press using either platen or cylinder to print from a flat form, as opposed to curved, type form.

FLAT COLOR Simplest form of spot color; each color stands alone, solid or screened—colors do not overlay each other to form additional colors.

FLEXOGRAPHY A relief printing method using liquid fast-dry ink on rubber plates.

FLOP To reverse art laterally—image, when printed, is opposite from original.

FOLIO A page number.

FOLO HEAD Headline over a small story related to and placed directly following the main story.

FONT All the letters and characters in one size of a type face.

FORM Type and engravings locked in a chase, ready for printing or duplicating.

FORMAT The shape, size, and style of a publication.

FOUNDRY TYPE   Hand-set type.

FULLFACE   The standard or normal weight and width of a type face.

FURNITURE   Metal or wooden material used to fill in large nonprint areas of a letterpress form.

GALLEY   A metal tray for storing type.

GALLEY PROOF   Proof from type in a galley; after correction, stored type is made into pages.

GANG   To run several jobs on one press at a time. Also, to make several engravings—all at same enlargement or reduction—at one time.

GAUGE   *See* line gauge.

GOLDENROD   Opaque golden-orange paper that serves as the vehicle for an offset flat.

GOTHIC TYPE   Those faces with, generally, monotonal (noncontrast) strokes and no serifs; also called sans-serif, contemporary, or block letter.

GRIPPER EDGE   The edge of a sheet held by the gripper on the impression cylinder of a cylinder press or sheet-fed rotary; it represents an unprintable ⅜ to ½ inch.

GUTTER   The inside margin of a page at the binding.

HALFTONE   A printing plate made from a photograph, wash drawing, etc. Gradation of tone is reproduced by a pattern of dots produced by interposition of a screen during exposure.

HED SKED   A headline schedule, the newspaper inventory sheet showing all headlines the newspaper normally uses.

HIGHLIGHT   The lightest portion of a photo or other art or reproduction of same. To highlight a halftone is to remove mechanically or photographically the dots in certain areas. Such a halftone is called a highlight or drop-out halftone.

HOT METAL   *See* hot type.

HOT-METAL PASTE-UP   Methods of ad make-up for letterpress newspapers in which stripped type slugs and plates are affixed to a plastic base; base plus slugs, plates, and stereo casts are type-high. The plastic base is marked off in grids to delineate columns and facilitate location of elements. The paste-up is placed in the page forms for mat rolling.

HOT TYPE   Type composed by machine from molten metal; sometimes includes foundry type.

IMPOSITION   The location of pages in a form or on a sheet so that when the printed sheet or signature is folded, pages will fall in proper order.

IMPRESSION   The pressure of type or plate against paper in printing. Also, "impressions per hour" refers to number of sheets being delivered.

INITIAL   A large, decorative letter used to start a copy area.

INSERT   A separately printed piece placed in a publication at time of binding.

INTAGLIO   Process of printing from depressed areas carrying ink.

INTERTYPE   A keyboard-operated, circulating mat linecaster.

ITALIC   Type which slants right; counterpart to roman posture, which is upright.

JIM DASH   A short dash (about three ems long) used between headline decks in some newspapers.

JUMP   To carry over a portion of a story from one page to another. Also the continued portion of the story.

JUSTIFY   To space or quad out a line of type to make it full to the right margin.

KEY PLATE   The printer (plate) in color printing which is laid first and to which others must register.

KICKER   A short line of type above and/or below the main part of a headline; used mainly for feature story headlines.

LAYOUT   Often used as synonym for dummy. A pattern, roughly or carefully drawn, to show placement of elements on a printed piece.

LEADERS   A row of dots used to guide vision across open areas of tabular material.

LEADS (pronounced "leds")   Thin metallic strips used to provide extra space between type lines.

LEGIBILITY   That degree of visibility which makes printed matter read easily and rapidly.

LETTERPRESS   The traditional system of printing from raised (relief) areas.

LIGATURE   Two or more letters joined together as a single unit, such as ffl, fi.

LINE   In advertising, an agate line; in illustrations, it refers to art work and plates composed only of extreme tones as opposed to halftone illustrations.

LINECASTER   A machine, such as Linotype, which casts type in line units.

LINE CONVERSION   A relatively new technique of converting photographs to line illustrations for special effect.

LINE CUT   An engraving, usually on zinc, containing no gradation of tone unless applied by Ben Day or similar means.

LINE GAUGE   Printer's ruler marked off in picas and other printing units of measure.

LINOTYPE   A keyboard-operated circulating mat linecasting machine.

LITHOGRAPHY   A system of printing from a flat surface using principle that grease and water don't mix. *See also* offset.

LOCK UP   Securing type, engraving, and furniture in a form prior to plating.

LOGOTYPE   Several letters, words, or a slogan cast in one piece of type such as an advertiser's signature or a newspaper name plate.

LOWER CASE   Small letter, as distinguished from a capital.

LUDLOW TYPOGRAPH   A typecasting machine usually used for display type; molds are hand set in lines and then the line is cast as a single slug.

MAKE-READY   Preparation of page forms or plates which involves padding and other means of adjusting the contact between printing surfaces and paper to produce uniform impression during printing.

MAKE-UP   Arrangement according to design of type, illustrations, and other elements into pages.

MARK UP   To put composition instructions on copy or layout. As a noun refers to ad layouts so marked.

MASK   A sheet of opaque paper used to prevent light from striking the plate while making offset or engraving plates; areas are cut from the mask so desired image will be exposed on the plate. Masks may also be made photographically on film.

MATRIX   A mold of a typecasting machine from which a type character or other element is cast. Also the sheet of papiér mâché or composition material used as a mold in stereotyping.

MEASURE   Page, line, or column width expressed in picas.

MECHANICAL   A paste-up with all elements in proper position, marked, and ready to be photographed and made into a plate.

MECHANICAL BINDING   Type of binding using plastic, metal spirals, or rings instead of traditional sewing or stapling.

MINIATURE   A small layout prepared as a preliminary to executing a full-scale layout.

MOIRÉ   A pronounced screen pattern that results from the clash of dot patterns when two or more screens are used; corrected in full-color and duotone work by changing screen angles.

MONOTYPE   A typecasting machine; casts single letters rather than lines and uses a tape-punching unit and a casting unit to do this.

MONTAGE   A combination of several distinct pictures into a composite picture; usually called a collage unless the edges of the component pictures are made to blend into each other.

MORTISE An engraving containing a cut-out area to permit insertion of type or other matter; if the cut-out is from outside edges, it is usually called a notch.

NAME PLATE The name of a newspaper, usually at the top of page one.

NEGATIVE In photography, engraving, and photographic printing processes, the film containing a reversed (in tone) image of copy being photographed.

NONPAREIL A size of type, 6-point.

OFFSET A lithographic printing method in which the inked image transfers from plate to rubber blanket to paper. Often called indirect or photo-offset lithography. Also a process in book making whereby pages (text and illustrations) are photographed and then printed from the plates made from these photographs.

OVERHANG COVER A cover that, after trimming, projects beyond the dimensions of inside pages.

OVERLAY Transparent or translucent sheets of paper or acetate used over art and photos to show location or shape of special treatments. Camera copy that combines on the same plate with the art or photo underneath, or overprints it in another color, may also be placed on an overlay.

OVERSET Type that is set but not used.

PAGE PROOF Proof of type matter in page form together with illustrations or with holes left for them.

PERFECT BINDING A method of binding books with paper in lieu of case and flexible glue instead of stitching.

PERFECTING PRESS A press capable of printing on both sides of a sheet or web at the same time.

PHOTOCOMPOSING Automatic, repeated exposure of a flat on a single offset or wrap-around plate. Each printing impression from the plate, when it is run, results in several copies of the same image. Also, synonym for photocomposition.

PHOTOCOMPOSITION Type composed by exposing negatives of the characters on film or paper.

PHOTOENGRAVINGS Original letterpress plates used to reproduce line and halftone illustrations.

PHOTOGELATIN A screenless printing process using gelatin plates, especially suitable for reproducing tone illustrations; also called collotype.

PHOTOSTAT A photocopy, either positive or negative (reversed in tone), same size, enlarged, or reduced.

PI Type that is mixed up and hence unusable.

PICA Standard unit of linear measurement (12 points); approximately 1/6 of an inch.

PLATEN PRESS   A flat-surfaced relief press. Paper is supported on one surface, type on the other. The two are brought together for impression.

PRESS PROOF   One of the first copies off the press; it offers final opportunity to make changes in the job.

POINT   Printer's unit of measuring size of type and of rules, border, spacing material; there are 12 points to a pica and approximately 72 points to an inch. As unit of measurement for board equals 1/1000 of an inch.

PROCESS COLOR   The reproduction of continuous-tone color originals by separating out each color and recording it on film; then plates are made from these films to carry the respective colors to paper.

PROGRESSIVE PROOFS   Proofs of process color plates; each color is shown separately, then in combination with each other. For four-color process a set of "progs" would show seven printings.

PROOF   A trial printing of type, negatives, or plates, to be checked for possible errors.

QUAD   A less-than-type-high spacing material used within lines; an em-quad is the square of the type size, a 2-cm quad is twice as wide as the type size. An en-quad is half as wide as the type size.

QUIRE   Twenty-four or 25 sheets of paper of the same size and quality.

READABILITY   The quality of rhetorical and graphic presentation of material that produces ease in reading. *See also* Legibility.

REAM   Either 480 or 500 sheets of paper of the same size and quality.

REGISTER   Placement of forms, plates, or negatives so that they will print in precise relation to or over other forms, plates, or negatives, as in color printing.

REPRODUCTION PROOF   A proof on special paper of exceptional cleanness and sharpness to be used as camera copy for offset, rotogravure, or relief plates.

REVERSE   Printing so that whites in original are black and blacks are white.

ROMAN   A type characterized by serifs, also refers to vertical type commonly used for typesetting as distinguished from italic.

ROTARY PRESS   Prints as paper passes between a cylindrical impression surface and a curved printing plate (letterpress).

ROTOGRAVURE   Printing and printing presses using the rotary and gravure principles; intaglio process.

ROUGH   A preliminary layout not in finished form.

ROUTING   Cutting away of excess metal from nonprinting areas of engravings or duplicates.

RULE   Strips of metal that are type-high and produce a line on paper; they vary in thickness and length.

RUN   The number of copies to come off the press.

RUNNING HEADS   Titles or heads repeated at the top of book and publication pages usually followed by or preceded by folio.

SADDLE-STITCH   To fasten a booklet together by stitching or stapling through the middle fold of the sheets.

SANS-SERIF   Type having no serifs. *See* Gothic.

SCALE   To find any unknown dimension when enlarging or reducing original art for reproduction to size.

SCAN-A-GRAVER   A machine that electronically reproduces plates as halftones on plastic for newspaper use.

SCORE   To crease paper or cover stock to facilitate folding without breaking.

SCREEN   Cross-ruled glass or film used in cameras to break continuous-tone copy into halftone dots. The number of lines per linear inch on the screen governs fineness of engraving. Also a tint block or flat tone.

SCRIPT   Types which stimulate handwriting in which letters appear to join.

SELF-COVER   A cover which is part of one of the signatures of a booklet and of the same paper.

SERIES   The range in sizes of a type face.

SERIF   The finishing cross stroke at the end of a main stroke in a type letter.

SHEET-FED   Referring to presses that accept sheets, not rolls (webs).

SHEETWISE   An imposition calling for printing half the pages in a signature on one side of the sheet, the other half on the other side.

SIDE-STITCH   To fasten sheets together sideways through the fold.

SIGNATURE   A number of pages printed on one sheet of paper; when folded and trimmed, pages fall in numerical order. A book signature may contain 8, 16, 32, or 64 pages.

SILHOUETTE   Reproduction of art or photo with background removed.

SILK-SCREEN   A process of printing by which ink or paints is "squeegeed" through a stencil-bearing silk screen to the paper beneath.

SLUG   A line of type from a linecasting machine. Also, between-line spacing material of metal 6 points or greater in thickness. Also, the word or two to identify a story.

SMALL CAPS   *See* caps and lower case.

SPLIT-FOUNTAIN PRINTING   In letterpress printing the ink receptacle (fountain) can be separated into compartments corresponding to segments of the ink roller which has also been split. By putting different colors in each fountain segment, more than one color can be printed from a form during one press run.

SPLIT PAGE   A magazine page that is part advertising and part editorial.

SPLIT-ROLLER   See split-fountain printing.

SPOT COLOR   Any color printing other than process printing.

SQUARE INDENTION   A newspaper headline pattern in which all lines are uniformly indented from the left; a modification of the flush-left headline.

SQUARE-SERIF   Types basically Gothic in nature but carrying also monotonal serifs.

STEREOTYPE   A letterpress duplicate metal plate (flat or curved) made from a cardboardlike mold.

STOCK   Paper or cardboard.

STRAIGHT MATTER   Text copy composed in normal paragraph form, as contrasted with tabular matter.

STRIPPED SLUG   A type slug that is shaved underneath; it can then be mounted at any angle on base material that brings it type-high.

STRIPPING   Affixing film negatives or positives to a flat. Also, cutting linecast slugs to less than type height. (See stripped slug and also hot-metal paste-up.)

SUBSTANCE   A term for the basis weight for paper.

SURPRINT   A combination plate made by exposing line and halftone negatives in succession on the same plate.

TELETYPESETTER   An attachment that automatically operates a mat circulating linecasting machine from perforated tape.

TEXT   A type face with an "Old English" look. Also any body type (written with lower-case *t*). Also the body of a book excluding front and back matter.

THERMOGRAPHY   A printing process that produces a raised impression simulating an intaglio engraving. An image is put on paper in the usual way; it is powdered while wet, then heated so powder and ink fuse to a raised image.

THUMBNAIL   A miniature layout. Also a half-column photoengraving.

TINT BLOCK   A photoengraving used to print tints of any percentage of color. Also refers to the panel printed from a block.

TIP-IN   A single sheet or partial signature glued into a book or magazine. Often of smooth stock used for halftone printing while remainder of publication may be printed on a cheaper stock of paper.

TOMBSTONE   The typographical effect that results from side-by-side placement of two or more headlines too similar in size and face to stand as separate units.

TRANSPARENCY   A color photograph which may be viewed by transmitted light.

TYPE-HIGH   In letterpress printing, .918 inches, the desire height for all elements in a form.

TYPO   A typographical error.

UPPER CASE   Capital letter.

VELLUM   Originally a calfskin or lambskin prepared as a writing surface; now used to label a paper stock with a good writing surface.

VELOX   A screened photographic print similar to a photostat positive, but usually sharper in definition.

VIGNETTE   The treatment given a photograph or halftone so that edges fade away into the background without breaking sharply.

WATERMARK   A faint design or lettering pressed into paper during its manufacture that can be seen when the sheet is held up to light.

WEB-FED   Paper fed into a press from a roll.

WHITE PRINT   A photocopy (contact print or enlargement) from a negative (halftone or line).

WIDOW   A short line at the end of a paragraph; always to be avoided at the top of newspaper or magazine columns or book pages, but its presence elsewhere may or may not be disliked.

WORK-AND-TUMBLE   A system resembling work-and-turn (below) except that the sheet is turned so that a new edge is grabbed by the grippers.

WORK-AND-TURN   A system of printing both sides of a printing piece on one side of a sheet, then turning so its gripper edge remains constant and printing is done on reverse side.

WORK-UP   A fault in relief printing that causes a spot to be printed because spacing materials or blank portions of type slugs have risen high enough to gather ink.

WRAP   An insert into a magazine or book. Unlike a tip-in, it is wrapped around a signature.

WRAP-AROUND PRESS   A relief press (sheet- or web-fed) that utilizes a shallow-etch curved plate made from a flat similar to that used in offset.

WRONG FONT   A letter or character that is of different size or face from the type that was specified.

XEROGRAPHY   A dry system of printing based on electrostatic principles.

ZINC   A photoengraving, line or halftone, made of zinc.

INDEX